Adaptive Behavior and Its Measurement

Implications for the Field of Mental Retardation

EDITED BY

ROBERT L. SCHALOCK, PHD
Hastings College

DAVID L. BRADDOCK, PHD
Books and Research Monographs Editor

AAMR

American Association on Mental Retardation

© 1999 American Association on Mental Retardation

Published by
American Association on Mental Retardation
444 North Capitol Street, NW, Suite 846
Washington, DC 20001-1512

The points of view herein are those of the authors and do not necessarily
represent the official policy or opinion of the American Association on
Mental Retardation. Publication does not imply endorsement by the editor,
the Association, or its individual members.

Printed in the United States of America.

Library of Congress Cataloging-in-Publication Data

Adaptive behavior and its measurements : implications for the field of
    mental retardation / edited by Robert L. Schalock, David Braddock.
                    p. cm.
            Includes bibliographical references.
            ISBN 0-940898-64-0
            1. Adaptability (Psychology)—Testing. 2. Mentally
handicapped—Pyschological testing. 3. Mental retardation—Diagnosis.
I. Schalock, Robert L. II. Braddock, David L.
RC570.2.A33   1999
616.85'88—dc21   99-26776
                                                     CIP

Contributors

Robert H. Bruininks, PhD
University of Minnesota
Minnetonka, MN

Brian R. Bryant, PhD
University Affiliated Program
Department of Special Education
The University of Texas at Austin
Austin, TX

Diane Pedrotty Bryant, PhD
University Affiliated Program
Department of Special Education
The University of Texas at Austin
Austin, TX

Steve Chamberlain, MS
University Affiliated Program
Department of Special Education
The University of Texas at Austin
Austin, TX

Ellis M. (Pat) Craig, PhD
Assistant Deputy Commissioner
Mental Retardation Services
Texas DMH/MR
Austin, TX

Stephen Greenspan, PhD
Educational Psychology
University of Connecticut
Storrs, CT

Laird W. Heal, PhD (Deceased)
Formerly at University of Illinois
at Urbana
Champaign, IL

Kevin S. McGrew, PhD
Department of Applied Psychology
St. Cloud State University
St. Cloud, MN

Kazuo Nihira, PhD
Department. of Psychology and
Behavioral Sciences
University of California, Los Angeles
Los Angeles, CA

Robert L. Schalock, PhD
Department of Psychology
Hastings College
Hastings, NE

Penny Crews Seay, PhD
University Affiliated Program
Department of Special Education
The University of Texas at Austin
Austin, TX

Scott Spreat, EdD
Wood's Services, Inc.
Allentown, NJ

Marc J. Tassé, PhD
Department of Psychology
Université du Québec à Montréal
Montreal, Québec
Canada

James R. Thompson, PhD
Department of Specialized Educational
Development
Illinois State University
Normal, IL

Dedication

Laird Heal was our friend, colleague, and mentor.

We dedicate this book to Laird and his legacy that reflects

a life of family, scholarship, and commitment to the welfare of others.

Contents

Tables

Figures

Preface

This book has developed over the last 5 years in conjunction with the American Association on Mental Retardation (AAMR) Ad Hoc Committee on Adaptive Behavior, appointed in 1994 by AAMR President David Braddock. The Committee was charged with integrating the concept of adaptive behavior more fully into the 1992 AAMR definition of mental retardation (Luckasson, et al.), relating the emerging concept of the multidimensional structure of adaptive behavior with the parallel development in the area of intelligence, and pursuing reliable and valid ways to assess adaptive behavior from a cross-cultural perspective.

Six goals directed the development of this book, *Adaptive Behavior and Its Measurement: Implications for the Field of Mental Retardation*:

1. Summarize the critical role that adaptive behavior has played in the definition of mental retardation.
2. Update the reader regarding the most recent work in the conceptualization of the construct of adaptive behavior, including its factor structure.
3. Review the various measurement strategies that are available to measure or assess one's adaptive behavior.
4. Sensitize the reader to the critical role that one's culture plays in the definition and use of the adaptive behavior construct.
5. Demonstrate how a clear understanding of adaptive skills, combined with prosthetic devices, can be used to enhance people's adaptive behavior and meaningful involvement in their communities.
6. Relate the changing conception of adaptive behavior to the similarly changing conception of intelligence, and suggest how these two critical concepts may well merge in future definitions of mental retardation.

There are a number of reasons why this book is so timely. First, the concept of adaptive behavior has been a major component in the definition of mental retardation since its inclusion in the sixth edition of the American Association on Mental Deficiency (AAMD; now AAMR) definition and classification manual (Heber, 1959, 1961). The concept of adaptive skills found in the 1992 AAMR *Mental Retardation: Definition, Classification, and Systems of Supports* (*System*; Luckasson et al.) is a continuation of the historical attention given to social competence in the definition of mental retardation. A necessary criterion in the 1992 AAMR definition of mental retardation is that significantly subaverage intellectual functioning exists concurrently with related limitations in two or more applicable adaptive skill areas: communication, self-care, home living, social skills, community use, self-direction, health and safety, functional academics, leisure, and work.

This focus on adaptive skills in the 1992 AAMR definition (Luckasson et al.), rather than adaptive behavior which was found in the 1983 AAMD definition (Grossman), represents a change due in part to the concerns surrounding the conceptual nature of adaptive behavior and the ensuing issues related to its operational use and measurement. Both of these concerns are central issues in this book and integral to other issues in the field of mental retardation, such as diagnosis, eligibility, and service considerations (Simeonsson & Short, 1996).

Second, the concept of adaptive behavior is also central to a number of significant developments within the field of mental retardation. Chief among these include: the movement of individuals with mental retardation into their communities and the development of support systems; the recent court decisions regarding fairness in special education and bias in assessment outcomes; the mainstreaming and inclusion of students with special needs into public schools; the recent legislation mandating early intervention for young children; and the increased movement toward a supports model and person-centered planning.

Because of the increased use of the adaptive behavior construct, it is important that consumers, advocates, professionals, decision makers, and the legal system be aware of the most current understanding of the conception, measurement, and use of the construct. As stated by Widaman, Borthwick-Duffy, and Little (1991):

We agree with others that adequate answers to definitional and theoretical problems concerning adaptive behavior have lagged behind measurement concerns. By continuing to focus attention to these problem areas and to address criticisms that are potentially directed at this research domain, significant strides will be made toward an adequate understanding of the domain of adaptive behavior and of the development and aging of these forms of behavior across the life span. (p. 2)

This book is also important because it begins to address environmental and cross-cultural issues as they relate generally to mental retardation and specifically to one's adaptive behavior. Increasingly, mental retardation is being viewed from a contextual perspective, which implies the need to recognize the role that both the individual and the individual's environment play in human functioning. Indeed, one of the key points in the 1992 AAMR definition (Luckasson, et al.) is that "the existence of a person's strengths and limitations in adaptive skills must be documented within the context of community environments typical of the individual's age peers and tied to the person's individual needs for supports" (p. 15).

Finally, this book is important because it addresses the need to develop a better understanding of how the concepts of adaptive behavior and intelligence relate to the con-

struct of mental retardation. We are seeing the rapid emergence of a multifaceted conception of both intelligence and adaptive behavior, which provides the current opportunity to integrate the cocriteria of intelligence and adaptive behavior into a heuristic model of mental retardation. This multifaceted conception is very consistent with the changing role that adaptive behavior has played over the last four decades in the definition of mental retardation and current changes occurring within the field. Key changes include (Luckasson et al., 1992; Schalock, Stark, Snell, Coulter, & Polloway, 1994):

- Approaching the construct of mental retardation not as an absolute trait expressed solely by the person, but as an expression of the functional impact of the interaction between the person with limited intellectual and adaptive skills and that person's environment. This new approach requires a better understanding of the significant role that one's environment and culture play in that interaction.

- Basing services and supports on the strengths and capabilities of the person, inclusive environments, and person-centered planning. This new emphasis on actual functioning requires greater clarity in describing those adaptive skills and limitations that influence everyday living, and identifying the specific adaptive skills considered critical for coping successfully with one's environment.

- Moving away from the tendency to relegate functioning to either separate parts of the brain or to central determiners such as "intelligence." This change has resulted in the expansion of both the concepts of intelligence and adaptive behavior to include multiple dimensions that underlie one's successful adjustment to environmental demands.

- Emphasizing the modularity of functioning and reconceptualizing disability severity in terms of the extent of needed supports rather than in the terms of decontextualized deficiencies.

Throughout the process of chairing the AAMR Committee on Adaptive Behavior and editing this book, it has been my privilege and joy to work with a group of wonderful, creative, conscientious, and valued colleagues. To each, I say, thank you for a job well done. Each of us hopes that this book will stimulate considerable discussion and creative endeavors related to the role that adaptive behavior plays in the definition of mental retardation, the interrelatedness of intelligence and adaptive behavior, and how best to measure adaptive behavior within a multicultural environment. I also express my appreciation and admiration to Ann Podraza for her tireless commitment to a quality product and her technical skills.

Robert L. Schalock, PhD
Hastings, Nebraska
October 1998

References

Grossman, H. J. (Ed.) (1983). *Classification in mental retardation*. Washington, DC: American Association on Mental Deficiency.

Heber, R. (1959). A manual on terminology and classification in mental retardation. *American Journal of Mental Deficiency Monograph, 64*(2).

Heber, R. (2nd ed.) (1961). A manual on terminology and classification in mental retardation. *American Journal of Mental Deficiency Monograph, 65*.

Luckasson, R., Coulter, D. L., Polloway, E. A., Reiss, S., Schalock, R. L., Snell, M. E., Spitalnik, D. M., & Stark, J. A. (1992). *Mental retardation: Definition, classification, and systems of supports* (9th ed.). Washington, DC: American Association on Mental Retardation.

Schalock, R. L., Stark, J. A., Snell, M. E., Coulter, D. L., & Polloway, E. (1994). The changing conception of mental retardation: Implications for the field. *Mental Retardation, 32*(3), 181-193.

Simeonsson, R. J., & Short, R. J. (1996). Adaptive behavior, survival roles, and quality of life. In J. W. Jacobson and J. A. Mulick (Eds.), *Manual of diagnosis and professional practice in mental retardation* (pp. 137-146). Washington, DC: American Psychological Association.

Widaman, K. F., Borthwick-Duffy, S. A. & Little, T. D. (1991). The structure and development of adaptive behavior. In N. W. Bray (Ed.), *International review of research in mental retardation, 17* (pp. 1-54). San Diego: Academic Press.

PART 1

The Concept of Adaptive Behavior

Introduction

Before the advent of the intelligence testing movement around the turn of the 20th century, mental retardation was described in terms of what we now call adaptive behavior. It was not until 1959, however, that adaptive behavior formally became part of the definition of mental retardation. Since then, it has been an integral part of the definition of mental retardation, the subject of considerable research and controversy, and the catalyst for the development of more than 200 scales of "adaptive behavior." Issues related to the changing conception of adaptive behavior and its measurement provide the focus of the first part of this monograph.

Over the years, we've seen a wide variety of definitions and categories of adaptive behavior. In the 1973 American Association on Mental Deficiency (AAMD; now American Association on Mental Retardation; AAMR) classification manual (Grossman), the concept was defined as "the effectiveness and degree with which the individual meets the standard of personal independence and social responsibility expected of his age and cultural groups" (p. 11). Analogously, adaptive behavior deficits were conceptualized as "significant limitations in an individual's effectiveness in meeting the standards of maturation, learning, personal independence, and/or social responsibility that are expected for his or her age level and cultural group, as determined by clinical assessment and, usually, standardized scales" (p. 11).

In the 1983 AAMD classification manual (Grossman), adaptive behavior referred to the quality of everyday performance in coping with environmental demands. The quality of general adaptation is mediated by level of intelligence; thus, the two concepts overlap in meaning. It is evident, however, from consideration of the definition of adaptive behavior, with its stress on everyday coping, that adaptive behavior refers to what people do to take care of themselves and relate to others in daily living rather than [to] the abstract potential implied by intelligence. (p. 42)

In the most recent revision of the AAMR manual, *Mental Retardation: Definition, Classification, and Systems of Supports* (Luckasson et al., 1992), the term *adaptive skills* replaced the older concept of adaptive behavior. In an effort to operationally define the term, 10 adaptive skills were included in the definition: communication, self-care, home living, social skills, community use, self-direction, health and safety, functional academics, leisure, and work. In the 1992 AAMR definition, these adaptive skills areas are considered central to successful life functioning; are related to the need for supports for the person with mental retardation; and, because the relevant skills within each adaptive skill area may vary with chronological age, assessment of functioning should be referenced to the person's chronological age.

In addition to these changes, the 1992 definition suggested that (a) practical and social intelligence act in concert to sustain the development of adaptive skills and (b) the adaptive difficulties in mental retardation derive from limitations in practical and social intelligence. In this notion (Luckasson et al., p. 15): (a) practical intelligence refers to the ability to maintain and sustain oneself as an independent person in managing the ordinary activities of daily living; and (b) social intelligence refers to the ability to understand social expectations and the behavior of other persons and to judge appropriately how to conduct oneself in social situations.

Although adaptive behavior is included currently in all of the major classification systems (including AAMR; *Diagnostic and Statistical Manual of Mental Disorders* [American Psychiatric Association, 1994]; *International Classification of Diseases* [World Health Organization, 1992]), there is no universal agreement on the factor structure of adaptive behavior, the best method to assess it, the role that adaptive behavior or skill deficits should play in the definition and diagnosis of mental retardation, and the relationship between the concepts of intelligence and adaptive behavior. These are the critical issues that the reader will be exposed to in part 1 of this monograph.

In chapter 1, Kaz Nihira reviews the history of the concept of adaptive behavior and summarizes the significant impact the concept and its measurement has had on the field of mental retardation, especially since the 1960s. It was during the 60s, for example, that the [then] American Association on Mental Deficiency revived adaptive behavior as a relevant concept that broadened the definition of mental retardation. Also during that decade, the definition and assessment of adaptive behavior became part of the national effort and professional practice to provide a basis for establishing training goals and programs for people with mental retardation. During the 1970s, the field experienced a significant shift toward consumer-referenced normalization and mainstreaming. Again, the concept of adaptive behavior and its measurement were helpful in facilitating fair placement decisions by identifying social development outside the academic setting. The 1980s and 1990s have been characterized by research into the factor structure of adaptive behavior, the proliferation of adaptive behavior assessment instruments, and the use of the adaptive behavior construct for (a) the development of instructional programs, (b) placement decisions, (c) research on the factor structure of adaptive behavior, and (d) the understanding of developmental trends in adaptive behavior.

Since the 1960s, we have experienced significant conceptual developments in regard to adaptive behavior, including reference to its factor structure and its relationship to the multidimensionality of intelligence.

In chapter 2, James Thompson, Kevin McGrew, and Bob Bruininks review the factor structure of adaptive and maladaptive behavior. They begin their chapter with an extensive review of the literature on adaptive behavior and then present the results of a factor analysis they completed of adaptive behavior data (86 samples) reported in 31 studies that used adaptive behavior instrument assessment of people with mental retardation. Based on that analysis, the authors conclude that:

- Adaptive behavior, as currently measured in existing instruments, is a multidimensional construct.
- Maladaptive behavior factors generally fall into the two broad categories of personal (intrapunitive) and social (extrapunitive) problem behaviors.
- The methodological factors of variable breadth (that is, subscales, item parcels, and items) contribute significantly to the variability in the number of adaptive or maladaptive factors identified in different studies.
- No single adaptive or maladaptive behavior instrument measures the complete range of adaptive and maladaptive behavior dimensions.

Based on these conclusions and a synthesis of existing adaptive behavior literature, the authors suggest that it is critical that future research be driven by conceptual models; without this conceptual organization, the continued isolated factoring of existing adaptive behavior instruments will not result in any "significant strides in understanding the constructs of adaptive and maladaptive behavior." Three heuristic models are then presented to stimulate conceptually driven research and scholarly discourse regarding adaptive behavior. These three models not only integrate the emerging hierarchical and multidimensional nature of both adaptive behavior and intelligence, but also relate the concepts of adaptive behavior and intelligence to the overarching notion of personal competence.

In chapter 3, Bob Schalock presents a possible future scenario related to the impact and implications for the field of mental retardation resulting from the currently changing conception, measurement, and use of the constructs of intelligence and adaptive behavior. The primary purpose of Dr. Schalock's chapter is to sensitize the reader to how the two primary components of mental retardation—intelligence and adaptive behavior—are merging, and what implications this merger might have on the future definition, measurement, and use of the mental retardation construct. The author suggests that the merging of the constructs of adaptive behavior and intelligence, along with the current ecological and functional perspectives on disability, requires a reconsideration of disability and mental retardation. Throughout the chapter, the author argues that if the concepts of intelligence and adaptive behavior are subsumed under the common framework of overall competence, we can implement a heuristic model of mental retardation that will better accommodate future ecological, functional, and accountability foci.

Two significant themes throughout this book are that (a) mental retardation should be viewed from a contextual perspective and (b) one cannot separate the changing conception of adaptive behavior from an analogous change in the conception of intelligence. Both notions are discussed in detail in chapter 4 by Steve Greenspan.

For readers who might not be aware of the currently popular notion of contextualism, its major aspects include: (a) an appreciation of the setting or context within which behavior occurs; (b) an emphasis on the reality of the active, ongoing, and changing process of becoming; (c) an appreciation for the study of social reality as it occurs in its everyday, practical state; (d) an understanding that individuals are active determiners of their own development and active selectors of their own setting; (e) and an emphasis on the "pragmatics" of life skills, knowledge, and expertise.

Throughout his chapter, Dr. Greenspan discusses the importance of understanding the context of behavior in determining the limits of one's competence and, by inference, the diagnosis of mental retardation. He describes further the recent use of contextualism as a guiding framework for research and clinical practice in the field of mental retardation. He concludes his chapter with a discussion of the ways in which the study and assessment of adaptive behavior could benefit from use of a contextualist perspective, using one aspect of social intelligence (credulity) as an example.

In chapter 5, Brian Bryant, Penny Crews Seay, and Diane Pedrotty Bryant describe the exciting trends in the use of assistive technology to enhance the adaptive functioning in people with mental retardation. The authors base their presentation and work on two important principles: (a) that variables related to independent living are closely related both to variables associated with adaptive behavior and to the 10 adaptive skill areas found in the 1992 AAMR definition of mental retardation, and (b) personal choice and assistive technology facilitate the attainment of skills related to adaptive behavior. Based on these two principles, the authors: (a) provide a brief introduction to the independent living movement and its relationship to adaptive behavior, (b) identify the relationship between personal choice and successful community integration, (c) discuss how assistive technology devices and services can be used by people with disabilities to live more independently, and (d) present and discuss a model for examining what tasks people do and identifies how adaptations can make such tasks possible.

Throughout part 1, the reader may sense the excitement of the current *zeitgeist* (mood of the time) as we look at where we were and where we might go with the concept of adaptive behavior and its measurement.

Key points to keep in mind in reading part 1:

- How has the concept of adaptive behavior changed during the last century?
- What do we now know about the factor structure of adaptive behavior that we did not know 10 years ago?
- How is adaptive behavior currently conceptualized?
- Why is contextualism such an important concept in how we define adaptive behavior and mental retardation?
- How close is the factor structure of adaptive behavior to the multidimensional nature of intelligence?

References

American Psychiatric Association. (1994). *Diagnostic and statistical manual of mental disorders* (4th ed.). Washington, DC: Author.

Grossman, H. J. (Ed.) (1973) *Manual on terminology and classification in mental retardation.* Washington, DC: American Association on Mental Deficiency.

Grossman, H. J. (Ed.) (1983). *Manual on terminology and classification in mental retardation.* Washington, DC: American Association on Mental Deficiency.

Luckasson, R., Coulter, D. L., Polloway, E. A., Reiss, S., Schalock, R. L., Snell, M. E., Spitalnik, D. M., Stark, J. A. (1992). *Mental retardation: Definition, classification, and systems of supports* (9th ed.). Washington, DC: American Association on Mental Retardation.

World Health Organization. (1992). *International classification of diseases* (10th ed.). Geneva: Author.

CHAPTER 1

Adaptive Behavior: A Historical Overview

KAZUO NIHIRA
University of California, Los Angeles

Introduction

In recent years, the concept of adaptive behavior that has been emphasized as being essential to the definition of mental retardation. It refers to "the effectiveness and degree with which the individual meets the standard of personal independence and social responsibility expected of his age and cultural group" (Grossman, 1973, p. 11). Although adaptive behavior has a long philosophical, literary, and medical history, its recent history in the field of mental retardation began in 1959 when the American Association on Mental Deficiency (AAMD) included the concept of adaptive behavior in the definition of mental retardation. Mental retardation was defined as "subaverage general intellectual functioning which originates during the developmental period and is associated with impairment in adaptive behavior" (Heber, p. 3). In the 1973 revision of the AAMD *Manual on Terminology and Classification*, even greater emphasis was placed on adaptive behavior. The manual defined mental retardation as "significantly subaverage intellectual functioning existing concurrently with deficits in adaptive behavior" (Grossman, p. 5).

The AAMD stressed that both IQ and adaptive behavior should be considered in defining mental retardation. This was a significant change from the exclusive dependence on the IQ measure in defining mental retardation for decades prior to 1960. Because of this dual criterion, a child with a low IQ who functioned well outside of school was not classified as mentally retarded. For example, a familiar phenomenon of that *zeitgeist* was the "6-hour [school-day] retarded child" who scored relatively low on IQ tests but had

learned to function adequately at home and in the neighborhood (President's Committee on Mental Retardation, 1970). According to the 1973 AAMD definition, such a child was not considered mentally retarded. The inclusion of adaptive behavior in the definition of mental retardation was an attempt to avoid labeling children who had IQs in the range of mental retardation but who were subsequently absorbed into the general population after the school years.

The AAMD definition did not survive unscathed or without criticisms, however. Some researchers argued that the definition implied a simplistic conception of human adaptation, and raised serious concern about operational difficulties in assessment of adaptive behavior (Baumeister & Muma, 1975); the amount of research activity related to the AAMD definition and adaptive behavior during the last two decades indicates appreciation of their concern.

Before addressing the impact of the adaptive behavior concept and its assessment in the field of mental retardation in recent history, it seems worthwhile to review how mental retardation was defined before the intelligence test was developed. Before the advent of the intelligence test movement around 1900, mental retardation was described in terms of what we now call adaptive behavior. Horton (1966) reported that Itard and Haslan (in 1819), Seguin (in 1837), Voisin (in 1843), Howe (in 1858), and Goddard (in 1914) all spoke about adaptive behavior, using terms such as "social competency," "skills training," "social norms," "the power of fending for one's self in life," and "adaptability to the environment." The relatively new intelligence test movement, in spite of its practical value for predicting school achievement, reinforced two age-old misconceptions regarding the nature of intelligence: (a) the unitary conception of intelligence and (b) the notion that intellectual ability is unchangeable throughout the life of an individual.

Adaptive Behavior Prior to the 1960s

Overreliance on the IQ score and misconceptions regarding the nature of IQ reinforced the notion of incurability and justification for custodial care of people with mental retardation during the first half of the 20th century. The first misconception, of monolithic intelligence, was given a scientific seal by the introduction of a single score for the measurement of intelligence. There is some recognition of the multiple aspects of intelligence as exemplified by the subscale systems of the *Wechsler Intelligence Scales* (Wechsler, 1981, 1991), but the multifaceted aspects of intelligence were all but lost in the more generally used composite scores. In practice, intelligence testing became merely a process for labeling individuals—mild, moderate, severe, and profound.

It should be noted that, in our recent history, mental deficiency has been considered a permanent condition. Doll (1941), for example, included constitutional origin, duration to adulthood, and essential incurability among his six criteria for mental deficiency. The development of the Intelligence Quotient (IQ), the expression of an individual's intelligence in terms of chronological age, appeared to have reinforced the second misconception, the immutability of intellectual ability throughout the life of an individual (i.e., the idea that once classified as mentally retarded, the individual remains retarded for life). The overreliance on IQ testing, coupled with the idea that mental retardation is essentially incurable, provided an implicit justification for custodial care of individuals with severe or profound retardation, and the life-long stigmatization of "special education" for individuals with mild

retardation. The misconceptions regarding the nature of intelligence, rather than IQ testing itself, strongly influenced the public's attitude toward mental retardation and seriously impeded needed changes in its remedial approaches.

The inclusion of adaptive behavior as part of its classification system of mental retardation gave the AAMD the distinction of reviving adaptive behavior as a relevant concept that broadened the very definition of mental retardation. In September 1964, the AAMD, in conjunction with Parsons State Hospital and Training Center, was awarded a grant from the National Institute of Mental Health to demonstrate the function of adaptive behavior, both as a psychiatric problem and as a means of establishing a new classification in mental retardation. The project yielded the *Adaptive Behavior Checklists* for children and for adults (Nihira, Foster, Shellhaas, & Leland, 1968), which was the predecessor of the AAMR *Adaptive Behavior Scale—Residential and Community Version* (Nihira, Leland, & Lambert, 1993) and the AAMR *Adaptive Behavior Scale—School Version* (Lambert, Nihira, & Leland, 1993). The adaptive behavior approach was originally intended to encourage one to look at the individuals with an eye toward remediation and prescriptive assessment, rather than merely classifying and labeling.

Adaptive Behavior During the 1960s

Several important social forces and trends during the 1960s stimulated the revival of the adaptive behavior approach. The 1960s were a decade of national awareness and concern for the treatment of individuals with mental retardation. Postwar economic prosperity helped shape public opinion that the federal government should assume greater responsibility for less-advantaged people. In 1961, President Kennedy appointed the first President's Committee on Mental Retardation; in February 1963, he recommended to the Congress "a national program to combat mental retardation." Never before had so many resources been focused on the problem of mental retardation. The inclusion of adaptive behavior in the AAMD definition of mental retardation increased the need for adaptive behavior instruments in routine assessment practices. In the climate of the 1960s, the definition and the assessment of adaptive behavior became part of the national effort and professional practice to provide rehabilitation training for individuals with mental retardation.

The concept and assessment of adaptive behavior provided the basis for describing the competencies of clients in specific behavioral terms. It also provided a basis for establishing training goals and programs, as well as for program evaluation. Adaptive behavior assessment offered a technical basis for implementing deinstitutionalization and community rehabilitation. The major contribution of the adaptive behavior approach during the 1960s was to provide socially relevant goals and aspirations for treatment and intervention efforts. In their historical review of adaptive behavior in assessment and intervention, Horn and Fuchs (1987) aptly stated, "We believe that, throughout history, when societies have displayed a willingness to develop treatment programs for mentally retarded people, there has been a concomitant increase in the use of the concept of adaptive behavior to help define the content of those intervention programs" (p. 11). The decade of the 1960s was the high point of adaptive behavior in the recent history of mental retardation.

Adaptive Behavior During the 1970s

The decade of the 1970s witnessed a major shift in national concern. Issues changed, from providing treatment for individuals with mental retardation to providing services that were in the best interest of the individuals and asking whether their legal rights were being violated. The principal ideologies of this period were normalization and its educational counterpart, *mainstreaming*. The assessment and training of adaptive behavior was integral to these principles, in that people with mental retardation must have the basic skills and awareness required to function in the least restrictive environment. To this end, considerable research efforts were devoted to the identification of skills needed for successful integration into the community. Literature of this period has been summarized in a number of sources (e.g., Meyers, Nihira, & Zetlin, 1979; Whitman & Scibak, 1979).

State and federal legislation implementing normalization and mainstreaming was enacted during this period. For example, California State Senate Bill 33, enacted in 1971, required that children shall have an evaluation of adaptive behavior, developmental history, cultural background, and school achievement along with a standard measure of intelligence before they can be assigned to special-education classes. Similar legislation was enacted in Florida, Texas, and North Carolina. Mainstreaming and normalization increased the need to assess and train behaviors that are important in the transition of individuals with handicaps into integrated learning and living environments.

In 1975, The Education for all Handicapped Children Act required that a state must establish nondiscriminatory testing procedures in the evaluation and placement of children with mental retardation. This legislation reflected an attempt to resolve the controversy regarding the appropriateness of the intelligence test and its use in making differential placements in public schools. The passage of this law created a national need to develop assessment instruments and testing procedures that assure nondiscriminatory testing. Central to the issue of nondiscriminatory assessment has been the use of procedures that avoid the disproportionate identification and placement of ethnic minority children in special-education classes. Within this context, adaptive behavior assessment has facilitated the fairness of placement decisions by identifying the social development of children outside the academic setting.

The assessment of adaptive behavior came to be viewd as part of the diagnostic solution for protecting potential EMR (educable mentally retarded) children from erroneous classification. Thus, adaptive behavior has become involved in the legal and educational controversy over IQ testing and its use in differential placements in public schools. In some states—California, for example, in the 1972 *Larry P. v. Riles* court case—the use of IQ testing for EMR placement has been prohibited altogether. In other states, legislation has mandated the inclusion of adaptive behavior appraisal as part of multidimensional evaluation for potential EMR children.

While the original intention for introducing the concept and measurement of adaptive behavior was for treatment and programming, rather than custodial care, for individuals with mental retardation, the use of adaptive behavior as a potential diagnostic tool in nondiscriminatory testing during the 1970s resulted in a second orientation: identification and labeling of school children for administrative purposes (Mercer, 1973). These two very different orientations (i.e., programming for treatment and identification for labeling) are of historical importance. What's more, they have had a profound effect upon subsequent development of the concept of adaptive behavior and scales for measuring it.

Adaptive Behavior During the 1980s

By the late 1970s, the controversies over IQ, adaptive behavior, and school classification moved from the court rooms to research. The 1980s witnessed a substantial body of research using adaptive behavior measures for subject descriptions in professional literature (Hawkins & Cooper, 1990). The number of adaptive behavior assessment instruments proliferated. In their review of adaptive behavior, Meyers et al. (1979) counted 136 checklists and scales of adaptive behavior. The proliferation of scales indicated the need for a variety of instruments

to assess adaptive behavior that have different values and meanings at different ages, for individuals having different types and degrees of disabilities, in different settings, and for different assessment objectives. The two different orientations (i.e., programming for treatment vs. identification for labeling) dictated the selection of different items and domains, as well as norm-referenced and criterion-referenced assessments.

During the 1980s, adaptive behavior assessment measures continued to be an effective means for developing instructional programs to prepare individuals for living in less-restrictive environments and structuring transitional programs (Silverman, Silver, Sersen, Lubin, & Schwartz, 1986). Using adaptive behavior scales to help make educationally relevant placement decisions has been troublesome, primarily because skills taught or assessed in special-education settings frequently fail to transfer to mainstream settings. The reader wanting more comprehensive reviews of the literature on the application of adaptive behavior assessment measures during this period should consult Harrison (1987), Horn and Fuchs (1987), and Witt and Martens (1984).

As adaptive behavior assessment has become more prominent, its shortcomings have been increasingly criticized. Some researchers have found adaptive behavior information to be too vague and of questionable validity for classification purposes (Zigler, Balla, & Hodapp, 1984) and of limited use at school (Witt & Martens, 1984). In opposition to the decades-old tradition of the AAMD definition of mental retardation, Zigler et al. proposed that mental retardation should be defined solely by subaverage performance on measured intellectual abilities. In spite of these criticisms, or perhaps because of them, the 1980s witnessed a substantial increase in the number of research efforts directed toward comprehensive understanding of the nature of adaptive behaviors, their structure, and their development.

The decade of the 1980s was very active with respect to investigation of the factor structure of adaptive behavior. A number of exploratory factor analyses conducted using different populations and different measures of adaptive behavior provided somewhat confusing results with regard to the number of factors, as well as the nature of each factor (Bruininks, McGrew, & Maruyama, 1988; Widaman, Gibbs, & Geary, 1987). A recent review by Widaman and McGrew (1996) proposes that the factor structure of adaptive behavior is hierarchical in nature—with broader or more general factors at high levels in the hierarchy, and narrower or more specific factors at the lower levels. The apparent disparities among factor analytic studies reported in the 1980s may suggest that the investigators were looking at different hierarchical levels of the factor structure of adaptive behavior.

Another significant topic of research in this decade was the investigation of convergent and discriminant validities of different scales of adaptive behavior. The nature of traits or domains common to different scales of adaptive behavior have been identified in the investigation of convergent and discriminant validities. For example, applying Campbell and Fiske's criteria, Middleton, Keene, and Brown (1990) reported that the domains of personal living skills, communication skills, and community living skills were assessed commonly in the *Vineland Adaptive Behavior Scale* (Doll, 1953). Researchers and practitioners in the field should be given information regarding both commonalities among different scales of adaptive behavior and the uniqueness of each scale. Such information should lead to consolidation and more parsimonious operational models of adaptive behavior.

Investigations of developmental trends in adaptive behavior during the 1980s provided important information for understanding the nature of adaptive behavior. Cross-sectional and longitudinal studies on adaptive behavior indicated clearly differing developmental

projectories in adaptive behavior for different degrees of mental retardation. Furthermore, different domains of adaptive behavior were characterized by differing developmental trajectories. For example, individuals with mild levels of mental retardation show rapid development in personal living skills during early childhood, whereas communication skills and community living skills continue to develop during adolescence and young adulthood (Nihira, 1976; Janicki & Jacobson, 1986; Eyman & Widaman, 1987). These developmental studies of adaptive behavior helped us identify specific requirements for continuing services and supports across different ages and degrees of mental retardation.

The 1980s also witnessed some conceptual developments related to adaptive behavior, as well as controversy regarding the definition of mental retardation. Some researchers called for a broader conceptualization of intelligence by including practical or everyday intelligence in the definition of mental retardation (Greenspan, 1979, 1981; Sternberg, 1984). The revival of social intelligence in the definitional controversy is reminiscent of Doll's effort (Doll, 1966) to define mental deficiency on the basis of demonstrated social incompetence. The controversy over the definition of mental retardation is intricately related to the age-old controversy over the definition of intelligence. It appears, however, that it will be some time before practical or everyday intelligence can be defined and assessed for classification purposes.

Conclusion

Throughout recent history, with the exception of the first half of the 20th century, adaptive behavior (or social competency) has been integral to the definition, diagnosis, and treatment of people with mental retardation. The concept of adaptive behavior received special attention during the 1960s because of national awareness and concern for the treatment of individuals with mental retardation. In the 1970s, the assessment of adaptive behavior became a part of the controversy over IQ, educational placement, and the definition of mental retardation. This controversy resulted in a proliferation of adaptive behavior measures. The 1980s witnessed a number of interesting developments in adaptive behavior research. Research in construct validity, based on factor analysis and convergent and discriminant analysis, was an attempt to consolidate different assessment measures of adaptive behavior and a search for a unified structural theory of adaptive behavior. Research in developmental processes of adaptive behavior expanded our understanding of the nature of adaptive behavior domains in terms of human development. Such research helps us identify specific requirements of the process of service delivery for evaluation, functional assessment, and program development across different ages and degrees of mental retardation. Research into a broader conception of intelligence may be promising as an alternative to current adaptive behavior approaches, although the operational use of such a concept of intelligence would appear to be years away.

References

Baumeister, A. A., & Muma, J. R. (1975). On defining mental retardation. *Journal of Special Education*, 9, 293-306.

Bruininks, R., McGrew, K., & Maruyama, G. (1988). Structure of adaptive behavior in samples with and without mental retardation. *American Journal of Mental Retardation*, 3, 265-272.

Doll, E. A. (1941). The essentials of an inclusive concept of mental deficiency. *American Journal of Mental Deficiency*, 46, 214-219.

Doll, E. A. (1953). Measurement of Social Competence: A Manual for the Vineland Social Maturity Scale. Minneapolis: Educational Test Bureau.

Doll, E. A. (1966). Recognition of mental retardation in the school-age child. In I. Philips (Ed.), *Prevention and treatment of mental retardation* (pp. 59-68). New York: Basic Books.

Eyman, R. K., & Widaman, K. F. (1987). Lifespan development of institutionalized and community-based mentally retarded persons, revisited. *American Journal of Mental Deficiency*, 91, 559-569.

Greenspan, S. (1979). Social intelligence in the retarded. In N. R. Ellis (Ed.), *Handbook of mental deficiency: Psychological theory and research* (2nd ed., pp. 483-531). Hillsdale, NJ: Lawrence Erlbaum.

Greenspan, S. (1981). Social competence and handicapped individuals: Implications of a proposed model. *Advances in Special Education*, 3, 41-82.

Grossman, H. J. (Ed.). (1973). *Manual on terminology and classification in mental retardation* (Rev. ed.). Washington, DC: American Association on Mental Deficiency.

Harrison, P. L. (1987). Research with adaptive behavior scales. *Journal of Special Education*, 21, 37-68.

Hawkins, G. D., & Cooper, D. H. (1990). Adaptive behavior measures in mental retardation research: Subject description in AJMD/AJMR articles. *American Journal of Mental Retardation*, 94, 654-660.

Heber, R. A. (1961). A manual on terminology and classification on mental retardation (2nd ed.). *American Journal of Mental Deficiency Monograph*, 65.

Horn, E., & Fuchs, D. (1987). Using adaptive behavior in assessment and intervention: An overview. *Journal of Special Education*, 21, 11-26.

Horton, L. (1966, May). The historical development of the concept of adaptive behavior. Paper presented at the annual meeting of American Association on Mental Deficiency, Chicago.

Janicki, M. P., & Jacobson, J. W. (1986). Generation trends in sensory, physical, and behavioral abilities among older mentally retarded persons. *American Journal of Mental Deficiency*, 90, 490-500.

Lambert, N., Nihira, K., & Leland, H. (1993). AAMR *adaptive behavior scale—school version* (2nd edition). Austin, TX: Pro-Ed.

Larry P. v. Riles, 343 F. Supp. 1306 (N.D. Cal. 1972).

Mercer, J. R. (1973). *Labeling the mentally retarded: Clinical and social system perspectives on mental retardation*. Berkeley: University of California Press.

Meyers, C. E., Nihira, K., & Zetlin, A. (1979). The measurement of adaptive behavior. In N. R. Ellis (Ed.), *Handbook of mental deficiency: Psychological theory and research* (2nd ed., pp. 431-481). Hillsdale, NJ: Lawrence Erlbaum.

Middleton, H. A., Keene, R. C., & Brown, G. W. (1990). Convergent and discriminant validities of the scales of independent behavior and the revised Vineland Adaptive Behavior Scales. *American Journal of Mental Retardation, 94,* 669–673.

Nihira, K. (1976). Dimensions of adaptive behavior in institutionalized mentally retarded children and adults: Developmental perspective. *American Journal of Mental Deficiency, 81,* 215-226.

Nihira, K., Foster, R., Shellhaas, M., & Leland, H. (1968). *Adaptive behavior checklist.* Washington, DC: American Association on Mental Deficiency.

Nihira, K., Leland, H., & Lambert, N. (1993). AAMR *adaptive behavior scale—residential and community version* (2nd ed.). Austin, TX: Pro-Ed.

President's Committee on Mental Retardation. (1970). Mental Retardation: 1970. Washington, DC: U.S. Government Printing Office.

Silverman, W. P., Silver, E. J., Sersen, E. A., Lubin, R. A., & Schwartz, A. A. (1986). Factors related to adaptive behavior changes among a mentally retarded, physically disabled person. *American Journal of Mental Deficiency, 90,* 651-658.

Sternberg, R. J. (1984). Macrocomponents and microcomponents of intelligence: Some proposed loci of mental retardation. In P. H. Brooks, R. Sperber, & C. McCauley (Eds.), *Learning and cognition in the mentally retarded* (pp. 89-114). Hillsdale, NJ: Lawrence Erlbaum.

Wechsler, D. (1981) *Manual for the Wechsler adult intelligence scale—revised.* New York: Psychological Corporation.

Wechsler, D. (1991). WISC-III *manual.* San Antonio, TX: Psychological Corporation.

Whitman, T. L., & Scibak, J. W. (1979). Behavior modification research with severely and profoundly retarded. In N. R. Ellis (Ed.), *Handbook of mental deficiency: Psychological theory and research* (2nd ed., pp. 289-340). Hillsdale, NJ: Lawrence Erlbaum.

Widaman, K. F., Gibbs, K. W., & Geary, D. C. (1987). Structure of adaptive behavior: I. Replication across fourteen samples of nonprofoundly mentally retarded people. *American Journal of Mental Deficiency, 91,* 348-360.

Widaman, K. F., & McGrew, K. S. (1996). The structure of adaptive behavior. In J. W. Jacobson & J. Mulick (Eds.), *Manual of diagnosis and professional practice in mental retardation* (pp. 97-110). Washington, DC: American Association on Mental Retardation.

Witt, J., & Martens, B. (1984). Adaptive behavior: Tests and assessment issues. *School Psychology Review, 13,* 478-484.

Zigler, E., Balla, D., & Hodapp, R. (1984). On the definition and classification of mental retardation. *American Journal of Mental Deficiency, 89,* 215-230.

CHAPTER 2

Adaptive and Maladaptive Behavior: Functional and Structural Characteristics

JAMES R. THOMPSON
Illinois State University

KEVIN S. McGREW
St. Cloud State University

ROBERT H. BRUININKS
University of Minnesota

Introduction

Concepts associated with adaptive behavior have been presented and discussed since the earliest study of mental retardation. Pioneers in the field of mental retardation, including Itard, Seguin, Voisin, and Howe, referred to concepts associated with adaptive behavior long before the phrase was defined formally and incorporated into the definition of mental retardation (Lambert, 1978). Early legal and professional definitions of mental retardation typically referred to deficits in learning and community adaptation (Bruininks, Thurlow, & Gilman, 1987).

Despite the more recent explicit inclusion of adaptive behavior in the definition of mental retardation and the proliferation of adaptive behavior assessment instruments over the past four decades, there is still no consensus regarding what the construct represents. In the 1992 AAMR definition and classification manual (Luckasson et al.), adaptive behavior was said to comprise 10 specific *adaptive skill areas*: communication, self-care, home living, social skills, community use, self-direction, health and safety, functional academics, leisure, and work. In contrast, and perhaps in response to the AAMR manual, the American Psychological Association published a manual of diagnosis and professional practice that presented *adaptive functioning* as a unidimensional construct (Jacobson & Mulick, 1996). Still others have argued that adaptive behavior criteria should be abandoned altogether for purposes of definition and classification, because confusion over the construct has rendered it meaningless and invalid (e.g., Clausen, 1972; Zigler, Balla, & Hodapp, 1984). More recently, Greenspan (1997) proposed dropping both adaptive behavior and the traditional operational use of intelligence (i.e., the IQ score) from definitional criteria. He suggested a mental retardation definition based on a "tripartite model" of intelligence, where intelligence comprises social, practical, and conceptual dimensions. While practical and social intelligence have traditionally been imbedded in adaptive behavior, in Greenspan's model social, practical, and conceptual intelligence are all included under the umbrella of intellectual functioning.

Whether adaptive behavior is multidimensional or unidimensional and can be separated from intelligence or a concept whose key features are best conceptualized within a broader domain of personal competency, it is evident that the extent to which "individuals meet the standards of personal independence and social responsibility expected for age and cultural group" (Grossman, 1983, p. 1) lies at the essence of mental retardation. While history shows that the conception and operational use of adaptive behavior are in continual states of change, history also reveals that adaptive behavior has remained central to identifying, instructing, and supporting people with mental retardation.

The past two decades have seen an explosion of interest and research on adaptive behavior. In many ways, the recent research on adaptability and mental retardation is reminiscent of the intense research on the construct of intelligence during the first half of the 20th century, when psychologists developed and applied instruments and theories, including increasingly complex statistical methodologies, to map and define intelligence. The early theories defined a simple structure of intelligent behavior, with primary emphasis on a broad, general (g) factor (cf. Spearman, 1904; Thurstone, 1938, 1947; Thurstone & Thurstone, 1941). Through decades of research, the construct of intelligence was refined and differentiated (cf. Carroll, 1993; Cattell, 1971; Guilford, 1967; Horn & Noll, 1997; Vernon, 1956). Much of the progress regarding cognition and the construct of intelligence can be traced to increased precision in measurement and advances in statistical methodology.

Similarly, the past two decades have witnessed increased refinement in the assessment of adaptive behavior and the application of more complex conceptual analyses and statistical procedures. We feel that further research and development will lead to refinement in theory, conceptual models, and delineation of meaning regarding adaptive behavior. These advances in measurement and research will likely lead to a broader and deeper understanding of human adaptation and a much broader and more precise definition of adaptive behavior.

The purpose of this chapter is to review the literature regarding the factor structure of adaptive behavior and provide recommendations to guide future research. Specifically, we will explain statistical research methods used to complete factor studies and summarize literature pertaining to the structure of adaptive behavior. Additionally, we will analyze factor studies completed over the past 30 years. Finally, we will discuss directions for future research in light of past findings and current trends.

The Search for Structure

Defining adaptive behavior has challenged researchers for years. Coulter and Morrow (1978) compared 10 definitions of adaptive behavior published between 1968 and 1976. While noting that no two definitions were exactly alike, they concluded there were considerable similarities between the sources. Bruininks et al. (1987) captured the essence of adaptive behavior in reporting that the term describes the "achievement of skills needed for successful adaptation and often the reduction or elimination of behaviors that interfere with effective adjustment in typical environments" (p. 73). Emphasis has consistently been placed on: a person's independent functioning in regard to physical needs and community participation, an individual's ability to maintain responsible social relationships, and an individual's display of behaviors within the context of his or her age and culture. There has also been general agreement that adaptive behavior and intelligence are separate but related constructs. Whereas adaptive behavior reflects an individual's typical, everyday behavior, intelligence reflects a person's abstract reasoning skills and thought processes (Coulter & Morrow, 1978; Grossman, 1983; Meyers, Nihira, & Zetlin, 1979).

Despite a relatively high level of agreement in defining adaptive behavior, there has been little consensus regarding its structure. In reviewing 13 adaptive behavior assessment scales, Holman and Bruininks (1985) identified five major classifications of content areas. These were self-help skills and personal appearance, communication, consumer skills, domestic skills, and vocational skills. Additional content areas included physical development or gross motor skills, community orientation, cognitive functioning, and health care and personal welfare. In similar reviews Meyers et al. (1979) and Kamphaus (1987) noted comparable patterns of content areas. Holman and Bruininks (1985) reported considerable variation among instruments in terms of content areas and the extent of coverage within particular areas; they concluded that "coverage of adaptive behavior skills in available tests is often uneven and quite limited" (p. 100).

The incongruity of content in the instruments that purportedly measure the same construct is linked to the absence of a clear theoretical foundation concerning the structure of adaptive behavior. Thus, there are several compelling theoretical and practical reasons why identifying psychometrically valid domains of adaptive behavior is desirable to advance research and practice. These include:

- *The need objectively to differentiate individuals by disability categories in order to provide them special assistance and support (e.g. special education, supported employment services, etc.).* Clear and psychometrically defensible criteria regarding what constitutes adaptive behavior deficits would produce fewer false positives and negatives when assessing individuals for purposes of eligibility, classification, and access to services. Decreasing false positives would reduce the overrepresentation of individuals from minority populations who receive services as individuals with mental retardation. Decreasing false negatives would enable many individuals to receive support who currently "fall through the cracks" of the service system. Furthermore, a more precise understanding of the structure of adaptive behavior would enable policy makers to make funding decisions based on more definitive population estimates and a more explicit understanding of the types and nature of support services people with mental retardation truly need.
- *The need to provide planning teams with a clearer understanding of human development.* A valid conceptual structure would provide planning teams with an empirically defensible basis on which to prioritize educational and habilitation goals and activities for individuals. Areas of relative strength could be enhanced and capitalized on while areas of relative weakness could be targeted for improvement and support.
- *The need to give service providers a sound means to evaluate the effectiveness of programs and investigate the efficacy of interventions.* Identifying empirically supported, essential domains of adaptive behavior would enable educators and adult provider organizations to monitor the progress of individuals and make decisions regarding their program's effectiveness. Additionally, areas for program improvement and staff development could be more effectively identified.

While identifying and describing valid domains of adaptive behavior has much to offer the field of mental retardation and developmental disabilities, accepting erroneous domains that are not truly distinct from one another can do significant harm. As Thackery (1991) pointed out, it is critical that "interpretive hypotheses be formulated within the context of the known psychometric properties of the assessment instrument" (p. 214). Assessment decisions based on empirically insupportable domains will lead to inconsistent application of eligibility criteria and unequal treatment across populations. Moreover, education and training goals based on false domains run the risk of being totally misguided. Finally, research efforts based on faulty domains may be fundamentally flawed and ultimately useless. For example, research findings showing that an intervention resulted in the development of adaptive behavior skills in the domains of community use, leisure, and work would be helpful if these three domains were independent of one another. However, if the items measuring the three domains were measures of a single adaptive behavior domain, the results of the research would be misleading.

Factor Analysis: The Primary Structural Tool

In his review of conceptual and psychometric issues in the assessment of adaptive behavior, Kamphaus (1987) called for additional factor analytic research using a large variety of adaptive behavior scales; if certain factors consistently emerged from data collected across a variety of scales and with a variety of populations, there would be a scientific basis on which to propose a structure for the adaptive behavior construct. Like intelligence (general (*g*) versus multiple intelligences), it is conceivable that adaptive behavior may be unidimensional or consist of many dimensions.

A systematic review of factor analytic studies of adaptive behavior that have been completed over the past 30 years is provided in a later section of this chapter. To appreciate the factor analytic research that has been completed in the adaptive behavior area, the reader needs a basic understanding of the assumptions underlying factor analysis.

Factor analysis is based on the premise that there are variables of theoretical interest that cannot be directly observed. Information concerning unobservable variables, typically referred to as latent factors or common factors, must be obtained indirectly by examining their effects on observed variables, such as items or subscales on an adaptive behavior scale. The fundamental assumption of factor analysis is that the covariation (i.e., shared variance) among observed variables is due to latent factor(s) that the observed variables have in common (Harman, 1976; Long, 1983).

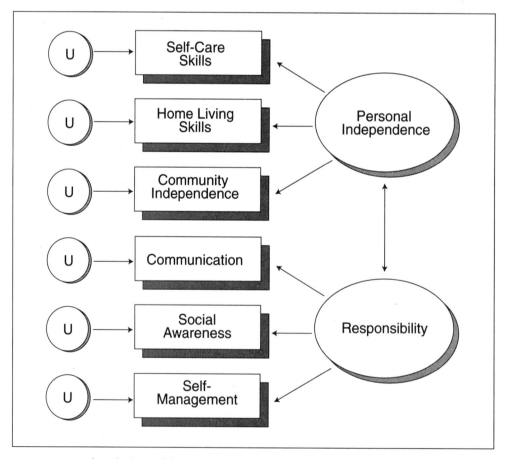

Figure 2.1. *Hypothetical adaptive behavior factors and variables.*

Table 2.1
Factor Analytic Studies Included in Review

Source	Scale	Level	Number/Type of Samples
Levin & Elzey (1968)	SFVCS	Item	1 – Adults With MR
Nihira (1978)	ABS-Reg	Item	2 – Children With MR 1 – Adults With MR
Sparrow & Cicchetti (1978)	BRIR	Item	1 – Children With MR
Reynolds (1981)	PCS	Item	1 – Adults With MR
Silverman, Silver, Lubin, & Sersen (1983)	MDPSBS	Item	2 – Children With MR 2 – Adults With MR
Matson, Epstein, & Cullinan (1984)	BPC	Item	1 – Children With MR 1 – Children Without MR
Sparrow & Cicchetti (1984)	BIRD	Item	1 – Children With MR
Aman, Richmond, Stewart, Bell, & Kissel (1987)	ABC	Item	2 – Adults With MR
Newton & Sturmey (1988)	ABC	Item	1 – Adults With MR
Bihm & Poindexter (1991)	ABC	Item	1 – Adults With MR
Freund & Reiss (1991)	ABC	Item	2 – Children With MR
Rojahn & Helsel (1991)	ABC	Item	1 – Children With MR
Marshburn & Aman (1992)	ABC	Item	1 – Children With MR
Aman, Burrow, & Wolford (1995)	ABC	Item	1 – Adults With MR
Nihira (1976)	ABS-Reg	Parcel	6 – Children With MR 2 – Adults With MR
Widaman, Gibbs, & Geary (1987)	CDER	Parcel	6 – Children With MR 8 – Adults With MR
Nihira (1969a)	ABCL	Subscale	1 – Adults With MR
Nihira (1969b)	ABCL	Subscale	3 – Children With MR
Owens & Bowling (1970)	PAR	Subscale	1 – Children With MR
Guarnaccia (1976)	ABS-Reg	Subscale	1 – Adults With MR
Lambert & Nicoll (1976)	ABS-Psv	Subscale	2 – Children With MR 1 – Children Without MR
Hug, Barclay, Collins, & Lamp (1978)	PAR	Subscale	1 – Children Without MR
Cunningham & Presnall (1978)	ABS-Reg	Subscale	1 – Adults With MR
Katz-Garris, Hadley, Garris, & Barnhill (1980)	ABS-Reg	Subscale	1 – Adults With MR
Song, Jones, Lippert, Metzgen, Miller, & Borreca (1984)	WBRS	Subscale	1 – Children & Adults With MR 1 – Children Without MR

Continued on next page

Source	Scale	Level	Number/Type of Samples
Millsap, Thackery, & Cook (1987)	ABIC	Subscale	1 – Children (disability status unclear)
Bruininks, McGrew, & Maruyama (1988)	SIB	Subscale	1 – Children With MR 1 – Adults With MR 4 – Children Without MR 1 – Adults Without MR
Silverstein, Wothke, & Slabaugh (1988)	MDPSBS	Subscale	1 – Children & Adults With MR
McGrew, Ittenbach, & Bruininks (1989)	ICAP-PBS	Subscale	6 – Children With MR 6 – Adults With MR
Thackery (1991)	CTAB	Subscale	3 – Children With MR 3 – Adults With MR
Widaman, Stacy, & Borthwick-Duffy (1993)	CDER	Subscale	1 – Adults With MR

Note. Scale Abbreviations: SFVCS = *San Francisco Vocational Competency Scale*; ABS = AAMD *Adaptive Behavior Scale* (*Reg* = Regular, *Psv* = Public School Version); BRIR = *Behavior Rating Inventory for the Retarded*; PCS = *Personal Competency Scale*; MDPSBS = *Minnesota Developmental Programming System Behavioral Scales*; BPC = *Behavior Problem Checklist*; BIRD = *Behavior Inventory for Rating Development*; ABC = *Aberrant Behavior Checklist*; CDER = *Client Development Evaluation Report*; ABCL = *Adaptive Behavior Checklist*; PAR = *Preschool Attainment Record*; WBRS = *Wisconsin Behavior Rating Scale*; SIB = *Scales of Independent Behavior*; ICAP-PBS = *Inventory for Client and Agency Planning—Problem Behavior Scales*; CTAB = *Comprehensive Test of Adaptive Behavior*.

According to Harman, the chief aim of factor analysis is to "attain scientific parsimony or economy of description" (p. 4).

Factor analytic studies are completed by collecting data on a sample population and by applying a sequential series of statistical procedures to the data to identify variables that cluster together (i.e., are highly correlated with one another). A good factor model is parsimonious and accounts for a significant proportion of the covariance among the variables comprising a data set.

The factor analytic model is illustrated in Figure 2.1 with hypothetical factors and variables related to adaptive behavior. The rectangles represent observed variables (i.e., items or subscales from an adaptive behavior scale) while latent factors (i.e., dimensions of adaptive behavior) are represented by ovals. The arrows emerging from the factors to the observed variables indicate causation.

In factor analysis, it is assumed that an underlying factor/dimension *causes* perfor-

mance on the observed variables. In Figure 2.1, variables related to self-care skills (e.g., behaviors involving grooming, toileting, dressing), home living skills (e.g., behaviors involving household cleaning, food preparation, clothing care), and community independence (e.g., behaviors associated with travel around the community, use of public facilities, vocational skills) are highly interrelated. That is, in most instances someone who is relatively strong in self-help skills also tends to be relatively strong in home living skills and relatively strong in community independence. Therefore, it is assumed that self-help skills, home living skills, and community independence are all related to an underlying factor, which in the example is labeled "personal independence." In this case, personal independence might be defined as an individual's self-sufficiency in caring for personal needs, maintaining a household, and using community resources.

Figure 2.1 also shows that while behaviors related to self-care, home living, and community independence all share a common factor, they have little relationship to behaviors associated with communication (e.g., receptive and expressive language, interpersonal communication skills), social awareness (e.g., social amenities, sexual behavior, group participation skills), or self-management (e.g., personal safety, scheduling and time management, self-direction). However, communication, social awareness, and self-management are all highly correlated with one another. The underlying factor assumed to be responsible for the relationship among performance in these areas is here labeled "responsibility." This may be defined as the extent to which an individual is able to fulfill the interpersonal and social expectations necessary to interact and participate with others in society.

The small circles in Figure 2.1 represent unique (i.e., residual) variance. Unique variance comprises specific variance and random measurement error variance. Specific variance is the portion of the *observed* variance that is *not* accounted for by the common factors but can be reliably measured (Harman, 1976). It is important to note that unique variance is *not* related to the broader factor structure. Thus, in this example, the unique variance associated with self-care skills is variance that has nothing to do with the personal independence factor or any other factor in the model.

Factors may or may not be correlated with one another. (The factor correlation is represented by the two-headed curved arrow in Figure 2.1.) However, highly correlated factors *may* indicate that the factors do not represent independent dimensions. In such cases, a model may be questionable (Long, 1983).

There are several variations of factor analysis (e.g., maximum-likelihood factoring, weighted and unweighted least squares methods, image factor analysis, etc.), each with different purposes and strengths. While discussion of these methods is beyond the scope of this chapter, it is important to note

that different methods of analysis can provide support for different factor structures. Therefore, decisions regarding which method to employ must be made prior to the analysis and be based on the type of data and nature of the research questions. For example, the measurement level of the variables, the use of a correlation or covariance matrix, the sample size, and the need to perform statistical tests must all be considered prior to selecting a method to extract factors. Of course, due to the ease by which today's computers enable the completion of factor analysis, researchers must refrain from simply switching from method to method in hopes of finding a factor structure that corresponds to a preconceived hypothesis (Harman, 1976; Kim & Mueller, 1978a, 1978b).

Factor analysis is typically divided into exploratory and confirmatory procedures. The key distinctions between these two procedures are embedded in the differing purposes for which they are used and the underlying assumptions associated with each method. Exploratory methods provide a means by which to investigate the underlying factor structure when there is little basis for hypothesizing the parameters or structure of a model. Exploratory methods are especially valuable in the early stages of theory building and measurement development. Jöreskog and Sörbom (1993) reported that "The results of an exploratory analysis may have heuristic and suggestive value and may generate hypotheses which are capable of more objective testing by other multivariate methods" (p. 22).

The primary weakness of the exploratory approach stems from the wide range of models that can be obtained. Because there are no constraints placed on model parameters, researchers run the risk of discovering statistically plausible solutions that are theoretically and logically implausible (Kim & Mueller, 1978a; Long, 1983).

The limitations posed by the atheoretical nature of exploratory factor analysis can be overcome through the application of confirmatory methods. Long (1983) reports that confirmatory procedures require researchers to specify any or all of the following four restrictions prior to analyzing data: "(1) which pairs of common factors are correlated, (2) which observed variables are affected by which common factors, (3) which observed variables are affected by a unique factor, and (4) which pairs of unique factors are correlated" (p. 12).

Restrictions, specified by researchers in advance of the analyses, are based on hypotheses developed through a review of prior research and/or theory. The more restrictions imposed, the more rigorous the test. Confirmatory factor analysis procedures yield a variety of statistical tests based on the chi-square statistic to determine whether the sample data are consistent with the imposed restrictions and the a priori model (Long, 1983).

The Past: A Glance Back at Prior Factor Analytic Research

For nearly 30 years, researchers have used factor analytic methods to identify scientifically defensible dimensions of adaptive behavior. While this line of research has not progressed to the point of providing relatively definitive conclusions regarding the structure of adaptive behavior (as can be found in the area of intelligence; see Carroll, 1993), there is sufficient convergence of evidence from these investigations to provide an empirical basis on which theoretical models of adaptive behavior can be proposed.

Meyers, Nihira, and Zetlin (1979) Review

The first published review of factor analytic research in adaptive behavior was completed by Meyers et al. (1979). They reviewed eight factor analytic studies published prior to 1977. The samples in the studies were all composed of children and adults with mental retardation, except for the Lambert and Nicoll (1976) study, which included one sample of children without mental retardation. People who lived in their home communities and those who lived in institutional settings were represented in these samples, although most studies used samples from large residential facilities. Data from four separate adaptive behavior scales were represented.

Meyers et al. (1979) concluded that "no evidence exists that adaptive behavior can be described as a general or unitary trait. It would appear inappropriate to describe a subject in terms of only a single score that is secured on a broad-ranged instrument" (p. 465). They further concluded that adaptive behavior consisted of an adaptive domain and a maladaptive domain. Within the adaptive domain there were two factors—autonomy and responsibility. *Autonomy* encompassed behaviors related to personal independence and self-sufficiency, while *responsibility* included behaviors related to interpersonal skills and competence in a variety of social interactions. Within the maladaptive domain there was support for separate social and personal maladaptation factors. *Social maladaptation* included punitive, antisocial problem behaviors that were directed toward others or the environment. *Personal maladaptation* included punitive problem behaviors directed toward oneself.

In a special issue of the *Journal of Special Education* devoted to the subject of adaptive behavior (Harrison & Kamphaus, 1987; McCarver & Campbell, 1987), it was noted that the Meyers et al. conclusion that adaptive behavior was a multidimensional construct was not universally accepted. This observation is still correct today. While there is general agreement that an adaptive domain can be distinguished from a maladaptive domain, support for both unidimensional and multidimensional factor structures within each of these domains can be found in relatively recent as well as more dated literature (cf. Arndt, 1981; Lambert & Nicoll, 1976; Thackery, 1991; Widaman, Gibbs, & Geary, 1987).

McGrew and Bruininks (1989) Review

McGrew and Bruininks (1989) completed a more recent review of factor analytic research in adaptive behavior. Because they were interested in the theoretical factor structure of adaptive behavior, McGrew and Bruininks (1989) limited their review to studies that (a) identified factors without imposing any prespecified constraints on the factor structure and (b) included at least six variables for analysis. They located 16 studies that met these criteria.

McGrew and Bruininks (1989) found substantial variability in the number of factors identified by different researchers. They concluded that much of the variability was due to the measurement level of the factored variables. *Item level* studies were investigations where individual items were the unit of analysis. *Parcel studies* factored composite variables comprised of only a small number of items (i.e., an average of 5 or fewer per parcel). *Subscale studies* factored multivariate variables that averaged six or more items per unit of analysis. It was noted that item studies included a far greater number of variables for analyses than did the parcel studies. Likewise, parcel studies factored more variables than did subscale studies. McGrew and Bruininks concluded that "the highly related (and confounded) characteristics of the number of adaptive variables and measurement level appeared to account for almost all of the variance in the number of adaptive factors identified across studies" (p. 69).

Because factor analytic studies composed of individual items and parcel items tend to produce false factors (Kim & Mueller, 1978b; Thorndike, 1982), McGrew and Bruininks (1989) chose to focus on the subscale studies in drawing conclusions regarding the factor structure of adaptive behavior. They concluded there was considerable support for a *personal independence* factor and tentative support for separate responsibility, functional academic/cognitive, vocational/community, and physical development factors. McGrew and Bruininks acknowledged that item and parcel studies would be useful in investigating a hierarchical model where "specific skills (items) . . . reflect a smaller number of more general skills (item parcels), which in turn reflect a smaller number of more general traits (subscales), which in turn all reflect general adaptive functioning" (p. 69).

Widaman, Borthwick-Duffy, and Little (1991) Review

Widaman et al. (1991) focused on issues concerning sample characteristics, number and psychometric properties of variables, factoring methods, and findings of factor analytic studies in their literature review. They argued against focusing exclusively on the measurement level or breadth of adaptive behavior factors when reviewing factor analytic literature. They also indicated that sample size, the nature and scope of variables analyzed, and the analytic methods employed had substantial influence on the factor solutions derived from adaptive behavior data. While acknowledging that "there is as yet no final consensus on the dimensional structure of adaptive behavior" (p. 16), they concluded that "the results of the factor analyses of indices of adaptive behavior seem to support fairly strongly the presence of multiple factors for the domain" (p. 18). Furthermore, they stated "it is likely that the structure of the adaptive behavior domain is similar in form to the structure usually posited for the domain of mental abilities—a structure that is hierarchical in nature, with broader or more general factors at higher levels in the hierarchy and narrower or more specific factors at lower levels" (p. 18). For example, they suggested that the four adaptive behavior factors (i.e., motor development, independent living skills, cognitive competence, social competence) could be related to a higher-order personal independence factor and that the two maladaptive factors (i.e., social maladaptation, personal maladaptation) could be related to a higher-order general maladaptation factor.

Widaman and McGrew (1996) APA Review

The most recent review of findings on the structure of adaptive behavior was published in 1996. In their review, Widaman and McGrew cautioned against ignoring the findings of item-level studies, as this could mask the presence of lower-stratum factors in a hierarchical model. They concluded that there was strong support for a multiple factor structure of adaptive behavior. The four domains with the strongest support were "a) motor and physical competence; b) independent living skills, daily living skills, or practical intelligence; c) cognitive competence, communication, or conceptual intelligence; and d) social competence or social intelligence" (p. 109). They recommended that future researchers focus on identifying a hierarchical factor structure and noted that such a structure would provide converging evidence for seemingly contradictory research findings regarding unidimensional and multidimensional models.

Widaman and McGrew (1996) also suggested that the integration and synthesis of future research regarding the structure of adaptive behavior could be enhanced if researchers would agree on a set of unambiguous terminology and use the terminology consistently when reporting findings and conclusions. They noted that different terms are sometimes used to convey the same information and similar terms are used to convey different information.

The Present: Reexamining and Extending the Prior Research

Review Methodology

Because it has been several years since factor analytic studies were systematically reviewed, we completed an extension of the 1989 McGrew and Bruininks. The procedures for this review were as follows:

- Copies of studies were located through an electronic search of the ERIC (1966 to July 1997) and PsychInfo (1967 to September 1997) databases using the following key words: *behavioral assessment, factor analysis, factor structure, factorial validity, measurement,* and *mental retardation.* An ancestral search (Cooper, 1989) of the reference lists from articles identified through the electronic searches was also completed.

- Studies were selected that used an adaptive behavior assessment instrument that had been factored either on at least one sample of people with mental retardation or on a sample where the disability composition was unclear, but where the scale was clearly designed to be used with people with mental retardation. Studies that did not meet these criteria were excluded. For example, The Harvey, et al. (1997) analysis of the *Social-Adaptive Functioning Evaluation* (SAFE) was excluded, because data from this instrument had been factored only on a sample of individuals with schizophrenia.

- Only studies that factored six or more variables were included in the review, because at least six variables are needed to produce a two-factor solution (Kim & Muller, 1978a). Because studies (e.g., Arndt, 1981) with fewer than six variables cannot produce a valid multifactor solution, these studies were not considered helpful in identifying the extent of empirical evidence for competing factor structures.

- The individual samples reported in each study were treated as separate units of analysis. Samples were coded based on the measurement level of the variable used in the factor analysis. Item studies factored single items; item parcel studies factored composite variables that averaged 5 or fewer per unit of analysis; subscale studies factored composite variables that were comprised of six or more items per unit of analysis.

This review included the 31 studies listed in Table 2.1. The 13 studies in bold type were new (i.e., were not included in McGrew & Bruininks, 1989). In total, data from 86 samples were analyzed (34 more than McGrew & Bruininks).

Adaptive Behavior

Number of Adaptive Behavior Factors

A review of Figure 2.2 indicates that the conclusions of McGrew and Bruininks (1989) continue to ring true 8 years later. Namely, the number of factors identified in factor analytic studies of adaptive behavior instruments is directly related to methodological variables (viz., the number of variables and the level of measurement used in the analysis). Figure 2.2 shows that factor analytic studies (n = 30 samples) of subscale variables produced factor solutions with the smallest number of factors (M = 1.6). Most subscale studies typically identified one to two adaptive behavior factors. In contrast, parcel studies (n = 22 samples) typically identified three or four factors (M = 3.4), while item level studies (n = 11 samples) typically identified four to eight factors (M = 6.3). The strong relationship between measurement level and number of adaptive behaviors was reflected in a significant ($p. < .01$) measurement level effect, $F(2, 60)$ = 74.51, a finding that indicated that 74% of the variance (R = .84) in the number

of adaptive behaviors identified was due to the breadth of the variables factored (i.e., subscales, parcels, items).

The likelihood that the adaptive behavior instrument accounts for the number of adaptive behavior factors identified was not supported when examining results from the 21 samples (24% of all samples) that used the AAMD *Adaptive Behavior Scale* (Nihira, Leland & Lambert, 1993) and its precursor, the *Adaptive Behavior Checklist* (Nihira, Foster, Shellhaas & Leland, 1968). The pattern of number of factors by measurement level (subscale M = 1.9; parcel M = 2.5; item M = 7.3) and the pattern of histograms presented in Figure 2.3 directly parallel those found for the total sample (see Figure 2.2).

It is clear that a *"failure to recognize the importance of the measurement level of the factored variables may lead to inaccurate conclusions concerning the structure of adaptive behavior* [italics added] *"* (McGrew & Bruininks, 1989, p. 76). These results also suggest a possible hierarchical adaptive behavior factor structure (McGrew & Bruininks; Widaman et al., 1991; Widaman &

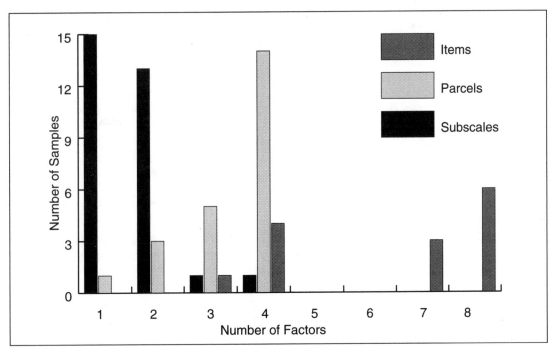

Figure 2.2. Frequency of samples identifying number of adaptive factors by scale level.

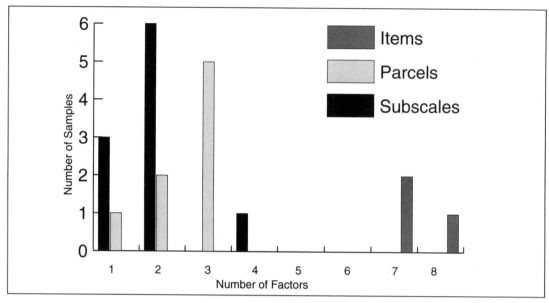

Figure 2.3. *Frequency of Adaptive Behavior Scale samples identifying number of adaptive factors by measurement level.*

McGrew, 1996) that will be discussed later in this chapter.

Type of Adaptive Behavior Factors

Using the same logic described by McGrew and Bruininks (1989), all adaptive behavior factors identified in subscale and parcel studies were categorized into the adaptive behavior domain categories that are most frequently mentioned in the literature (Gresham & Elliott, 1987; Reschly, 1982, 1987). These results are presented in Table 2.2. Given the methodological problems inherent in item studies described previously, item factor studies were not included in this summary. At variance from the McGrew and Bruininks review was the inclusion of both subscale and item parcel factors in this summary. (McGrew and Bruininks only summarized subscale studies.) The item parcel studies were included in the review because we wished to take a less conservative approach than McGrew and Bruininks and minimize the possibility of overlooking potential factors that were supported in prior research.

A review of the results in Table 2.2 suggests that *adaptive behavior is a multidimensional construct*. Although the results presented in Table 2.2 offer no new insights on the dimensions of adaptive

behavior (as currently measured) beyond those offered by McGrew and Bruininks (1989), the number of studies now provide stronger support for a multidimensional interpretation of adaptive behavior. The dimensions of personal independence (e.g., functional autonomy, self-sufficiency, independent functioning), responsibility (e.g., meeting expectations of others and/or getting along with others in social contexts), and cognitive/academic (e.g., functional time, number, and literacy skills) are most clearly supported; these are followed by physical/developmental (e.g., physical and health aspects of perceptual/motor skills; locomotion/ambulation) and vocational/community (e.g., effective skills in community, job, career, work settings).

Maladaptive Behavior

Number of Maladaptive Factors

The current review, which included 47 different samples that used five different instruments (i.e., ABCL, ABS/ABCL, CDER, ICAP-PBS), significantly extends our understanding of the factor structure of maladaptive behavior beyond that reported by McGrew and Bruininks (1989), which was based only on

Table 2.2

Adaptive Behavior Factors Emerging From Subscale and Parcel Studies

Scale	Personal Independence	Responsibility	Cognitive/ Academic	Vocational/ Community	Physical/ Developmental	Miscellaneous/ Uninterpretable
ABCL/ABS	AR (14) CR (17) CWOR (1)	AR (11) CR (11) CWOR (1)	CR (6) AR (8)	AR (3) CR (3)	CR (10) AR (8)	CR (6) AR (1)
ABIC	CU (1)					
CDER		AR (1)	AR (1)			
CTAB	AR (3) CR (3)					
MDPSBS	C&AR (1)		C&AR (1)			
PAR	CWOR (1)	CR (1)			CR (1)	
SIB	CWOR (4) AR (1) AWOR (1) CR (1)	CWOR (1)	CR (1) CWOR (1)	AWOR (1)		
WBRS			C&AR (1) CWOR (1)		C&AR (1) CWOR (1)	

Note. Scale abbreviations: ABCL = Adaptive Behavior Checklist; ABS = AAMD Adaptive Behavior Scale; ABIC = Adaptive Behavior Inventory for Children; CDER = Client Development Evaluation Report; CTAB = Comprehensive Test of Adaptive Behavior; MDPSBS = Minnesota Developmental Programming System Behavioral Scales; PAR = Preschool Attainment Record; SIB = Scales of Independent Behavior; WBRS = Wisconsin Behavior Rating Scale.

Sample abbreviations: AR = adults with mental retardation; CR = children with mental retardation; C&AR = children and adults with mental retardation; AWOR = adults without mental retardation; CWOR = children without mental retardation.

Numbers in parentheses are the number of samples in which the factor emerged.

seven samples and one instrument (i.e., ABS/ABCL; Nihira, Foster & Spencer, 1968). Similar to the adaptive factor analysis synthesis, a significant relation ($p. < .01$), F 3/44 = 19.780, was found between the number of maladaptive factors identified and measurement level. Approximately half of the variance (R = .69; 47%) in the number of maladaptive factors identified across studies was due to the level of measures factored. Subscale and parcel studies were similar in the identification of approximately 2+ factors (M = 2.5 and 2.0, respectively). Item level studies identified a significantly larger number of factors (M = 3.8). For the same reasons presented for the domain of adaptive behavior, item level studies were dropped from further consideration in the current review.

Results from subscale and parcel studies support the conclusion that, as currently operationalized in existing scales, *maladaptive behavior is largely a two-to three-factor domain of problem behaviors.*

Type of Maladaptive Behavior Factors

A review of Table 2.3 indicates that (according to our logical analysis) maladaptive behavior factors can largely be classified into two broad categories—personal (intrapunitive) and social (extrapunitive). General personal and general social maladaptive factors were most frequently identified. It is our opinion that the remaining maladaptive behavior factors identified represent more narrow forms of maladaptive behavior subsumed under the broader personal (intrapunitive) and social (extrapunitive) factors (see Table 2.3). This interpretation suggests a hierarchical maladaptive structure that could be further extended to include the even more narrow or specific item studies (e.g., all of the item studies with the ABC). This hierarchical interpretation will be treated later in this chapter.

Conclusions

In general, the extant factor analytic research continues to support the broad strokes painted in the recent reviews of McGrew and Bruininks (1989) and Widaman and McGrew (1996). The primary conclusions are

- Adaptive behavior, as currently measured in existing instruments, is a multidimensional construct consisting of five domains (viz., personal independence, responsibility, cognitive/academic, physical/developmental, vocational/community).
- Maladaptive behavior factors generally fall into the two broad categories of personal (intrapunitive) and social (extrapunitive) problem behaviors.
- The methodological factor of variable breadth (i.e., subscales, item parcels, and items) contributes significantly to the variability in the number of adaptive/maladaptive factors identified in different studies. Recognition of this finding is critical when attempting to integrate findings across studies. More important, this robust finding suggests that a strong argument could be made for the interpretation and synthesis of adaptive and maladaptive factor research within a hierarchical structural model where *specific* factors are subsumed by *narrow* factors which in turn are subsumed by more general *broad* factors. Such a structure has direct parallels to Carroll's (1993; 1997) three-stratum theory of cognitive abilities, which reflects a massive integration of more than 50 years of factor analytic research in the area of intelligence.
- No single adaptive-maladaptive behavior assessment instrument completely measures the entire range of adaptive and maladaptive behavior dimensions. This conclusion is based on an examination of Tables 2.2 and 2.3. It is clear that different scales place different degrees of emphasis on different adaptive behavior domains. No one instrument produced a factor structure that included all of the domains.

Table 2.3
Maladaptive Behavior Factors Emerging
From Subscale and Parcel Studies

Scale	Personal (intrapunitive) maladaptive			Social (extrapunitive) maladaptive						
	General personal maladaptive	Withdrawal	Destructive—internal	General—Social Maladaptive	Destructive—general	Destructive—external	Destructive—internal	Socially disruptive	Sexually aberrant	Miscellaneous Uninterpretable
ABCL/ ABS	CR (5) CWOR (1) AR (2)	CR (2) AR (1)		CR (5) CWOR (1) AR (1)				AR (1)	CR (1)	AR (1) CR (3)
CDER	AR (1)			AR (1) CR (6)						
ICAP-PSB	CR (6) AR (6)		AR (4)	CR (5) AR (1)	CR (1) AR (2)	AR (2)	AR (4)	CR (1) AR (5)		

Note. Scale abbreviations: ABCL = *Adaptive Behavior Checklist*; ABS = AAMD *Adaptive Behavior Scale*; CDER = *Client Development Evaluation Report*; ICAP-PSB = *Inventory for Client and Agency Planning – Problem Behavior Scales*.

Sample abbreviations: AR = adults with mental retardation; CR = children with mental retardation; A&CR = adults and children with mental retardation; CWOR = children without mental retardation.

Numbers in parentheses are the number of samples in which the factor emerged.

The Future: The Need for a "Big-Picture" Perspective

What do these conclusions about the structure of adaptive and maladaptive behavior mean for research and practice? Do we now have sufficient empirical evidence that will allow the field to design comprehensive and theoretically valid measures of adaptive and maladaptive behavior? Does the evidence provide definitive answers to how these constructs should be finalized in an enduring definition of mental retardation and other disabilities? Not quite. However, sufficient information is available to initiate steps toward these goals.

Although the current review continues to further our understanding of the structure of adaptive and maladaptive behavior (as measured by existing instruments), when compared to similar research in the area of cognitive abilities or intelligence (see Carroll, 1993), "the adaptive behavior research is in its stage of infancy . . . we are still at the stage of developing a working legend from which to start the initial mapping of the terrain" (McGrew & Bruininks, 1989, p. 79). In fact, we would argue that a number of different interpretations of the factor structure results are possible, each with a somewhat different implication for research and practice.

For construct-related adaptive behavior research to result in systematic incremental progress, we believe it is critical that future research be driven by theoretical and conceptual models and frameworks. The continued isolated factoring of existing adaptive behavior instruments, although important for understanding each instrument, will not result in significant strides in understanding the constructs of adaptive and maladaptive behavior unless these studies are conceptually organized. To facilitate this achievement, we offer three different but related conceptual frameworks for understanding the construct of adaptive behavior. These models are offered primarily as heuristic frameworks to stimulate conceptually driven research and scholarly discourse. Given the limited construct-related research on adaptive behavior (when compared to that on intelligence), these models are to a large extent speculative. They are intended to "push the edge of the envelope" on thinking and research regarding the constructs of adaptive and maladaptive behavior.

Adaptive and Maladaptive Behavior as Hierarchical Constructs

As discussed earlier, a number of the adaptive behavior factor analysis reviews (McGrew & Bruininks, 1989; Widaman et al., 1991; Widaman & McGrew, 1996) suggest that the robust relation between the number of factors identified (across studies) and the breadth of the variables factored (viz., items, parcels, subscales) points to hierarchical adaptive and maladaptive models. To demonstrate possible hierarchical models, the adaptive and maladaptive factors identified across studies in the current review (see Tables 2.2 and 2.3) are placed within a hierarchical framework that is encompassed within an even larger conceptual framework (i.e., a version of Greenspan's model of personal competence that has received empirical support; see McGrew, Bruininks, & Johnson, 1996). This model is presented in Figure 2.4.

Much can be learned from the decades of factor analytic research on cognitive abilities that has recently converged on a hierarchical *Gf-Gc* theory of intelligence (Carroll, 1993; Horn & Knoll, 1997; McGrew, 1997; McGrew & Flanagan, 1998). We also believe that the empirically supported hierarchical structure of cognitive abilities (i.e., conceptual intelligence) can and should be an exemplar for the domains of adaptive and maladaptive behavior. In Figure 2.4, an adapted version (McGrew; McGrew & Flanagan) of Carroll's three-stratum model of cognitive abilities is presented, a model based on the Carroll's seminal review and integration of nearly 60 years of factor analytic research. At the apex or most *general* level (stratum III) is *g* or general intelligence ("conceptual intelligence" in Greenspan's model of personal competence). Subsumed under *g* are 10 *broad* or stratum II Gf-Gc abilities, which in turn are subsumed by approximately 70 different *narrow* or stratum I abilities.

Stratum is an important concept embedded in the hierarchical Gf-Gc; *stratum* differs from the factor analytically based term *order*. According to Carroll (1993), "The order of a factor refers to the purely operational level of analysis at which it is found. The stratum of a factor would refer to an absolute measure of its degree of generality over the domain of cognitive abilities" (p. 577). Therefore, the order at which a factor has been operationally isolated in a given factor analysis is independent of the stratum to which it is assigned. Thus, the placement of cognitive abilities within the hierarchical Gf-Gc model was based on the breadth or generality of a factor over a domain of behaviors. Using the same logic, we have made a first attempt to categorize the adaptive and maladaptive factors found in this review (see Tables 2.2 and 2.3) at their appropriate stratum within hierarchical structures under the categories of practical intelligence, social intelligence, and emotional competence.

Within the domain of maladaptive behavior, a general maladaptive factor may exist at stratum III (see Figure 2.4). Subsumed under *maladaptive g* (for want of a better term) are the broad (stratum II) dimensions of personal (intrapunitive) and social (extrapunitive) behavior. In turn, more narrow or specific (stratum I) problem behaviors (e.g., withdrawal and destructive: internal under personal maladaptation) could be placed under the two respective broad maladaptive behaviors. In contrast, four of the five adaptive behavior factors that have been identified might be considered to represent broad (stratum II) dimensions under a general adaptive behavior domain (practical intelligence). The responsibility factor (which often has "social" connotations) might similarly be placed at the broad (stratum II) level under the general domain of social intelligence. (It is interesting to note that the presence of only one possible factor

under social intelligence is consistent with Greenspan's lament of the omission of this construct in measures of adaptive behavior and in the definition of mental retardation; see Greenspan, this volume; Greenspan & Driscoll, 1997).

In sum, important lessons can be gleaned from the rich history of attempts to define an empirically based (largely factor analytic) taxonomy of cognitive abilities. Foremost is the need to evaluate the breadth or degree of generality of dimensions identified in adaptive and maladaptive behavior factor analytic research. Furthermore, it is particularly important that the results of factor analytic studies be interpreted within hierarchical adaptive and maladaptive frameworks, which in turn could be embedded in even larger frameworks (e.g., Greenspan's model of personal competence) that include other important human competencies (e.g., intelligence).

Adaptive and Maladaptive Behavior as "Typical Performance"

Although the hierarchical models just described have considerable theoretical and logical appeal (particularly for those with strong psychometric backgrounds and those who subscribe to the belief that adaptive and maladaptive behavior represent distinct constructs similar to that of intelligence), an alternative interpretation of the same research is possible. This model is derived largely from Widaman and McGrew's (1996) review in which they reconciled the results from factor analytic research of adaptive and maladaptive behavior with that of broader models of personal competence.

Drawing on Cronbach's (1984) distinction between measures of maximal and typical performance, Widaman and McGrew (1996) suggested that measures of adaptive behavior measure typical performance, which is the "level of skill a person typically displays when responding to challenges in his or her environment" (p. 98). This contrasts with measures of maximal performance (e.g., intelligence tests)

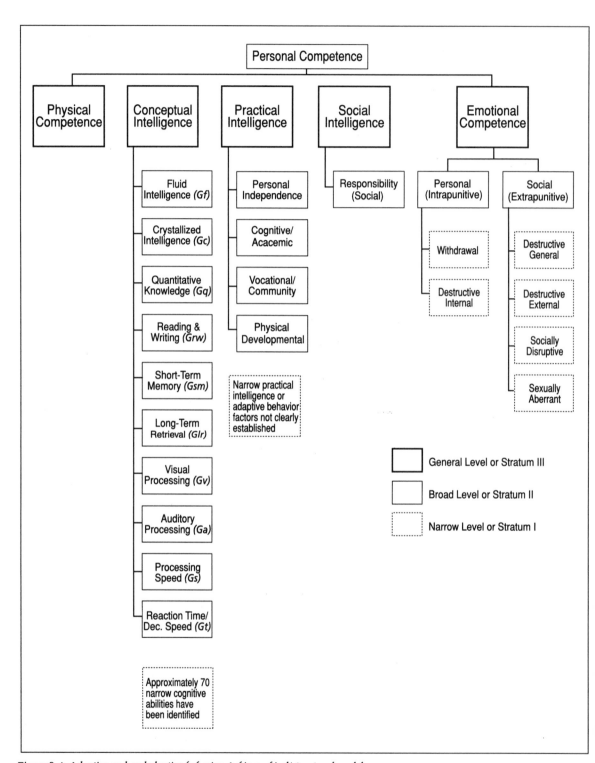

Figure 2.4. *Adaptive and maladaptive behavior*: A *hierarchical/structural model.*

where the focus is on determining "the optimal level of performance of which a person is capable" (p. 98). Although this distinction is not a clear dichotomy, in general, maximal performance measures typically focus on describing forces internal to the person (i.e., traits). The emphasis is on ability or what the *person has the potential to do*. In contrast, typical performance measurement focuses more on observable behavior with few, if any, internal trait or ability inferences. Typical performance focuses more on what the person actually does (Cronbach).

An "ability as maximal performance" interpretation of the adaptive behavior factor analytic research would be similar to that described in the hierarchical or structural model depicted in Figure 2.4. That is, adaptive behavior would be seen as being analogous to a practical intelligence ability or trait under which different broad and narrow abilities could be organized (similar to intelligence). However, a nontrait or nonability interpretation of adaptive behavior (i.e., typical perfor-

mance) would argue against the traditional psychometrically based hierarchical structural. Instead, as suggested by Widaman and McGrew (1996), the factors that have been identified in the research literature may simply describe typical performance across the very broad or general domains of personal competence. This possibility is presented in Figure 2.5.

In this model, the same five factors that were listed at the broad (stratum II) level under practical intelligence (adaptive behavior) in the hierarchical model (see Figure 2.4) now describe typical performance in the very broad domains of physical competence and conceptual, practical, and social intelligence. This model shifts the focus away from adaptive behavior as an independent construct, entity or "thing" inside a person, to a person's typical performance or achievement across the major domains of personal competence. Proponents of this model would argue for a movement away from continued attempts to identify the nature or characteristics (e.g., factors) of the

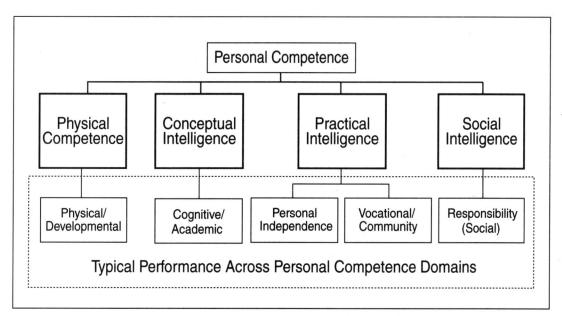

Figure 2.5. Adaptive behaviors as "typical performance."

entity or trait of adaptive behavior to delineating those skills or achievements in the major domains of personal competence that are important for describing how a person is adapting to an environment.

The Edge of the Envelope: A "Big-Picture" Heuristic Framework

In the spirit of stimulating dialogue and research on adaptive and maladaptive behavior, in Figure 2.6 we present the initial broad strokes of a "big-picture" framework that we hope will result in more conceptually driven research. Similar to Figures 2.4 and 2.5, a version of Greenspan's model of personal competence is the overarching framework. The most important feature of this model (for the current discussion) is the distinction between maximal and typical performance frameworks or models. We first start with a brief explanation of the conceptual intelligence portion of the model given the maturity of the research (in a relative sense) in this area.

As discussed earlier, the development and factor analysis of maximal performance psychometric measures of intelligence has resulted in convergence on a hierarchically organized Gf-Gc model of intelligence. In addition to serving as the most promising framework for measuring and assessing intellectual abilities (cf. Flanagan & McGrew, 1995; McGrew, 1997; McGrew & Flanagan, 1998), we suggest that this model could be used to organize thinking about how best to measure typical or functional conceptual intelligence performance (viz., the functional cognitive or academic component of adaptive behavior).

Most current conceptions of adaptive behavior include the notion of functional academics, which in Figure 2.6 could be considered to be a person's typical application of quantitative knowledge (Gq) and reading/writing (Grw) in everyday settings. By and large, this is the extent to which typical conceptual intellectual functioning has been incorporated into definitions or measures of adaptive behavior. Given the strong support

for the contemporary Gf-Gc theory, our big-picture model implies the notion that functional conceptual intelligence may also need to include functional knowledge (Gc) (breadth and depth of important environmental knowledge necessary for independent functioning), functional thinking or problem solving abilities (e.g., Gf —a person's typical use of inductive and deductive reasoning when faced with everyday practical problems), functional memory (Gsm, Glr) (e.g., how effectively an individual employs short- and long-term memory abilities in daily functioning), and functional cognitive speed (Gs, Gt) (e.g., how quickly and efficiently an individual can think in everyday situations). Thus, we feel that by distinguishing between maximal and typical performance within broad domains of personal competence, and by using the more established and researched maximal performance personal competence taxonomies as guides, significant advances can be realized in attempts to define and measure adaptive and maladaptive behavior.

Emotional competence is another domain for which there is growing support for a possible empirically based taxonomy of traits. In particular, the big-5 or five-factor model of personality has recently emerged as a potentially useful hierarchical framework for understanding affective functioning. In Figure 2.6 we have listed (for illustrative purposes) the five dimensions described by Costa and McCrae (1992). These dimensions are analogous in breadth to the broad (stratum II) Gf-Gc abilities. Many of the adjectives used to describe these personality traits (e.g., anxiety, impulsiveness, aggressiveness, stubborn, withdrawn, excitable, distractible, etc.) sound very similar to many of the behaviors used to describe an individual's personal or social maladaptation (i.e., an individual's typical emotional or behavioral functioning).

Space, as well as existing research, does not allow for a discussion of all of the maximal and typical relations portrayed in Figure 2.6. The examples listed under physical competence, practical intelligence, and social

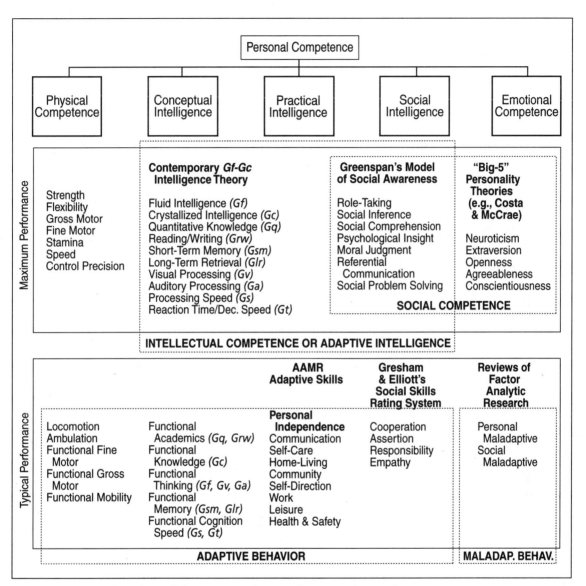

Figure 2.6. *Understanding adaptive behavior: Using a heuristic "big-picture" framework.*

intelligence are just that—examples. For example, there is no obvious link (as was the case with conceptual intelligence) between the components of Greenspan's model of social awareness (Greenspan & Granfield, 1992) and Gresham and Elliott's (1987) social skills rating system. Greenspan's social awareness model is largely speculative and is only one of a number of different possible social cognition or intelligence taxonomies. However, such models could be used to delineate the important social behaviors that should be measured by typical social skill performance measures (which are often labeled as measures of social skills).

According to this overarching big-picture conception, practical intelligence is the personal competence domain most in need of research. This is a significant conclusion given that practical intelligence is the construct most often related to current notions of adaptive behavior. Recently there has been an increased interest in "practical know-how," "street smarts," "successful intelligence," or "tacit knowledge" (Wagner, 1994). Although there is not yet a consensus on a suitable definition of practical intelligence, these terms all deal with "the ability to solve the ill-defined problems that arise in daily life, for which there may be no clear-cut answers" (Wagner, p. 823).

When a workable taxonomy of practical intellectual abilities is developed, it could serve as a template to operationalize those adaptive skills that represent typical performance in this domain (in a manner similar to that previously described for conceptual intelligence and emotional competence). This interpretation suggests that it may be especially important for researchers in the field of mental retardation to actively research the construct of practical intelligence. For the purpose of illustration, we have listed the eight AAMR adaptive skills areas (Luckasson et al., 1992) under the typical performance category.

Implications of the Big Picture

The implications of the framework presented in Figure 2.6 are many. At least four major implications relate to furthering our understanding of the constructs of adaptive and maladaptive behavior. First, as just described, the primary value of the big-picture heuristic framework is the recognition that adaptive and maladaptive behavior should not be considered to be similar to other constructs that are based on the ability-as-maximal-performance model (e.g., intelligence; personality traits). Rather, adaptive and maladaptive behavior represent typical performance across the major domains of personal competence.

Second, rather than continuing to focus exclusively on attempts (that largely use the maximal performance trait research methodology) to identify *the* dimensions (factors) of adaptive and maladaptive behavior that might be used to specify a hierarchical structural taxonomy, it might be more important to focus efforts on translating the implications of available maximal performance taxonomies (e.g., Gf-Gc theory in conceptual intelligence; big-5 personality theory in emotional competence) into the operational measurement of typical performance of the major domains of these taxonomies (e.g., developing measures of functional knowledge, thinking, memory, and cognitive speed).

Third, the concepts of conceptual, practical, and social intelligence have deep historical roots in the fields of psychology and mental retardation. Reflecting the theoretical writings of Greenspan (Greenspan, 1979; Greenspan & Driscoll, 1997; Greenspan & Granfield, 1992), in Figure 2.6 we indicated (via a dashed rectangle) that the combination of these three domains may represent the construct of intellectual competence or adaptive intelligence. (We have similarly indicated Greenspan's notion of social competence.) Intellectual competence differs from the traditional use of the term *intelligence*, which is represented by conceptual intelligence in this model. Furthermore, it is important to recognize that reviews of the literature and empirical studies (e.g., see summaries in Harrison, 1987; McGrew, Bruininks, & Johnson, 1996) clearly indicate that intelligence (conceptual intelligence) and adaptive behavior are moderately related but distinctly different constructs. If the concept of intellectual competence or adaptive intelligence makes sense (as Greenspan has argued in reference to the definition of mental retardation), we propose that typical intellectual competence (i.e., adaptive behavior) may best be represented by these three domains. Given that most current concepts of adaptive behavior focus on personal independence skills, this would suggest that new research efforts need to include a broader range of functional conceptual and social intelligence behaviors. Furthermore, an argument could be made to exclude physical competence domains (e.g., motor skills) from the definition and measurement of adaptive behavior. Physical competencies would still be considered important, but would stand alone as distinct from adaptive behavior.

The fourth implication of the "big picture" is that researchers and scholars in the field of mental retardation need to cast a much wider net for important ideas and concepts emanating from other behavioral sciences. For example, as presented above, contemporary Gf-Gc cognitive theory and the various big-5 personality theories represent some of the most mature and empirically supported taxonomies of important domains of personal competency. These maps of important human traits could be used to guide the development of parallel typical performance measures, resulting in a far broader conceptualization of adaptive and maladaptive behavior. In addition, researchers in the field of mental retardation need to actively contribute to, or at a minimum monitor the results of, research regarding the constructs of practical and social intelligence. Attempting to understand and define adaptive and maladaptive behavior primarily from the analysis of available measures of adaptive and maladaptive behavior is too restricted and will not (in our opinion) result in meaningful advances in understanding and measuring adaptive and maladaptive behavior. Future researchers must become much more knowledgeable of research in related fields in order to couch research and dialogue in the context of conceptual models.

In conclusion, we recognize that the three different frameworks we have advanced are based on a limited amount of research (especially when compared to that used to develop the hierarchical Gf-Gc framework). No pretense is made that these models are anything more than reasoned hypotheses. We hope that practitioners, researchers, and scholars working in the area of adaptive and maladaptive behavior and mental retardation will use the frameworks presented as heuristics from which to advance the measurement and understanding of the constructs of adaptive and maladaptive behavior. If this occurs, we believe reviews of the factor analytic and construct-related research in 5 to 10 years will provide a far more complete and possibly different picture of the nature of adaptive and maladaptive behavior.

References

Aman, M. G., Burrow, W. H., & Wolford, P. L. (1995). The aberrant behavior checklist—Community: Factor validity and effect of subject variables for adults in group homes. *American Journal on Mental Retardation*, 100, 283-292.

Aman, M. G., Richmond, G., Stewart, A. W., Bell, J. C., & Kissel, R. C. (1987). The Aberrant Behavior Checklist: Factor structure and the effect of subject variables in American and New Zealand facilities. *American Journal on Mental Retardation*, 91, 570-578.

Arndt, S. (1981). A general measure of adaptive behavior. *American Journal of Mental Deficiency*, 85, 554-556.

Bihm, E. M., & Poindexter, A. R. (1991). Cross-validation of the factor structure of the Aberrant Behavior Checklist for persons with mental retardation. *American Journal on Mental Retardation*, 96, 209-211.

Bruininks, R. H., McGrew, K. S., & Maruyama, G. (1988). Structure of adaptive behavior in samples with and without mental retardation. *American Journal on Mental Retardation*, 93, 265-272.

Bruininks, R. H., Thurlow, M., & Gilman, C. J. (1987). Adaptive behavior and mental retardation. *Journal of Special Education*, 21, 69-88.

Carroll, J. B. (1993). *Human cognitive abilities: A survey of factor-analytic studies*. Cambridge: Cambridge University Press.

Carroll, J. B. (1997). The three-stratum theory of cognitive abilities. In D. P. Flanagan, J. L. Genshaft, & P. L. Harrison (Eds.), *Contemporary intellectual assessment: Theories, tests, and issues* (pp. 122-130). New York: Guilford Press.

Cattell, R. B. (1971). *Abilities: Their structure, growth, and action*. Boston: Houghton Mifflin.

Clausen, J. (1972). The continuing problem of defining mental deficiency. *Journal of Special Education*, 6, 97-106.

Cooper, H. M. (1989). *Integrating research: A guide for literature review* (2nd ed.). Newbury Park, CA: Sage.

Costa, P. T. Jr., & McCrae, R. R. (1992). Four ways five factors are basic. *Personality and Individual Differences*, 13, 653-655.

Coulter, W. A., & Morrow, H. W. (1978). A contemporary conception of adaptive behavior within the scope of psychological assessment. In W. A. Coulter & H. W. Morrow (Eds.), *Adaptive behavior: Concepts and measurements* (pp. 3-20). New York: Grune & Stratton.

Cronbach, L. J. (1984). *Essentials of psychological testing* (4th ed.). New York: Harper & Row.

Cunningham, T., & Presnall, D. (1978). Relationship between dimensions of adaptive behavior and sheltered workshop productivity. *American Journal of Mental Deficiency*, 82, 386-393.

Flanagan, D. P., & McGrew, K. S. (1995). A cross-battery approach to intelligence test interpretation. NASP *Communique*, 24(4).

Freund, L. S., & Reiss, A. L. (1991). Rating problem behaviors in outpatients with mental retardation: Use of the Aberrant Behavior Checklist. *Research in Developmental Disabilities*, 12, 435-451.

Greenspan, S. (1979). Social intelligence in the retarded. In N. R. Ellis (Ed.), *Handbook of mental deficiency: Psychological theory and research* (2nd ed., pp. 483-532). Hillsdale, NJ: Lawrence Erlbaum.

Greenspan, S. (1997). Dead manual walking? Why the 1992 AAMR definition needs redoing. *Education and Training in Mental Retardation and Developmental Disabilities*, 32, 179-190.

Greenspan, S., & Driscoll, J. (1997). The role of intelligence in a broad model of personal competence. In D. P. Flanagan, J. L. Genshaft, and P. L. Harrison (Eds.), *Contemporary intellectual assessment: Theories, tests, and issues* (pp. 131-150). New York: Guilford Press.

Greenspan, S., & Granfield, J. M. (1992). Reconsidering the construct of mental retardation: Implications of a model of social competence. *American Journal on Mental Retardation, 96,* 442-453.

Gresham, F. M., & Elliott, S. N. (1987). The relationship between adaptive behavior and social skills: Issues in definition and assessment. *Journal of Special Education, 21,* 167-181.

Grossman, H. J. (Ed.). (1983). *Classification in mental retardation.* Washington, DC: American Association on Mental Deficiency.

Guarnaccia, V. J. (1976). Factor structure and correlates of adaptive behavior in noninstitutionalized retarded adults. *American Journal of Mental Deficiency, 80,* 543-547.

Guilford, J. P. (1967). *The nature of human intelligence.* New York: McGraw-Hill.

Harman, H. H. (1976). *Modern factor analysis* (3rd ed., rev.). Chicago: University of Chicago Press.

Harrison, P. L. (1987). Research with adaptive behavior scales. *Journal of Special Education, 21,* 37-68.

Harrison, P. L., & Kamphaus, R. W. (1987). *Journal of Special Education, 21* (1).

Harvey, P. D., Davidson, M., Mueser, K. T., Parrella, M., White, L., & Powchick, P. (1997). Social-Adaptive Functioning Evaluation (SAFE): A rating scale for geriatric psychiatric patients. *Schizophrenia Bulletin, 23,* 131-145.

Holman, J. G., & Bruininks, R. H. (1985). Assessing and training adaptive behaviors. In K. C. Lakin & R. H. Bruininks (Eds.), *Strategies for achieving community integration of developmentally disabled citizens* (pp. 73-104). Baltimore: Paul H. Brookes.

Horn, J. L., & Knoll, J. (1997). Human cognitive capabilities: Gf-Gc theory. In D. P. Flanagan, J. L. Genshaft, and P. L. Harrison (Eds.), *Contemporary intellectual assessment: Theories, tests, and issues* (pp. 53-91). New York: Guilford Press.

Hug, N., Barclay, A, Collins, H., & Lamp, R. (1978). Validity and factor structure of the Preschool Attainment Record in Head Start children. *Journal of Psychology, 99,* 71-74.

Jacobson, J., & Mulick, J. (Eds.). (1996). *Manual on diagnosis and professional practice in mental retardation.* Washington, DC: American Psychological Association.

Jöreskog, K., & Sörbom, D. (1993). LISREL 8: *Structural equation modeling with the* SIMPLIS *command language.* Hillsdale, NJ: Lawrence Erlbaum.

Kamphaus, R. W. (1987). Conceptual and psychometric issues in the assessment of adaptive behavior. *Journal of Special Education, 21,* 27-35.

Katz-Garris, L., Hadley, T. J., Garris, R. P., & Barnhill, B. (1980). A factor analytic study of the Adaptive Behavior Scale. *Psychological Reports, 47,* 807-814.

Kim, J., & Mueller, C. W. (1978a). *Factor analysis: Statistical methods and practical issues.* Beverly Hills, CA: Sage.

Kim, J., & Mueller, C. W. (1978b). *Introduction to factor analysis: What it is and how to do it.* Beverly Hills, CA: Sage.

Lambert, N. M. (1978). The Adaptive Behavior Scale—Public School Version: An overview. In W. A. Coulter & H. W. Morrow (Eds.), *Adaptive behavior: Concepts and measurements* (pp. 157-184). New York: Grune & Stratton.

Lambert, N. M., & Nicoll, R. C. (1976). Dimensions of adaptive behavior of retarded and nonretarded public-school children. *American Journal of Mental Deficiency*, 18, 135-146.

Levin, S., & Elzey, F. F. (1968). Factor analysis of the San Francisco Vocational Competency Scale. *American Journal of Mental Deficiency*, 73, 509-513.

Long, J. (1983). *Confirmatory factor analysis*: A *preface to* LISREL. Beverly Hills, CA: Sage.

Luckasson, R., Coulter, D. L., Polloway, E. A., Reiss, S., Schalock, R. L., Snell, M. E., Spitalnik, D. M., & Stark, J. A. (1992). *Mental retardation: Definition, classification, and systems of support* (9th ed.). Washington, DC: American Association on Mental Retardation.

Marshburn, E. C., & Aman, M. G. (1992). Factor validity and norms for the Aberrant Behavior Checklist in a community sample of children with mental retardation. *Journal of Autism and Developmental Disorders*, 22, 357-373.

Matson, J. L., Epstein, M. H., & Cullinan, D. (1984). A factor analytic study of the Quay-Peterson Scale with mentally retarded adolescents. *Education and Training of the Mentally Retarded*, 19, 150-154.

McCarver, R. B., & Campbell, V. A. (1987). Future developments in the concept and application of adaptive behavior. *Journal of Special Education*, 21(1), 197-207.

McGrew, K. S. (1997). Analysis of the major intelligence batteries according to a proposed comprehensive *Gf-Gc* framework. In D. P. Flanagan, J. L. Genshaft, & P. L. Harrison (Eds.), *Contemporary intellectual assessment: Theories, tests, and issues* (pp. 151-179). New York: Guilford Press.

McGrew, K. S., & Bruininks, R. H. (1989). The factor structure of adaptive behavior. *School Psychology Review*, 18, 64-81.

McGrew, K. S., Bruininks, R. H., & Johnson, D. R. (1996). A confirmatory factor analysis investigation of Greenspan's model of personal competence. *American Journal on Mental Retardation*, 100, 533-545.

McGrew, K. S., & Flanagan, D. P. (1998). *The intelligence test desk reference (ITDR): Gf-Gc cross-battery assessment*. Boston: Allyn & Bacon.

McGrew, K. S., Ittenbach, R. F., & Bruininks, R. H. (1989). Factor structure of maladaptive behaviors across the lifespan of persons with mental retardation. Research in Developmental Disabilities, 12, 181-199.

Meyers, C., Nihira, K., & Zetlin, A. (1979). The measurement of adaptive behavior. In N. R. Ellis (Ed.), *Handbook on mental deficiency: Psychological theory and research* (2nd ed., pp. 431-481). Hillsdale, NJ: Lawrence Erlbaum.

Millsap, P. A., Thackery, M., & Cook, V. J. (1987). Dimensional structure of the Adaptive Behavior Inventory for Children (ABIC): Analyses and implications. *Journal of Psychoeducational Assessment*, 5, 61-66.

Newton, J. T., & Sturmey, P. (1988). The Aberrant Behavior Checklist: A British replication and extension of its psychometric properties. *Journal of Mental Deficiency Research*, 32, 87-92.

Nihira, K. (1969a). Factorial dimensions of adaptive behavior in adult retardates. *American Journal of Mental Deficiency*, 73, 868-878.

Nihira, K. (1969b). Factorial dimensions of adaptive behavior in mentally retarded children and adolescents. *American Journal of Mental Deficiency*, 74, 130-141.

Nihira, K. (1976). Dimensions of adaptive behavior in institutionalized mentally retarded children and adults: Developmental perspective. *American Journal of Mental Deficiency*, 81, 215-226.

Nihira, K. (1978). Factorial descriptions of the AAMD Adaptive Behavior Scale. In W. A. Coulter & H. W. Morrow (Eds.), *Adaptive behavior: Concepts and measurements* (pp. 45-58). New York: Grune & Stratton.

Nihira, K., Foster, R., Shellhaas, M., & Leland, H. (1968). *Adaptive behavior checklist*. Washington, DC: American Association on Mental Deficiency.

Nihira, K., Foster, R., & Spencer, L. (1968). Measurement of adaptive behavior: A descriptive system for mental retardates, *American Journal of Orthopsychiatry, 38*, 622-634.

Nihira, K., Leland, H., & Lambert, N. (1993). AAMR *adaptive behavior scale— residential and community version*. (2nd ed.). Austin, TX: Pro-Ed.

Owens, E. P., & Bowling, D. H. (1970). Internal consistency and factor structure of the Preschool Attainment Record. *American Journal of Mental Deficiency, 75*, 170-171.

Reschly, D. J. (1982). Assessing mild mental retardation: The influence of adaptive behavior, sociocultural status, and prospects for nonbiased assessment. In C. R. Reynolds & T. B. Gutkin (Eds.), *The handbook of school psychology* (pp. 209-242). New York: Wiley Interscience.

Reschly, D. J. (1987). *Adaptive behavior in classification and programming with students who are handicapped*. St. Paul: Minnesota Department of Education.

Reynolds, W. M. (1981). Measurement of personal competence of mentally retarded individuals. *American Journal of Mental Deficiency, 85*, 368-376.

Rojahn, J., & Helsel, W. J. (1991). The Aberrant Behavior Checklist with children and adolescents with dual diagnosis. *Journal of Autism and Developmental Disorders, 21*, 17-28.

Silverman, W. P., Silver, E. J., Lubin, R. A., & Sersen, E. A. (1983). Structure of the Minnesota Developmental Programming System Behavioral Scales, Alternate Form C. *American Journal of Mental Deficiency, 88*, 170-176.

Silverstein, B., Wothke, W., & Slabaugh, R. (1988). Toward parsimony with comprehensiveness: Management applications of MDPS factor scores. *Mental Retardation, 26*, 145-153.

Song, A., Jones, S., Lippert, J., Metzgen, K., Miller, J., & Borreca, C. (1984). Wisconsin Behavior Rating Scale: Measure of adaptive behavior for the developmental levels of 0 to 3 years. *American Journal of Mental Deficiency, 88*, 410-420.

Sparrow, S. S., & Cicchetti, D. V. (1978). Behavior rating inventory for moderately, severely, and profoundly retarded persons. *American Journal of Mental Deficiency, 82*, 365-374.

Sparrow, S. S., & Cicchetti, D. V. (1984). The Behavior Inventory for Rating Development (BIRD): Assessments of reliability and factorial validity. *Applied Research in Mental Retardation, 5*, 219-231.

Spearman, C. (1904). "General intelligence" objectively determined and measured. *American Journal of Psychology, 15*, 201-293.

Thackery, M. (1991). A principal components analysis of the Comprehensive Test of Adaptive Behavior. *American Journal on Mental Retardation, 96*, 213-215.

Thorndike, R. L. (1982). *Applied psychometrics*. Boston: Houghton Mifflin.

Thurstone, L. L. (1938). *Primary mental abilities*. Chicago: University of Chicago Press.

Thurstone, L. L. (1947). *Multiple factor analysis*. Chicago: University of Chicago Press.

Thurstone, L. L., & Thurstone, T. G. (1941). *Factorial studies of intelligence*. Chicago: University of Chicago Press.

Vernon, P. E. (1956). *The measurement of abilities*. London: University of London Press.

Wagner, R. K. (1994). Practical intelligence. In R. J. Sternberg (Ed.), *The encyclopedia of human intelligence* (Vol. 2), (pp. 821-828). New York: Macmillan.

Widaman, K. F., Borthwick-Duffy, S. A., & Little, T. D. (1991). The structure and development of adaptive behaviors. In N. W. Bray (Ed.), *International review of research in mental retardation*, 17, 1-54.

Widaman, K. F., Gibbs, K. W., & Geary, D. C. (1987). Structure of adaptive behavior: I. Replication across fourteen samples of nonprofoundly mentally retarded people. *American Journal of Mental Deficiency*, 91, 348-360.

Widaman, K. F., & McGrew, K. S. (1996). The structure of adaptive behavior. In J. W. Jacobson & J. A. Mulick (Eds.), *Manual of diagnosis and professional practice in mental retardation* (pp. 97-110). Washington, DC: American Psychological Association.

Widaman, K. F., Stacy, A. W., & Borthwick-Duffy, S. A. (1993). Construct validity of dimensions of adaptive behavior: A multitrait-multimethod evaluation. *American Journal on Mental Retardation*, 98, 219-234.

Zigler, E., Balla, D., & Hodapp, R. (1984). On the definition and classification of mental retardation. *American Journal of Mental Deficiency*, 89, 215-230.

CHAPTER 3

The Merging of Adaptive Behavior and Intelligence: Implications for the Field of Mental Retardation

ROBERT L. SCHALOCK
Hastings College

Introduction

Chapters 1 and 2 discuss the transition taking place in the construct of adaptive behavior in reference to its conception, measurement, and use in the field of mental retardation. The construct of intelligence is undergoing a similar transition. This chapter discusses a possible future scenario reflecting the implications of these transitions that seem to be leading toward a merging of the constructs of intelligence and adaptive behavior.

As the reader is undoubtedly aware, the field of mental retardation is also in a state of transition characterized by:

- a transformed vision of what constitutes the life possibilities of individuals with mental retardation; this view includes an emphasis on self-determination, strengths and capabilities, inclusion, provision of individualized support systems, enhanced adaptive behavior and role status, and equity;
- a supports paradigm that focuses on supported living and employment and inclusive education;
- an interfacing of the concept of quality of life with quality enhancement, quality assurance, quality management, and outcome-based evaluation; and
- a changing conception of disability, moving away from a focus on pathology to a contextual perspective in which a person's disability results from an interaction among limitations and the person's social and physical environment.

As important as this transition is to both people with mental retardation and workers in the field, its success relies largely on how the future construct of mental retardation will be conceptualized, measured, and used. The primary purpose of this chapter is to discuss (a) how the two primary components of mental retardation—intelligence and adaptive behavior—are merging and (b) what implications this merger might have on the future definition, measurement, and use of the mental retardation construct. To accomplish this purpose, the chapter is divided into three sections discussing: (a) the merging of the constructs of intelligence and adaptive behavior; (b) the impact of this merger on the concept of disability, the definition of mental retardation, and the focus of assessment; and (c) the implications of the merger for the field of mental retardation.

I will suggest that the merging of the constructs of adaptive behavior and intelligence, along with the current ecological and functional perspectives on disability, calls for a reconsideration of disability and mental retardation along the following lines: (a) that disability be characterized as involving functional limitations in overall competence and (b) that mental retardation be characterized by limitations in practical, conceptual, and social skills.

Throughout the chapter, this is my working hypothesis: If intelligence and adaptive behavior are subsumed under the common framework of overall competence, we can implement a heuristic model of mental retardation that will better accommodate what we know about the condition and thus better prepare the field for the ecological, quality-of-life-oriented, and accountability foci of the future.

The Merging of the Constructs of Intelligence and Adaptive Behavior

The Multifactorial Approach to Intelligence

Arvey, Bouchard, Carroll, Cattell, & Cohen (1994) give a good definition of intelligence:

> a very general mental capability that, among other things, involves the ability to reason, plan, solve problems, think abstractly, comprehend complex ideas, learn quickly, and learn from experience. (p. B1).

As reflected in this definition, intelligence represents an attempt to clarify, organize, and explain the fact that individuals differ in their ability to understand complex ideas, to adapt effectively to their environments, to learn from experience, to engage in various forms of reasoning, to overcome obstacles by taking thought, and to communicate (Nesser, Bode, Bouchard, Boykin & Cohen, 1996). Similarly, Anastasi (1986) suggests that "intelligent behavior is essentially adaptive, insofar as it represents ways of meeting the demands of a changing environment" (pp. 19-20).

Unfortunately, there is little agreement today on what intelligence is. Indeed, when two dozen prominent theorists were asked a few years ago to define intelligence, they gave two dozen different definitions (Sternberg & Detterman, 1986). Similarly, in a review of intelligence by Carroll (1993), more than 70 different abilities were identified by currently available "intelligence tests." Despite this lack of consensus, the Arvey et al. (1994) definition suggests that we have moved away from the notion that there is a general factor of intelligence (what Spearman (1923) called g) and have moved to the notion that intelligence should be viewed as multifactorial and hierarchical, with g potentially at the apex (Carroll; Nesser et al., 1996). This multifactorial nature of intelligence is evident in the following three prevalent models of intelligence: (a) fluid and crystallized intelligence,

(b) multiple intelligences, and (c) personal-social competence.

Fluid and Cystallized Intelligence

Cattell (1963, 1971) and Horn (1979) suggested that intelligence is composed of "fluid" and "crystallized" components. Fluid intelligence involves reasoning ability, memory capacity, and speed of information processing, whereas crystallized intelligence involves the ability to apply acquired knowledge and skills in problem solving. This distinction between fluid and crystallized intelligence is central to the most recent revision of the *Stanford-Binet Intelligence Scale* (Thorndike, Hagen, & Sattler, 1986), which groups its 15 subtests under the broader categories of crystallized abilities, fluid-analytical abilities, and short-term memory. These three are then grouped under composite IQ, reflective of g. Similarly, in the third edition of the *Wechsler Intelligence Scale for Children* (Wechsler, 1991), four factor scores are found: verbal comprehension, perceptual organization, processing speed, and freedom from distractibility (Daniel, 1997).

Multiple Intelligences

Thurstone (1938) argued that intelligence involves seven distinct factors: word fluency, verbal comprehension, spatial ability, perceptual speed, numerical ability, inductive reasoning, and memory. More recently, Gardner (1993) proposed a theory of multiple intelligence that comprises seven distinct types, here listed along with tasks reflective of each type:

- *linguistic*: reading, writing, receptive language;
- *logical-mathematical*: solving math problems, logical reasoning;
- *spatial*: getting from one place to another, sequential activities;
- *musical*: expressive and receptive musical behaviors;
- *bodily kinesthetic*: dancing, playing ball, running, throwing;
- *interpersonal*: relating to other people, interacting with others; and
- *intrapersonal*: understanding oneself.

Similarly, Sternberg (1985, 1988) proposed three fundamental aspects of intelligence: analytical, creative, and practical. In analytical thinking, one tries to solve familiar problems by using strategies that manipulate the elements of a problem or the relationships among the elements. In creative thinking, one tries to solve new kinds of problems that require one to think about the problem and its elements in a new way. In practical thinking, one tries to solve problems that apply what we know to everyday contexts. According to this triarchic theory, people differ in how well they apply their intelligence to different kinds of problems. For example, some people may be more "intelligent" when they face problems in their studies in school, whereas others may be more "intelligent" when they face practical problems.

Personal-Social Competence

The personal and social competence approach to intelligence arises, in part, from the afore-mentioned multiple intelligences approach and the consistent finding that predictors of success in school, such as conventional psychometric intelligence (i.e., IQ) tests, are less predictive of success out of school (Sternberg, Wagner, Williams, & Horvath, 1995). In fact, "even the most charitable estimates of the relation between intelligence test scores and real-world criteria such as job performance indicate that approximately three fourths of the variance in real-world performance is not accounted for by intelligence test performance" (p. 912).

The personal-social competence approach to intelligence is not new. In fact, a tripartite model of intelligence comprising social, practical, and conceptual components was originally proposed by E. L. Thorndike in 1920. As generally understood, the personal-social competence approach to intelligence includes the following three components:

Conceptual intelligence. This component, also referred to as academic or analytic, involves the ability to solve abstract "intellec-tual" problems and to use and understand symbolic processes, including language. It includes the traditional notion of intelligence quotient and school-related competencies (Greenspan & Granfield, 1992; Greenspan, Switzky, & Granfield, 1996; Nesser, 1976; Sternberg, 1997). Nesser, for example, de-scribes academic intelligence tasks (common in the classroom and on intelligence tests) as being formulated by others, often of little or no intrinsic interest, having all needed infor-mation available from the beginning, disembedded from an individual's ordinary experience, and having but one correct answer.

Practical intelligence. This component involves the ability to deal with the physical and mechanical aspects of life, including self-maintenance, daily living competencies, and vocational activities (Sternberg et al., 1995). It can be viewed as "people's ability to adapt successfully to the real-world environments in which they find themselves, and to exercise at least some significant degree of mastery over their environment" (Sternberg, 1984, p. 93). Nesser (1976) describes practical intelligence tasks as often being unformulated or in need of reformulation, of personal interest, lacking in information necessary for a solution, related to everyday experience, poorly defined, and characterized by multiple "correct" solutions, each with liabilities as well as assets.

Social intelligence. This component involves the ability to understand and deal effectively with social and interpersonal objects and events, including the ability to act wisely in human relations, to exhibit appropri-ate social skills, be empathetic and self-reflective, and achieve desired interpersonal outcomes (Bennet, 1993; Cantor & Kihlstrom, 1987; Greenspan, 1979; S. I. Greenspan, 1997; Keating, 1994; McGrew, Bruininks, & Johnson, 1996; Sternberg & Wagner, 1986; Taylor & Cadet, 1989). The concept of emotional intelligence is sometimes subsumed under this broader social intelligence (Goleman, 1995).

Conclusion

The three approaches to intelligence just discussed briefly—fluid and crystallized, multiple, and personal-social competence—have many common elements, including that they:

- reflect a multifactorial approach to understanding and measuring intelligence;
- indicate a significant difference between conceptual and other types of intelligences (such as practical and social);
- propose that human intelligence can best be understood from a contextual perspective; and
- suggest that intelligence can be subsumed under a broader framework of personal and social competence that is reflected in adaptive behaviors exhibited when dealing with environmental demands.

I contend that intelligence is composed of multiple factors, including practical, conceptual, and social components, and that it can best be approached within the field of mental retardation from an overall competency perspective (Schalock, 1997). This concept is shown graphically in Figure 3.1, the left side of which depicts the multidimensional aspects of intelligence just described. The right portion of Figure 3.1 will be described in the following section. The heuristic model shown in Figure 3.1 is based heavily on the work of Bruininks, McGrew & Maruyama (1988), Greenspan & Driscoll (1997), Greenspan & Granfield (1992), Greenspan et al. (1996), Ittenbach, Spiegel, McGrew, & Bruininks (1992), McGrew & Bruininks (1990), Nesser (1976), Sternberg (1985, 1988), Sternberg et al. (1995), Widaman, Borthwick-Duffy, & Little (1991), Widaman, Gibbs, & Geary (1987), and Widaman & McGrew (1996).

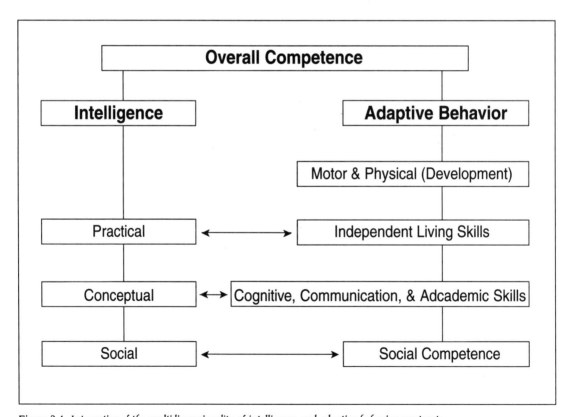

Figure 3.1. Integration of the multidimensionality of intelligence and adaptive behavior constructs.

The Multifactorial Approach to Adaptive Behavior

The concept of adaptive skills found in the 1992 American Association on Mental Retardation (AAMR) definition and classification manual (Luckasson, et al.) is a continuation of the historical attention given to social competence in the diagnosis of mental retardation. A necessary criterion in the 1992 AAMR definition of mental retardation is that significantly subaverage intellectual functioning exists concurrently with related limitations in two or more applicable adaptive skill areas: communication, self-care, home living, social skills, community use, self-direction, health and safety, functional academics, leisure, and work. This focus on "adaptive skills," rather than "adaptive behavior" (which was found in the 1983 American Association on Mental Deficiency [AAMD; now AAMR] definition [Grossman]) represents a change due in part to the pre-1992 concerns surrounding the conceptual nature of adaptive behavior and the ensuing issues related to its measurement. It is also consistent with the movement toward considering adaptive behaviors as "the behavioral skills that people typically exhibit when dealing with the environmental demands they confront" (Widaman & McGrew, 1996, p. 97).

The concept of adaptive skills implies an array of competencies, and thus provides a firmer foundation to several of the key points of the 1992 AAMR manual (Luckasson et al.):

- Adaptive skill limitations often coexist with strengths in other adaptive skill areas of personal competence.
- A person's strengths and limitations in adaptive skills should be documented within the context of community environments typical of the person's age peers and tied to the person's individualized needs for supports.
- The developmental relevance of the specific skills reference within the 10 adaptive skill areas.
- There is a need to focus on a broader range of functional conceptual and social intellectual behaviors.

In a review of adaptive behavior and adaptive behavior scales, Harrison (1989) summarized a number of common elements characterizing recent models and measures. He found that (a) most of the definitions suggest that adaptive behavior is developmental and increases in complexity as people grow older; (b) most definitions emphasize self-help, interpersonal, communication, vocational, and domestic skill domains; (c) the adaptive behavior construct is recognized as being dependent upon the expectations of culture groups and demands of particular situations and significant others with whom the person interacts; and (d) adaptive behavior is generally defined as the day-to-day performance of activities required for personal and social self-sufficiency, rather than ability to perform the activities (Bruininks, Thurlow, & Gilman, 1987; Kamphaus, 1987; Meyers, Nihira, & Zetlin, 1979; Reschly, 1982).

Based on these commonalities, chapter 2 (this volume) by Thompson, McGrew, and Bruininks, and other literature (Greenspan & Granfield, 1992; Kamphaus, 1987; Widaman & McGrew, 1996; Widaman, Stacy, & Borthwick-Duffy, 1993), there is an emerging consensus on the multifactorial structure of adaptive behavior. This structure includes:

- *motor or physical competence* (or development) that involves gross and fine motor skills, ambulating, basic eating, and toileting skills;
- *independent living* skills that involve household chores, dressing, bathing, preparing food, and washing dishes;
- *cognitive, communication, and academic* skills that involve receptive and expressive language, reading and writing skills, and handling money; and
- *social competence* skills that involve friendship (formation and maintenance), interaction with others, social participation, social reasoning, comprehension, and reasoning.

Figure 3.1 shows these multidimensional factors as being parallel to those suggested earlier for intelligence. The reader should note especially the *conceptual* similarity between the taxonomies of intellectual abilities and adaptive skills and the *specific* similarities between (a) practical intelligence and independent living skills, (b) conceptual intelligence and cognitive, communication, and academic skills, and (c) social intelligence and social competence. Initial support for this formulation comes from the confirmatory factor analytic work of Mathias and Nettelbeck (1992), McGrew et al. (1996), and Widaman and McGrew (1996) and from the conceptual work of Thompson et al. (this volume; cf. especially Figures 2.5 & 2.6).

Maladaptive behavior is not included in the integrative model presented in Figure 3.1. The current consensus (McGrew, Ittenbach, Bruininks, & Hill, 1991; Meyers et al., 1979; Widaman & McGrew, 1996; Widaman et al., 1993) is that maladaptive behavior includes two aspects: social maladaptation (e.g., externally directed aggression, destructiveness, resistance, destruction of others' property, and temper tantrums) and personal maladaptation (e.g., self-aggression, hyperactivity, repetitive body movements). As important as maladaptive behavior is to the person and to service providers, there are concerns about whether it should be considered in the diagnosis of mental retardation, whether it should be incorporated into the area of social intelligence or social competence, and/or whether it should be considered a "moderating variable" (cf. Schalock, this volume; Thompson et al., this volume).

In summary, not only is the field of mental retardation undergoing a transition, but the historical core-criteria of the definition of mental retardation—subaverage intelligence combined with limitations in adaptive behavior or adaptive skills—are also undergoing considerable reformulation. To this author, these changes are best summarized in Figure 3.1, which represents the integration of the multidimensionality of intelligence and adaptive behavior.

The next section of the chapter discusses three ways the merging of the concepts of intelligence and adaptive behavior might impact the field of mental retardation: (a) defining disability on the basis of functional limitations in overall competency (as per Figure 3.1); (b) reconceptualizing mental retardation as being limitations in practical, conceptual, and social skills; and (c) focusing on the measurement of performance domains related to practical, conceptual, and social skills.

Impact of the Merging of Intelligence and Adaptive Behavior

Concept of Disability

As with intelligence and adaptive behavior, the concept of disability is also undergoing significant change. For example, in 1980 the World Health Organization defined a handicap or disability as "arising from failure or inability to conform to the expectations or norms of the individual's universe . . . and characterized by a discordance between the individual's performance or status and the expectations of the individual himself or the particular group of which he is a member" (p. 183). More recently, Bradley (1995), the Institute of Medicine (1991), and the World Health Organization (1993) stress that since one's disability results from an interaction between disease and one's physical and social environment and resources, habilitation personnel need to focus on the impairment of functional skills (i.e., adaptive behaviors) and the environmental supports that lessen the impairment and thereby enhance the person's overall competence.

The focus on ecological factors and functional (i.e., adaptive) skills leads to the suggestion that disability is best defined as involving functional limitations in overall competence. This suggestion has implications for a contextual approach to mental retardation. Among the most important:

- Disability is neither fixed nor dichotomized; rather, it is fluid, continuous, and changing, depending upon the person's functional limitations and the supports available within a person's environment.
- One lessens functional limitations (and hence a person's disability) by providing interventions or services and supports that focus on prevention, adaptive behaviors, and role status.
- Evaluation focuses on the extent to which the functional limitations have been reduced and the person's adaptive behavior and role status enhanced.

Definition of Mental Retardation

Defining mental retardation as characterized by limitations in practical, conceptual, and social performance skills continues our attempts to better understand this important construct. Indeed, the concept of mental retardation and its definition have undergone numerous changes in terminology, IQ cutoff levels, and the diagnostic role of adaptive behavior over the last four decades (Grossman, 1973, 1977, 1983; Heber, 1959, 1961; Reschly, 1988; Sarason, 1985; Schalock, Stark, Snell, Coulter, & Polloway, 1994; Smith, 1997; Trent, 1994). The movement toward a contextual and functional definition of mental retardation is reflected in the 1992 AAMR definition and its related assumptions; in the 1992 manual (Luckasson et al.), the term *mental retardation* refers to substantial limitations in present functioning. It is characterized by significantly subaverage intellectual functioning, existing concurrently with related limitations in two or more of the following applicable adaptive skill areas: communication, self-care, home living, social skills, community use, self-direction, health and safety, functional academics, leisure, and work. Mental retardation manifests before age 18 (p. 5).

The definition is predicated on four assumptions essential to its application. First, valid assessment considers cultural and linguistic diversity as well as differences in communication and behavior. Second, limita-

tions in adaptive skills occur within the context of community environments typical of the individual's age peers; limitations are indexed to the person's individualized needs for supports. Third, specific adaptive limitations often coexist with strengths in other adaptive skill areas. Fourth, with appropriate supports over a sustained period, the life functioning of the person with mental retardation will generally improve (Luckasson et al., 1992, p. 5).

The 1992 AMMR manual (Luckasson et al.) reflects the significant change in our conception of mental retardation in which the condition is viewed not as an absolute trait expressed solely by the person, but as an expression of the functional impact of the interaction between the person with limited intellectual and adaptive skills and the person's environment. The overall competence model outlined in Figure 3.1 suggests the need to reconceptualize (and potentially redefine) mental retardation to be consistent with this notion of functional limitations in the performance domains of practical, conceptual, and social skills.

This suggestion is consistent with a number of recent attempts (e.g., Greenspan, 1997; Greenspan & Granfield, 1992; Haywood, 1997) to reformulate the construct of mental retardation within the context of the multifactorial approach to intelligence and adaptive behavior. Within this movement one finds the following key points:

- The definition of mental retardation should incorporate what is known about the behavior and development of people with mental retardation.
- Mental retardation is not a single entity.
- The key to devising an adequate definition of mental retardation is to base it on a broader model of intelligence, one that relies heavily on measures of everyday (i.e., social and practical) intelligence and not so exclusively on measures of academic intelligence (Greenspan et al., 1996, p. 127).
- People with mental retardation have demonstrated deficits in everyday intelli-

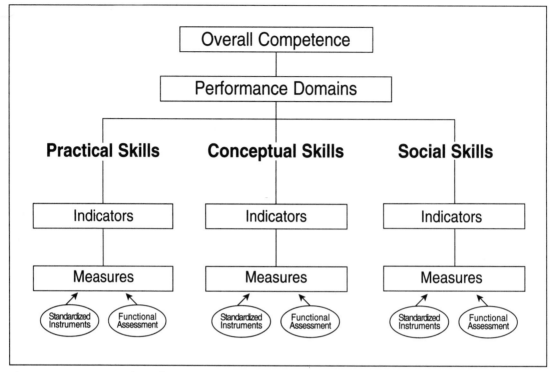

```
                    Overall Competence

                    Performance Domains

   Practical Skills      Conceptual Skills      Social Skills


      Indicators            Indicators           Indicators


       Measures             Measures             Measures

  Standardized Functional  Standardized Functional  Standardized Functional
  Instruments  Assessment  Instruments  Assessment  Instruments  Assessment
```

Figure 3.2. Measurement of overall competence.

gence (Greenspan, 1979; Greenspan & Granfield, 1992).

- Eight of the 10 adaptive skills listed in Luckasson et al. are more or less measures of adaptive intelligence (8 are practical, 1 ("functional academics") is a measure of conceptual intelligence, and 1 ("social skills") is a measure of social intelligence) (Greenspan, 1997).

- Deficits in social intelligence lie at the heart of the concept of mental retardation and may, in fact, provide a more justifiable basis for making the diagnosis of mental retardation (Greenspan, this volume; Reynolds, 1991).

- Social deficits account for many of the problems that people with mental retardation experience at work, in the community, and in school (Chadsey-Rusch, 1992; Schalock & Kiernan, 1990).

- The construct of mental retardation, like all constructs, is embedded in a historical-contextualist perspective. This implies that

humans are embedded in a social context; human behavior is effective or sophisticated in relation to goals, values, and resources operative within that context; and one's level of development can be understood only by looking directly at that person's process of learning and change and that person's ability to benefit from mediating interactions, not by looking only at the products of learning.

Focus of Assessment

If disability is defined on the basis of functional limitations in overall competence, and if mental retardation is defined as limitations in practical, conceptual, and social performance skills, then the focus of assessment (and by inference diagnosis, which will not be discussed in this chapter) must be related to the performance domains of practical, conceptual, and social skills. A model for doing so is presented in Figure 3.2. As shown in the model, overall competence is defined operationally on the basis of the three *performance domains* (practical, conceptual, and social skills), which are further defined in terms of *indicators* that are assessed via a combination of *measures* including standardized instruments and functional assessment.

Performance Domains

The three performance domains (practical, conceptual, and social skills) listed under overall competence in Figure 3.2 reflect the initial step in the operational use of a construct. The three domains define what is included in overall competence. The earlier material relating to the discussion of Figure 3.1 provided the theoretical and practical bases for including these three domains within the broader construct of overall competence. They are also the three domains found within the 10 adaptive skill areas used currently to define operationally the adaptive behavior criterion of mental retardation.

Indicators

Once the performance domains are identified, one turns to the second step in the operationalization of a construct. This second step involves selecting behaviorally based or performance indicators that represent the measurable components of the construct. This second step involves two aspects. The first is to identify clearly the focus of the indicators. For this construct, identified foci are the following:

- *for practical skills*: the ability to deal with the physical and mechanical aspects of life, including both self-maintenance and material activities (Greenspan, 1979, p. 510);
- *for conceptual skills*: the ability to solve abstract problems and use and understand symbolic processes, including language (Greenspan, 1981, p. 30); and
- *for social skills*: a person's ability to understand and deal effectively with social and interpersonal objects and events, including both awareness and skills (Greenspan & Granfield, 1992, p. 483).

The second aspect is to develop specific skill indicators that can be measured. A number of exemplary indicators are listed in Table 3.1.

Table 3.1
Exemplary Skill Indicators

Practical Skills
(Independent Living Skills)
- ADL
- IADLs
- Motor Functioning
- Community Living
- Self-Help Skills
- Occupational Skills

Conceptual Skills
(Cognitive Competencies)
- Receptive and Expressive Language
- Reading and Writing Skills
- Handling Money
- Nonverbal Communication

Social Skills
- Forming and Maintaining Friendships
- Interactions With Others
- Participation in Group Activities
- Emotional Competence
- Personal Adaptation and Social Adaptation
- Problem Solving
- Self-Direction
- Responsibility
- Socialization
- Self-Control and Self-Esteem
- Sensitivity and Insight

Measures

Figure 3.2 suggests that indicators of practical, conceptual, and social skills can be measured through one of two techniques: standardized instruments and/or functional assessment. Each is described below.

Standardized instruments. As the name implies, standardization involves uniformity of procedures in administering and scoring a test. Anastasi (1982) lays out the following critical components of a standardized measure of behavior: (a) provision of detailed directions for administration, including exact materials employed, time limits, oral instructions, preliminary demonstrations, and ways to handle queries from examinees; (b) establishment of norms that allow one to compare the person's test results with the standardization samples scores; (c) demonstration of the test's reliability and validity (see Spreat, this volume); and (d) use of trained examiners competent in test selection, administration and scoring, and score interpretation.

Functional assessment. The most typical format used in a functional assessment documents a person's functioning across one or more overall competence domains. To accomplish this, the assessment instrument employs some form of ordinal rating scale to yield a profile of individual functioning. One significant advantage of functional assessments is that, if developed and used properly, they have a higher probability of being nondiscriminatory and culturally sensitive than standardized instruments (Craig & Tassé, this volume; Lim & Browder, 1994; Mercer, 1973). In addition, they not only provide a reliable and valid way to assess functional skills, but they also can be used for diagnosis (Frattali, 1993; Granger, Cotter, Hamilton, & Fiedler, 1993; Heal & Tassé, this volume; Simeonsson & Short, 1996); instructional planning (Brown et al., 1979); implementing support strategies (Luckasson et al., 1992; Schalock, 1995); developing criterion-referenced assessments (Heal & Tassé, this volume); and evaluating

(re)habilitation outcomes (Bonwich & Reid, 1991; Schalock, 1998).

There are significant differences between functional assessments and standardized instruments. The most important include reliance on clinical judgment, use of criterion-referenced items, and the ordinal scaling of items (Heal & Tassé, this volume, Schalock & Karan, 1979; Simeonsson & Short, 1996). There is good reason to predict that functional assessments will be used even more in the future to assess performance skills related to both disability and mental retardation. Their use, and the accompanying greater use of clinical judgment, are consistent with current "best practices" recommendations found within the *Diagnostic and Statistical Manual for Mental Disorders* (American Psychiatric Association, 1994) and the *Standards for Educational and Psychological Testing* (American Psychological Association, 1985).

Implications for the Field

Thus far in the chapter I have suggested that the reformulation and merging of the constructs of adaptive behavior and intelligence will have a significant impact on:

- defining disability as functional limitations in personal overall competence;
- conceptualizing mental retardation as characterized by limitations in practical, conceptual, and social performance skills; and
- using a combination of standardized instruments and functional assessments to measure indicators of practical, conceptual, and social skills.

If these predictions are true, I foresee profound implications for the field of mental retardation. This section discusses three of these implications: (a) identifying the definitive features of mental retardation, (b) providing an organizing framework for our understanding of the construct of mental retardation, and (c) focusing the field on ecological and contextual factors.

Definitive Features of Mental Retardation

Many recent theorists (e.g., Greenspan, 1997; McGrew et al., 1996; Reschly, 1985) have suggested that mental retardation is a condition marked by deficits in three broad areas of competence: social, practical, and conceptual. The advantage of this broad conception is that it:

- reemphasizes the broad cognitive underpinnings of the disorder, while giving equal emphasis to social and instrumental competence;
- seems to better capture the essence of mental retardation by more closely aligning mental retardation with its taxon, which reflects deficits in everyday intelligence (Haywood, 1997; Reynolds, 1991; Zigler, Balla, & Hodapp, 1984);
- combines the intellectual component with other aspects of personal and social competence;
- relies on overall competence, a concept inclusive of cognitive and noncognitive abilities;
- reflects the fact that limitations in social and practical intelligence account for many of the problems encountered by people with mental retardation living and working in the community; and
- deemphasizes IQ and recaptures the natural basis of mental retardation reflective of earlier conceptions (Nihira, this volume; Thorndike, 1920).

Organizing Framework

Figures 3.1 and 3.2 provide a conceptual framework to guide the development and empirical validation of our future work. Such an organizational framework reflects policy changes, ideological changes, research findings, and theory that are providing a basis for consistent approaches to disability and mental retardation and their measurement (Simeonsson & Short, 1996). There are several advantages to such an organizing framework.

- It provides an overall competence focus that is consistent with an ecological and functional model of disability.
- It allows one to focus on the factor structure of adaptive behavior. As stated by Simeonsson and Short (1996), "one of the key conceptual dilemmas . . . is whether adaptive behavior should be conceptualized in its own right, as adaptive skills, or as social or social-developmental maturity and sophistication" (p. 138). Thus, by focusing on the multidimensionality of intelligence and adaptive behavior (see Figure 3.1), one can clarify what should be measured, reduce the overlapping nature of domains found in both measures and services, and solidify and focus on methodology, items, and samples.
- An overall competency model has been confirmed through confirmatory factor analysis, including the domains of physical and emotional competence (McGrew et al., 1996; Thompson et al., this volume).
- An organizing framework should result in better development and empirical validation of instruments for assessing multiple intelligences and the multidimensional nature of adaptive behavior.
- The organizing frameworks suggested in Figures 3.1 and 3.2 should help clarify and resolve the problems of variable terms and definitions in regard to both adaptive behavior and intelligence.

Ecological and Contextual Focus

There is a strong movement within the field of mental retardation to minimize the trait approach to the conception and measurement of mental retardation, focusing instead on the context of behavior, the interface between people and their environments, the measurement of functional skills related to important social outcomes, and the provision and evaluation of services based primarily on the support needs of the person (Castellani, 1987). This movement away from a trait approach and toward an ecological or contextual focus with the person at the apex has significant implications for the field. It has been my observation, for example, that such an approach provides a significant "common language" for consumers, advocates, and service or support providers. This common language allows for: the increased involvement of all players, the appreciation of the growth potential of the person with mental retardation, the viability of person-centered planning across environments, the implementation of appropriate support systems, and the evaluation of change.

Conclusion

In conclusion, I have suggested in this chapter that the reformulation and merging of the concepts of intelligence and adaptive behavior—and the corresponding changes in the concepts of disability and mental retardation—can have a number of significant positive impacts on the field of mental retardation. These principally include: identifying the definitive features of mental retardation, providing an organizing framework for our current and future work, and causing the field to focus on ecological and contextual factors. These potential impacts will involve significant changes to the field and, thus, represent significant challenges to each of us. How we respond to these challenges is a test of our creativity, ingenuity, persistence, and collaboration.

References

American Psychiatric Association. (1994). *Diagnostic and statistical manual for mental disorders* (4th ed.). Washington, DC: Author.

American Psychological Association. (1985). *Standards for educational and psychological testing.* Washington, DC: Author.

Anastasi, A. (1982). *Psychological testing* (5th ed.). New York: Collier Macmillan.

Anastasi, A. (1986). Intelligence as a quality of behavior. In R. J. Sternberg and D. K. Detterman (Eds.), *What is intelligence? Contemporary viewpoints on its nature and definition* (pp. 19-22). Norwood, NJ: Ablex.

Arvey, R. D., Bouchard, T. J., Carroll, J. B., Cattell, R. B., & Cohen, D. B. (1994, December 13). Mainstream science on intelligence. *Wall Street Journal,* p. B1.

Bennet, M. (Ed.). (1993). *The development of social recognition.* New York: Guilford Press.

Bonwich, L., & Reid, J. C. (1991). Medical rehabilitation: Issues in assessment of functional change. *Evaluation Practice, 12,* 205-215.

Borthwick-Duffy, S. (1994). [Review of *Mental retardation: Definition, classification, and systems of supports*]. *American Journal on Mental Retardation, 98,* 541-544.

Bradley, E. (1995). The ICIDH: Format, application in different settings, and distinction between disability and handicap. *International Disability Studies, 9,* 122-125.

Bruininks, R. H., McGrew, K., & Maruyama, G. (1988). Structure of adaptive behavior in sample with and without mental retardation. *American Journal on Mental Retardation, 93* (3), 265-272.

Brown, L., Branston, M. B., Hamre-Nieptupski, S., Pumpian, I., Certo, N., & Bruenewald, L. (1979). A strategy for developing chronological-age appropriate and functional curricular content for severely handicapped adolescents and young adults. *Journal of Special Education, 13,* 81-90.

Bruininks, R. H., Thurlow, M., & Gilman, C. J. (1987). Adaptive behavior and mental retardation. *Journal of Special Education, 21,* 69-88.

Cantor, N., & Kihlstrom, J. F. (1987). *Personal and social intelligence.* Englewood Cliffs, NJ: Prentice-Hall.

Carroll, J. B. (1993). *Human cognitive abilities*: A *summary of factor analytic studies.* Cambridge: Cambridge University Press.

Castellani, P. (1987). *The political economy of developmental disabilities.* Baltimore: Paul H. Brookes.

Cattell, R. B. (1963). Theory of fluid and crystallized intelligence: A critical experiment. *Journal of Educational Psychology, 54,* 1-22.

Cattell, R. B. (1971). *Abilities: Their structure, growth and action.* Boston: Houghton Mifflin.

Chadsey-Rusch, J. (1992). Toward defining and measuring social skills in employment settings. *American Journal on Mental Retardation, 96,* 405-418.

Daniel, M. H. (1997). Intelligence testing. *American Psychologist, 52* (10), 1038-1045.

Frattali, C. M. (1993). Perspectives on functional assessment: Its use for policy making. *Disability and Rehabilitation, 15* (1), 1-9.

Gardner, H. (1993). *Multiple intelligences: The theory in practice.* New York: Basic Books.

Goleman, D. (1995). *Emotional intelligence.* New York: Bantam.

Granger, C. V., Cotter, A. C., Hamilton, B. B., & Fiedler, R. C. (1993). The Functional Independence Measure (FIM) and the Sickness Impact Profile (SIP). *Archives of Physical Medicine and Rehabilitation, 74,* 133-138.

Greenspan, S. (1979). Social intelligence in the retarded. In N. Ellis (Ed.), *Handbook of mental deficiency: Psychological theory and research* (2nd ed.; pp. 483-531). Hillsdale, NJ: Lawrence Erlbaum.

Greenspan, S. (1981). Defining childhood social competence: A proposed working model. In B.K. Keough (Ed.), *Advances in Special Education* (Vol. 3, pp. 1-29). Greenwich, CT: JAI Press.

Greenspan, S. (1997). Dead manual walking? Why the 1992 AAMR definition needs redoing. *Education and Training in Mental Retardation and Developmental Disabilities, 32*(3), 179-190.

Greenspan, S., & Driscoll, J. (1997). The role of intelligence in a broad model of personal competence. In D. P. Flanagan, G. Genshaft, and P. L. Harrison (Eds.), *Contemporary intellectual assessment: Theories, tests, and issues* (pp. 131-150). New York: Guilford Press.

Greenspan, S., & Granfield, J. M. (1992). Reconsidering the construct of mental retardation: Implications of a model of social competence. *American Journal on Mental Retardation, 96*(4), 442-453.

Greenspan, S., Switzky, H. N., & Granfield, J. M. (1996). Everyday intelligence and adaptive behavior: A theoretical framework. In J. W. Jacobson and J. A. Mulick (Eds.), *Manual of diagnosis and professional practice in mental retardation* (pp. 127-135). Washington, DC: American Psychological Association.

Greenspan, S. I. (1997). *The growth of the mind: And the endangered origins of intelligence.* New York: Addison-Wesley.

Grossman, H. J. (Ed.). (1973). *Manual on terminology and classification in mental retardation.* Washington, DC: American Association on Mental Deficiency.

Grossman, H. J. (Ed.). (1977). *Manual on terminology and classification in mental retardation.* Washington, DC: American Association on Mental Deficiency.

Grossman, H. J. (Ed.). (1983). *Classification in mental retardation.* Washington, DC: American Association on Mental Deficiency.

Harrison, P. L. (1989). Adaptive behavior: Research to practice. *Journal of School Psychology, 23,* 301-313.

Haywood, H. C. (1997, May 28). Global perspectives on mental retardation. Keynote address, 121st annual meeting of the American Association on Mental Retardation, New York.

Heber, R. (1959). A manual on terminology and classification in mental retardation. *American Journal of Mental Deficiency Monograph 64.*

Heber, R. (1961). A manual on terminology and classification in mental retardation (2nd ed.). *American Journal of Mental Deficiency Monograph 65.*

Horn, J. L. (1979). Trends in the measurement of intelligence. In R. J. Sternberg and D. K. Detterman (Eds.), *Human intelligence: Perspectives on its theory and measurement* (pp. 237-278). Norwood, NJ: Ablex.

Institute of Medicine. (1991). *Disability in America: Toward a national agenda for prevention.* Washington, DC: National Academy Press.

Ittenbach, R. F., Spiegel, A. N., McGrew, K. S., & Bruininks, R. H. (1992). A confirmatory factor analysis of early childhood ability measures within a model of personal competence. *Journal of School Psychology, 30,* 307-323.

Kamphaus, R. W. (1987). Conceptual and psychometric issues in the assessment of adaptive behavior. *Journal of Special Education, 21*, 27-35.

Keating, D. P. (1994). Contextualist theories of intelligence. In R. J. Sternberg (Ed.), *Encyclopedia of human intelligence* (Vol. 1, pp. 293-298). New York: Macmillan.

Lim, L. H. F., & Browder, D. M. (1994). Multicultural life skills assessment of individuals with severe disabilities. *Journal of The Association for Persons With Severe Handicaps, 19*(2), 130-138.

Luckasson, R., Coulter, D. L., Polloway, E. A., Reiss, S., Schalock, R. L., Snell, M. E., Spitalnik, D. M., & Stark, J. A. (1992). *Mental retardation: Definition, classification, and systems of supports* (9th ed.). Washington, DC: American Association on Mental Retardation.

Mathias, J. L., & Nettelbeck, T. (1992). Validity of Greenspan's models of adaptive and social intelligence. *Research in Developmental Disabilities, 13*, 113-129.

McGrew, K. S., & Bruininks, R. H. (1990). Defining adaptive and maladaptive behavior within a model of personal competence. *School Psychology Review, 19*, 53-73.

McGrew, K. S., Bruininks, R. H., & Johnson, D. R. (1996). Confirmatory factor analytic investigation of Greenspan's model of personal competence. *American Journal on Mental Retardation, 100*(5), 535-545.

McGrew, K. S., Ittenbach, R. F., Bruininks, R. H., & Hill, B. K. (1991). Factor structure of maladaptive behavior across the lifespan of persons with mental retardation. *Research in Developmental Disabilities, 12*, 181-199.

Mercer, J. R. (1973). *Labeling the mentally retarded.* Berkeley: University of California Press.

Meyers, C., Nihira, K., & Zetlin, A. (1979). The measurement of adaptive behavior. In N.R. Ellis (Ed.), *Handbook of mental deficiency: Psychological theory and research* (2nd ed.), (pp. 431-481). Hillsdale, NJ: Lawrence Erlbaum.

Nesser, U. (1976). General, academic, and artificial intelligence. In L. Resnick (Ed.), *Human intelligence: Perspectives on its theory and measurement* (pp. 179-189). Norwood, NJ: Ablex.

Nesser, U., Bode, G., Bouchard, T. J., Boykin, A. W., & Cohen, D.W. (1996). Intelligence: Knows and unknows. *American Psychologist, 51* (2), 77-101.

Reschly, D. J. (1982). Assessing mild mental retardation. The influence of adaptive behavior, sociocultural status and prospects for nonbiased assessment. In C. R. Reynolds and T. B. Gutkin (Eds.), *The handbook of school psychology* (pp. 140-156). New York: Wiley Interscience.

Reschly, D. J. (1985). Best practices: Adaptive behavior. In A. Thomas and J. Grimes (Eds.), *Best practices in school psychology* (pp. 353-368). Washington, DC: National Association of School Psychology.

Reschly, D J. (1988). Assessment issues, placement litigation, and the future of mild mental retardation classification and programming. *Education and Training in Mental Retardation, 23*, 285-301.

Reynolds, M. C. (1991). Classification and labeling. In J. W. Lloyd, N. N. Singh, and A. C. Repp (Eds.), *The regular education initiative: Alternative perspectives on concepts, issues, and models* (pp. 29-41). Sycamore, IL: Sycamore.

Sarason, S. (1985). *Psychology and mental retardation: Perspectives in change.* Austin: Pro-Ed.

Schalock, R. L. (1995). *Outcome-based evaluation*. New York: Plenum.

Schalock, R. L. (1997, May 30). Defining mental retardation today: Implications for the field. Paper presented at the 121st annual meeting of the American Association on Mental Retardation, New York City.

Schalock, R. L. (1998). Traumatic brain injury: Implications for practice. *Applied and Preventive Psychology, 7*(4), 247-253.

Schalock, R. L., & Karan, O. C. (1979). Relevant assessment: The interaction between evaluation and training. In T. Bellamy and O. C. Karan (Eds.), *Vocational habilitation of the severely handicapped* (pp. 33-54). Baltimore: University Park Press.

Schalock, R. L., & Kiernan, W. E. (1990). *Habilitation planning for adults with disabilities*. New York: Springer-Verlag.

Schalock, R. L., Stark, J. A., Snell, M. E., Coulter, D., & Polloway, E. (1994). The changing conception of mental retardation: Implications for the field. *Mental Retardation, 32*(1), 25-39.

Simeonsson, R. J., & Short, R. J. (1996). Adaptive development, survival roles, and quality of life. In J. W. Jacobson and J. A. Mulick (Eds.), *Manual of diagnosis and professional practice in mental retardation* (pp. 137-146). Washington, DC: American Psychological Association.

Smith, J. D. (1997). Mental retardation as an educational construct: Time for a new shared vision? *Education and Training in Mental Retardation and Developmental Disabilities, 32*(3), 167-173.

Spearman, C. (1923). *The nature of 'intelligence' and the principles of cognition*. London: Macmillan.

Sternberg, R. J. (1984). Macrocomponents and microcomponents of intelligence: Some proposed loci in mental retardation. In P. H. Brooks, R. Speerber, and C. McCauley (Eds.), *Learning and cognition in the mentally retarded* (pp. 89-114). Hillsdale, NJ: Lawrence Erlbaum.

Sternberg, R. J. (1985). *Beyond IQ: A triarchic theory of human intelligence*. New York: Cambridge University Press.

Sternberg, R. J. (1988). *The triarchic mind*. New York: Viking.

Sternberg, R. J. (1997). The concept of intelligence and its role in lifelong learning and success. *American Psychologist, 52*(10), 1030-1037.

Sternberg, R. J., & Detterman, D. K. (Eds.). (1986). *What is intelligence? Contemporary viewpoints on its nature and definition*. Norwood, NJ: Ablex.

Sternberg, R. J., & Wagner, R. K. (1986). *Practical intelligence: Nature and origins of competence in the everyday world*. Cambridge: Cambridge University Press.

Sternberg, R. J., Wagner, R. K., Williams, W. M., & Horvath, J. A. (1995). Testing common sense. *American Psychologist, 50*(11), 912-927.

Taylor, E. H., & Cadet, J. L. (1989). Social intelligence: A neurological system? *Psychological Reports, 64*, 423-444.

Thorndike, E. L. (1920). Intelligence and its uses. *Harper's, 140*, 227-235.

Thorndike, E. L., Hagen, E. P., & Sattler, J. M. (1986). *The Stanford-Binet Intelligence Scale: Technical manual* (4th ed.). Chicago: Riverside.

Thurstone, L. L. (1938). *Primary mental abilities. Psychometric Monographs* (No. 1). Chicago: University of Chicago Press.

Trent, J. W. (1994). *Inventing the feeble mind: A history of mental retardation in the United States.* Berkeley: University of California Press.

Vernon, P. E. (1961). The structure of human abilities (2nd ed.).London: Methuen.

Wechsler, D. (1991). WISC-III manual. San Antonio, TX: Psychological Corporation.

Widaman, K. F., Borthwick-Duffy, S., & Little, T. D. (1991). The structure and development of adaptive behavior. In N. W. Bray (Ed.), *International review of research in mental retardation* (Vol. 17, pp. 1-54). New York: Academic Press.

Widaman, K. F., Gibbs, K. W., & Geary, D. C. (1987). Structure of adaptive behavior: I. Replication across fourteen samples on nonprofoundly mentally retarded people. *American Journal on Mental Retardation, 91,* 348-360.

Widaman, K. F., & McGrew, K. S. (1996). The structure of adaptive behavior. In J. W. Jacobson and J. A. Mulick (Eds.), *Manual of diagnosis and professional practice in mental retardation* (pp. 97-110). Washington, DC: American Psychological Association.

Widaman, K. F., Stacy, A. W., & Borthwick-Duffy, S. A. (1993). Construct validity of dimensions of adaptive behavior: A multitrait-multimethod evaluation. *American Journal on Mental Retardation, 98*(2), 219-234.

World Health Organization. (1980). *International classification of impairments, disabilities, and handicaps.* Geneva: Author.

World Health Organization. (1993). *The ICD-10 classification of mental and behavioural disorders. Diagnostic criteria for research.* Geneva: Author.

Zigler, E., Balla, D., & Hodapp, R. (1984). On the definition and classification of mental retardation. *American Journal of Mental Deficiency, 89,* 215-230.

CHAPTER 4

A Contextualist Perspective on Adaptive Behavior

STEPHEN GREENSPAN
University of Connecticut

Introduction

The adaptive behavior criterion was added to the definition of mental retardation nearly 40 years ago in response to the criticism that the IQ criterion was not substantially contextualized. It was felt, with some justification, that so serious a diagnosis should be based (at least in part) on performance in real-world contexts, rather than on a test administered in a psychologist's office. It is somewhat ironic, therefore, to note that one major limitation of existing adaptive behavior measures is the insufficient attention paid to the context in which the behavior takes place.

There is increasing understanding that context is important in determining the limits of one's competence. This is particularly critical in diagnosing people with mental retardation at the upper levels of the IQ cutoff, where one may function relatively competently in some (e.g., routinized) contexts but demonstrate significant incompetence in other (e.g., novel) contexts. If current adaptive behavior assessment instruments show contextual sensitivity, it is usually by adding items. For example, a more differentiated approach to "undressing" might ask whether one can undo a clothing item with snaps as well as one with zippers. But a contextualist perspective on adaptive behavior involves far more than item differentiation, as I hope to demonstrate.

I begin this chapter with a description of contextualism, one of the four worldviews used widely in the behavioral sciences. Then, I discuss how the fields of psychology and mental retardation have only recently begun to use contextualism as a guiding framework for research and clinical practice, pointing out the ways in which the study and assessment of

adaptive behavior could benefit from use of a contextualist perspective, using social intelligence (particularly the heretofore overlooked construct of credulity) as an example. I conclude the chapter with a discussion of a proposed action framework for social adaptation.

Contextualism Defined

Contextualism is one of the four scientific "worldviews" identified by S. Pepper (1942) in his path-breaking book, *World Hypotheses*. Contextualism, and the other three worldviews—organicism, mechanism, and formism—are broad metamodels within which narrower theorists and theories can be located. Until fairly recently, behavioral science in general, and the study of mental retardation in particular, was dominated largely by the other three worldviews, particularly mechanism. Within psychology, interest in contextualism has blossomed dramatically, as reflected in several publications exploring its implications for both research (Ford & Lerner, 1992; Gillespie, 1992; Keating, 1994; Rosnow & Georgoudi, 1986a, pp. 3-220) and clinical practice (Sarason, 1981; Sarbin & Juhasz, 1982).

Setting Within Which Behavior Occurs

An obvious central element in contextualism is an increased appreciation of the setting or context in which behavior occurs. Certainly, this is an important distinction, as many psychological frameworks (e.g., Freudian and Piagetian theory) attach almost no importance to context. Nevertheless, it is a mistake to think (as some do) that contextualism is nothing more than behavioral interaction. Obviously, an appreciation of setting is implicit in other metamodels, such as the emphasis in behaviorist psychology on the reinforcing value of settings and the emphasis in cognitive psychology on the role of setting as a source of task difficulty. But in contextualism, setting (including not just immediate setting but larger cultural and historical setting) provides "the wider context that 'allows' or 'invites' the occurrence of [an] event and renders it socially intelligible" (Rosnow & Georgoudi, 1986b, p. 5).

The Process of Becoming

A central part of contextualism is the "emphasis on reality as active, ongoing, changing; that is, an open process of 'becoming' " (Rosnow & Georgoudi, 1986b, p. 3). Thus, the social reality that an individual faces is transformed by that individual just as the individual is transformed by that social reality. This limits (although does not eliminate) a theoretician's ability to assert general laws; while patterns may still be discovered that have broad applicability, it is a mistake to assume, as in the past, that behavior is simply a function of linear relationships among variables. Instead, we must make a greater attempt to "unlock the mysteries of what makes an event meaningful" (Rosnow & Georgoudi, 1986b, p. 5) for individuals or groups.

The Pragmatics of Life

An important part of the contextualist approach is its assault on the division of science into "basic" and "applied" branches; it accepts the view that the best way to advance basic understanding is to study social reality as it occurs in its everyday, practical state. This emphasis has been especially important in the study of intelligence, where there has been increasing interest in natural categories (Rosch, 1988) and everyday cognition.

Central to the contextualist perspective is the notion of individuals as active determiners of their own development (Ford, 1987; Lerner

& Busch-Rossnagel, 1981) and as active selectors of their own settings. This reinforces the notion that behavior cannot be reduced to a linear aggregation of forces acting on the individual. Implicit in this view is an assault on what Dennett (1991) termed "boxology" (the tendency to localize functioning neatly into geographically separate parts of the brain) and also on the notion of a central processor or, for that matter, on a single decontextualized "intelligence." Rather, intelligence is viewed in terms of functional adaptation and survival in specific contexts.

Contextualist writings on intelligence have focused on the "pragmatics of life" (Dixon, 1986, p. 139) as reflected in Dewey's (1939) emphasis on skill, knowledge, and expertise aspects of intelligence. Life-span developmental psychologists, most notably Baltes and his colleagues (Baltes, Dittmann-Kohli, & Dixon, 1984), motivated by a desire to counter the view of aging as invariably debilitating, have formulated a dual-process view of intelligence, as "mechanics" (content-free processing) and "pragmatics" (experience-based action). Recent interest in "wisdom" (experience-based insight and judgment about complex aspects of everyday life) has been stimulated largely by efforts to demonstrate areas in which aging individuals are superior (or at least not inferior) to their younger counterparts (Sternberg, 1990). Each of these concepts reflects the importance of what I and others (e.g., Ford, 1986, 1994; Barnes & Sternberg, 1989) have termed "social intelligence."

Social Processes and Contexts

Radical critiques of clinical psychology (Sarason, 1981) and psychopathology (Sarbin, 1977, 1991) point out the absence in these fields of anything approaching a contextualist perspective. Because contextualism is in some respects more closely aligned with sociology than psychology, psychologists making such critiques are often found in community psychology, a branch of psychology that shares with sociology an emphasis on social processes and contexts.

Research and clinical approaches to adaptive (and maladaptive) behavior have been dominated largely by psychologists and have, for the most part, been devoid of contextualist influences. This has, however, begun to change, as reflected, for example, in the growing emphasis among behavior analysts on ecological (i.e., contextual) factors (Warren, 1977). An example of this in the mental retardation literature is the growing awareness of the communicative intent of maladaptive behavior in nonverbal individuals and the growing understanding that it is a mistake to treat behavior disorders solely as a function of an individual's internal pathology (Horner, 1994).

In summary, central to the contextualist metamodel is a view of persons as "self-organizing, self-constructing open systems fused with their environments" (Ford & Lerner, 1992, p. 222). Such a view runs counter to traditional scientific approaches in the mental retardation field in that contextualism view (a) individual behavior as nonlinear, complexly determined, and affected by self-regulatory processes and (b) environments as dynamic entities that challenge the adaptive schemas of individuals.

Contextualism and Mental Retardation

Contextualism has influenced efforts to define mental retardation and to measure adaptive behavior, although there has been relatively little explicit mention of contextualism in this literature. Leland (1992) has argued that the original approach to adaptive behavior was heavily influenced by Vygotsky's (1978; Wertsch, 1985) historical, contextualist perspective. This is reflected in the preference by Leland and the other authors of the first measure—the American Association on Mental Deficiency (AAMD; now American Association on Mental Retardation; AAMR) *Adaptive Behavior Scale* (Nihira, Foster, Shellhaas, Leland, 1968)—for a profile score approach rather than for a single summary index analogous to a full-scale IQ score. However

sympathetic one may be to this approach, it undoubtedly contributed to the ignoring of the adaptive behavior criterion. In spite of Nihira's lip-service to contextualism, however, one can question the extent to which the early (and certainly the later) approaches to adaptive behavior measurement reflect a contextualist or dynamic approach to assessment.

The so-called "paradigm shift" (Bradley & Knoll, 1995) reflected in the most recent AAMR classification manual (Luckasson et al., 1992) may be considered, in part, to be based on contextualist assumptions. Among the contextualist elements in that document are: (a) an emphasis on human plasticity (Gollin, 1981; Lerner, 1984)—a core concept in contextualism—reflected in the optimistic statement that people with mental retardation can grow out of their status; (b) an emphasis on the modularity of functioning (Fodor, 1983) in the view that one can have mental retardation and still be relatively competent, even normal, in numerous areas of functioning; and (c) perhaps the most important (and most noted) manifestation of contextualism in the 1992 AAMR manual, namely a presentation of disability severity in terms of extent of needed supports (i.e., adapted contexts) rather than in terms of decontextualized deficiencies.

Nevertheless, in spite of these contextualist elements, the field of adaptive behavior measurement is still, by and large, operating within noncontextualist assumptions. This is reflected in the continued reliance on IQ as the primary criterion for defining mental retardation, both in the AAMR (Luckasson et al., 1992) and APA (Jacobson & Mulick, 1996) manuals and in the continuing tendency to base measures of adaptive behavior on deductively generated "static" taxonomies, such as the community skills curriculum (Ford et al., 1989) underlying the construct of "adaptive skills." This new term is a synonym that was substituted for *adaptive behavior* in the 1992 AAMR manual, partly to shift the focus from pathology (as in maladaptive behavior) to competence.

An alternative, more contextualist, strategy suggested by Ceci (1996) for studying intelligence, but also applicable to adaptive behavior (which could be defined as intelligence applied to everyday life) is to examine the "natural" problems that are critical to adaptation in the real world. The original development of IQ measures was, in fact, guided by such a strategy, in that Binet and Simon devised their early scale by incorporating into it various items taken directly out of the elementary- and secondary-school curricula. (Their task, it should be remembered, was to devise a measure suitable for identifying children likely to fail in school.) Knowing this, Sternberg (1984) used the term "academic intelligence" to describe the content measured by IQ tests, most of which are modeled after the *Binet-Simon* scales. Sternberg distinguished academic intelligence from "everyday intelligence" (a term I now prefer to my own earlier "adaptive intelligence") to describe those aspects of intelligence that involve solving challenges faced in settings other than the classroom.

A basic problem with measures of adaptive behavior, as with the construct itself (under its various names), is the absence of any widely accepted or widely used comprehensive model of competence to guide development of measures or to put them into a broader context. This, of course, is true of most psychological constructs, including intelligence. In the absence of an initial guiding theoretical framework, a construct's content typically becomes defined by the items on the most widely used measures. Thus, the content structure of adaptive behavior, as of intelligence, has been derived from factor analyses of existing measures (Widaman & McGrew, 1996). This strategy underemphasizes, however, the importance of domains (such as social intelligence) that are poorly represented on existing measures and overemphasizes the importance of other domains (such as motor competence) that, although well-represented on such measures, may be less central to the natural "folk" construct of mental retardation.

Recent converging research on multidimensional aspects of intelligence and of adaptive behavior lends some support to the usefulness of a model of personal competence proposed some time ago (Greenspan, 1979, 1981) as a possible guiding framework for defining adaptive behavior and, by extension, mental retardation. In its most recent version (Greenspan & Driscoll, 1997), the model has eight components. As noted in Figure 4.1, these are grouped in pairs into four major domains. Physical competence is composed of organ competence and motor competence; affective competence is composed of temperament and character; everyday competence is composed of social intelligence and practical intelligence; while academic competence is composed of conceptual intelligence (IQ) and language.

Widaman and McGrew (1996) note that all four of the major domains are represented in factorial studies (except that social intelligence emerges as a separate subfactor only when relevant items are added to commonly used adaptive behavior measures). Everyday competence is undoubtedly the most widely tapped domain, especially practical intelligence, referred to typically as an "independence" or "activities of daily living" factor. Academic competence is included in measures of adaptive behavior, especially through various indices of communicative competence. Affective competence, involving both temperament and character, is represented in adaptive behavior instruments, under the rubric of the maladaptive behavior domain. Physical competence, especially a motoric competence (or development) factor is also found in most adaptive behavior measures.

A problem with a factor-analytic approach to adaptive behavior, however, is that while it makes sense of the content in existing measures (by grouping them hierarchically), it cannot indicate which content domains have no business being included or which missing content domains should be included. This judgment must be derived from some external validational technique, of either a quantitative

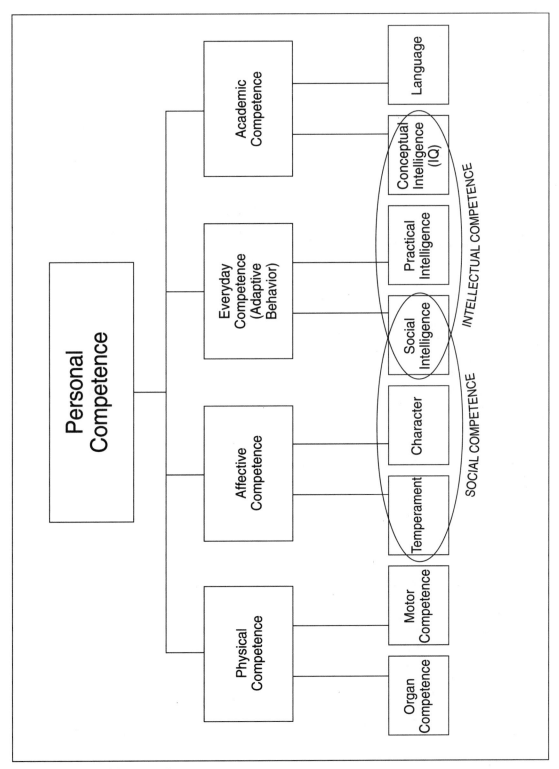

Figure 4.1. Static model of personal competence.

(e.g., discriminant function analysis) or qualitative (e.g., consensual validation) nature. Such a consensual approach underlay the decision by the AAMR (Luckasson et al., 1992) to conclude that maladaptive behavior (that is, psychopathology) has no place in the definition of mental retardation, regardless of how strong the empirical support for a psychopathology factor in existing measures of adaptive behavior.

The dropping of maladaptive behavior is in line with my earlier arguments (Greenspan, 1979, 1981) that presence of mental illness, while important for service provision, is irrelevant for the purpose of diagnosing people with mental retardation. This is because there are many individuals who have good mental health but who by consensus would be considered to have mental retardation. Maladaptive behavior was initially brought into the definition of adaptive behavior because of the quite accurate understanding that incompetence in the social domain is an important, indeed universal, aspect of mental retardation. However, given the absence of an orienting model of personal competence (especially one that contained a focus on multiple intelligences), the inventors of the first adaptive behavior measures assumed that social incompetence meant maladaptive behavior. In fact, the social intelligence construct provides a much more appropriate focus, one more in line with the natural prototype of mental retardation as a disorder characterized by "dumbness" (low everyday intelligence) rather than "badness" or "madness." Such a prototype approach, while once considered inferior to the polythetic (Chinese menu, or x symptoms out of y) approach underlying the APA *Diagnostic and Statistical Manuals* as well as the AAMR's approach to defining adaptive skills, is now considered by some scholars (Cantor & Genero, 1986) to provide a preferable basis for capturing the true essence of a behavioral disorder.

Various research studies (Greenspan & Delaney, 1983; Greenspan & McGrew, 1996; Greenspan & Shoultz, 1981; McGrew, Bruininks, & Johnson, 1996), using a variety of qualitative and quantitative methods, have provided evidence that low social intelligence (i. e., problems in interpersonal understanding) is, in fact, a critically important prototypic characteristic of people with mental retardation (see Greenspan & Love, 1997, for a recent review). Nevertheless, social intelligence continues to receive short shrift in measures of adaptive behavior.

While the 1992 AAMR definition of mental retardation, and of adaptive skills, was apparently influenced by my writings (see Luckasson et al., chap. 2), my main recommendation— the need to focus on intellectual aspects of adaptive behavior—was not followed. The construct of adaptive skills devised by Luckasson et al. was derived, instead, from a community skills curriculum (Ford et al., 1989) rather than from a model of multiple intelligences. In fact, of the 10 adaptive skills, 8 are mainly measures of practical competence; 1 is mainly a measure of academic competence; and 1 ("social skill") is defined in such a way that it is as much or more a measure of affective competence (temperament and character) than of social intelligence (see Greenspan, 1997; Greenspan, Switzky, & Granfield, 1996, for a fuller discussion).

Adaptive behavior measures have not been universally used, as reflected in the continued practice by the departments of mental retardation in several states of basing eligibility decisions solely on IQ. The main reason for this lack of universal use is the assumption by many clinicians and agencies— an assumption abetted by the AAMR definitions—that adaptive behavior is secondary to, and somehow separate from, deficiencies in "intelligence." Because many lay people perceive mental retardation to be a disorder marked by low intelligence, the key to making adaptive behavior central to the definition of mental retardation and more widely used in practice is to ground it in a broadened and multifaceted construct of intelligence.

Searching for Social Intelligence

The most widely used and best validated model of multiple intelligences is the one first proposed by E. L. Thorndike (1920) more than 75 years ago. The three intelligences in his model—abstract, mechanical, and social—are similar (except for names) to content domains in several other ability models, including those of Sternberg (1988), Carroll (1986), and Guilford (1967). Thorndike's model is incorporated into my competence model (see Figure 4.1), with social intelligence and mechanical (which I term "practical") intelligence making "everyday competence," and abstract (which I term "conceptual") intelligence incorporated (along with language) into "academic competence."

One interesting support for considering social intelligence in defining adaptive behavior and mental retardation is the finding from animal analog research that early neurological insult has greater impact on social and species-specific competencies than on academic or formally learned behaviors (Kolb, 1989, p. 1212). This is congruent with recent research suggesting that people with neurologically based disorder, such as Prader-Willi syndrome, Sotos syndrome, hydrocephalus, and Asperger disorder, invariably exhibit social decoding and encoding deficits, even when IQ is relatively normal (Greenspan & Love, 1997; Rourke, 1995).

An implication of social intelligence deficit in individuals with IQ at or above the 70 (or 75) IQ cutoff is that adaptive behavior assessment items need to be more relevant to the kinds of situations encountered in semi-independent community settings such as making complex everyday decisions. This emphasis in existing instruments reflects the fact that early measures of adaptive behavior were devised during a time when large numbers of people with mental retardation were institutionalized. In such contexts, it was understandable that daily living skills were emphasized more than complex social functioning. But if one looks at reasons why people

with mental retardation fail in community settings, such failures almost always involve mistaken or ineffective handling of difficult interpersonal situations. Examples of such mistakes (e.g., pulling a fire alarm when lonely, slashing someone's tires when angry, or failing to hide sexual arousal when playing with children) reflect an inability to understand the range of possible interpersonal consequences of one's actions.

Although I have been writing about social intelligence as a critical and overlooked aspect of adaptive behavior for almost 20 years, only relatively recently have I begun to understand the key to measuring social intelligence and, by extension, adaptive behavior: examining a person's ability to master intellectual demands of key interpersonal situations that are critical for community survival and may pose particular difficulty for a person with intellectual impairments. While the authors of the 1992 AAMR manual (Luckasson et al.) were justified in pointing out the wide variability among people in functioning, I believe that it is a mistake to conceptualize this solely in terms of variability across the 10 adaptive skill content areas. The overlooked phenomenon of variability within skill areas (as a function of specific contextual demands) may be even more important for understanding the extent to which one needs supports and protections and may have particular relevance for developing valid assessment instruments.

The literature on cognitive development (e.g., the work of Piaget) proposes that only under conditions of ambiguity and complexity (e.g., by creating perceptual illusions as in Piaget's famous water jar experiment) can one assess mastery of a concept (in that case, conservation of matter). Mastery of more routine and nonambiguous situations, while important sources of information about what someone can do in easy situations, will not provide critical information about the individual's limitations and vulnerabilities in more difficult situations that, no matter how infrequently they occur, may be relevant for viewing him or her as incompetent. For example, a person with mental retardation may be adequate in routine interpersonal situations (e.g., those that occur informally in a workplace or at a bus stop) but may well be much less adequate when dealing with more cognitively and affectively challenging situations (e.g., those that might occur when someone is trying to trick you into doing something you don't want to do or something that may not be in your best interest). Thus, the key to conceptualizing and measuring adaptive behavior may be to (a) identify situations particularly critical to achievement of a "competent" or "incompetent" status and (b) seek to understand better the reasons why people with mental retardation may be ineffective in coping with those situations.

Because measures of social intelligence have failed to incorporate problems that are modeled after critical microsituations found in the real world, it is not surprising that measures of social intelligence correlate highly with measures of IQ. This lack of sufficient differentiation from IQ subscales has, in fact, been one of the major sources of criticism of social intelligence measures (Keating, 1978; Walker & Foley, 1973). This has caused some critics to question not only the adequacy of the tests but the existence of the construct.

In opposition to this view, Goodnow (1986) pointed out the fallacy, especially common among psychologists, in thinking that something exists only if one can reliably attach a number to it. She notes, for example, that ugliness and shyness are widely accepted as important traits along which individuals differ, even though few feel the need to quantify judgments about these traits. In Goodnow's view, one cannot deny the existence of constructs such as social and practical intelligence (which, like ugliness and shyness, are so widely used in everyday parlance) just because of an absence of psychometrically sound instruments.

Again, measures of social intelligence correspond highly with measures of academic intelligence (i.e., IQ). This correlation most likely reflects the fact that, in spite of their interpersonal content, measures of social intelligence pose problems that require solutions highly similar in form to those used in measures of IQ. To overcome this limitation, it is necessary to frame problems derived from critical social situations, as they exist in their natural messy, or what Brunswick (1952) termed "tied," state. To devise a "cleaner" measure of social intelligence risks devising merely another measure of IQ.

Martin Ford (1986, 1992, 1994) has suggested that the goal of devising an adequate (i.e., differentiated-from-IQ) direct measure of social intelligence may be unattainable. He has proposed an alternate, contextualist, solution: to use actual behavior in critical tasks, rather than on formal tests, as an adequate indirect measure of one's social intelligence. This is in line with Goodnow's (1986) view that one can conclude that someone is lacking in social intelligence if that person behaves in a manner that causes others to view him or her as lacking in social intelligence (i.e., to view him or her as a person with mental retardation). This implies, as I have argued elsewhere (Greenspan, 1997), that there should be more of a role for integrative clinical judgment (the ultimate classificatory tool in most other psychoeducational disorders) in determining adaptive behavior deficits and in diagnosing mental retardation.

Abandonment of clinical judgment in practice reflects: (a) reification of the IQ test (in which an IQ score is treated as if it were more "real" than behavioral indices of intelligence); (b) concern about a history of abuse of clinical judgment, as in Goddard's human "moron detectors" who (mis)diagnosed people from a distance; and (c) a consequent belief among professionals in the field of mental retardation that false positives are worse than false negatives. Grossman (1983) called for return to a greater reliance on clinical judgment in diagnosing mental retardation, but his recommendation (like his related call for more flexibility in use if IQ scores) has not been followed universally.

Credulity and Gullibility as Core Deficits in Mental Retardation

Although the major focus of this volume is on the conceptualization and measurement of adaptive behavior, it is not possible for me to ignore the question that underlies most of the interest in this topic: What is mental retardation? This is because past failure to base measures of adaptive behavior more closely on core (i.e., cognitive) and critical deficits has resulted in less than universal use of the measures and in resistance to the construct as part of any definition of mental retardation.

An outgrowth of my growing interest in contextualism is an increased awareness that the core deficit in people who are validly viewed (regardless of their IQ) as having mental retardation may be their vulnerability to social exploitation through deception and psychological manipulation. In other words, their social intelligence deficit may manifest itself in relatively benign and minor forms in routine social situations, but may be quite disabling (i.e., risk creating) in situations of deliberate deception and manipulation.

The problem of victimization of people with mental retardation has received minimal attention and has been discussed mainly in terms of their being the target of criminal acts, such as assault or robbery (Luckasson, et al., 1992). However, victimization is a more central (and generally more subtle) problem that goes to the heart of why people with mental retardation are considered to need the protections (ranging from in-home services to conservators) associated with the label.

Anyone who has been involved in efforts to support people in inclusive community roles knows that exploitation by others is an ever-present possibility, one with the potential to unravel even the most promising of placements. Such exploitation can take many forms, from the relatively minor (e.g., the ubiquitous phone solicitor) to the relatively serious (e.g., being enticed into unwanted sex or criminal behavior), but they all involve some variant on the theme of someone pretending to be one's friend who is actually one's enemy. One particularly poignant example involved "Sue," a woman who had her young child taken away from her because she could not protect him sexually or herself financially from predatory friends and relatives.

The Richard Lapointe case (Greenspan, 1995) provides evidence that the related constructs of credulity (inability to see through untruthful assertions) and gullibility (ease with which one can be duped) may lie at the heart of explaining why people with mental retardation, and related developmental disorders, are so vulnerable to exploitation by others. Because the ability to see through ruses has clear cognitive (as well as personality) underpinnings, measures of credulity and gullibility have potential utility in development of contextually relevant measures of adaptive behavior.

Interestingly, one of the few references to credulity as a core deficit in people with mental retardation comes from a 19th century British psychiatry text by Sir Alexander Morrison (1824). In a chapter entitled "Degrees of Imbecility," Morrison noted that "when the judgment is remarkably deficient, there is a general and unusual degree of credulity" (as cited in Skultans, 1975, p. 243).

The case of Richard Lapointe illustrates the role of credulity and gullibility in placing people with developmental disabilities at risk of being ineffective in coping with crucial community challenges. Lapointe is a 50-year-old Connecticut man born with a congenital brain malformation, Dandy-Walker syndrome, causing hydrocephalus and a loss of cerebellar tissue (see Greenspan, 1998, for a description of the disorder). Although his IQ was considerably above the 70 cutoff score for mental retardation, Lapointe was perceived by fellow churchgoers, neighbors, coworkers (he was a dishwasher with solid work habits), and in-laws (his ex-wife has cerebral palsy, and they had a son) as a simple person with social skills that fit the natural prototype of someone with mild mental retardation. This is in line with recent literature suggesting that people with hydrocephalus and other developmental brain syndromes have a very high likelihood of having "nonverbal learning disabilities" (Rourke, 1995), a condition marked by moderate academic deficits (especially in math) and severe deficits in social intelligence (Semirud-Clikeman & Hynd, 1990).

In 1992, Lapointe, a man with no history of violence, was convicted of brutally raping and murdering Bernice Martin, his wife's elderly grandmother (5 years earlier). His conviction was based solely on three highly dubious confessions obtained during a 10-hour interrogation. The first confession said essentially, "I don't remember killing her, but if the evidence says I did it I guess I did." (Police interrogation handbooks encourage officers to suggest that the perpetrator blacked out, as explanation for their lack of memory.) The third confession contained details incongruent with forensic evidence presented by the prosecution at the trial. (The confessions were obtained from three different interrogators operating independently, and the third interrogator was a junior officer unfamiliar with many of the details of the crime.)

This case is very upsetting to disability advocates. Aside from the fact that Lapointe is a person with a disability who was likely convicted wrongly, the reality and relevance of his disability were minimized by the prosecution, who made much of the fact that his IQ score was above the cutoff score for mental retardation. This appears to be a reversal of the former tactic of many to use a too-low IQ score to institutionalize individuals who demonstrated no impairment in their everyday social behavior. In the Lapointe case, someone with universally noted social impairments who has a serious brain disorder now known to be associated with such impairments (Dennis, Jacennik, & Barnes, 1994) was given a life sentence (and very nearly executed) largely on the basis of an IQ score above an arbitrarily determined score.

Richard Lapointe, in spite of low-normal IQ, has always been considered to fit the natural prototype for mental retardation. One reason is that he has always exhibited remarkable credulity, as reflected in many anecdotes collected by Robert Perske (1997). Credulity is certainly germane to any effort to understand why his "confessions" should have been suppressed by the judge presiding over his trial. The key to making an innocent person confess in a police interrogation is making statements, threats, and promises that only a highly naive person would believe (Ofshe & Leo, in press).

Among the deceptive statements made to Lapointe are the following: (a) He was called into the police station on the false pretense of helping the police by sharing his expertise; he was not told at the outset that he was a suspect; (b) false charts (with the names of "Sergeant Friday and Detective Gannon") were displayed in the interrogation room, listing DNA and other nonexistent evidence, all intended to create a sense of being trapped; (c) Lapointe was told that the police had strong evidence that he committed the crime, and that from their experience his lack of memory meant he must have blacked out; (d) he was told that the police wanted to help him, but they could help only if he confessed; (e) Lapointe was told that there was a good chance his wife would go to jail and his son would be taken away if he did not cooperate; and (f) he was told he could go home if he confessed.

Lapointe, like many people with mild cognitive impairments, did relatively well in routine social situations where he could use what Spitz (1988) termed "learning" but less well in novel (especially ambiguous or threatening) social situations in which his limitations in what Spitz termed "thinking" became more evident. Lapointe's credulity (inability to decipher when he was being deceived) came into play in such situations, as on the many occasions when he was the butt of practical jokes. An example of such a joke occurred when he worked in a grocery store. Seeking to replenish the banana display, he asked where the bananas were kept. He was told to take them off the banana tree in the back room. Lapointe went looking for the banana tree, to the amusement of his coworkers (Perske, 1997).

Contextualism comes into play in understanding why Lapointe, who otherwise functioned successfully in many important social roles such as husband, father, and citizen, was so disastrously vulnerable to a police interrogation. Since the advent of protections against use of physical coercion in interrogations, police in the United States have become extremely skilled in using various forms of deceptive manipulation, which Ofshe and Leo (in press) have analogized to "a confidence scam" designed to extract confessions. The theory underlying use of such tactics is that only people with a guilty conscience would confess under these circumstances. But it is now widely understood that these techniques work on many innocent people and that innocent people with limited intelligence are especially susceptible (Gudjonsson, 1992).

The Assessment of Credulity and Gullibility

The behavior that characterizes overly credulous people such as Lapointe is typically referred to as gullibility. Credulity may be considered the cognitive underpinnings of gullibility, which (like all behaviors) is likely to be affected by personality factors, such as desire to please, or the "external" motivational orientation that Switzky (1997) and others have found to be widespread among people with mental retardation. Amazingly, although *gullibility* is a term widely used in everyday characterizations of others, it is virtually unmentioned in the psychology literature (this is also true of *credulity*), and what little does exist deals mainly with general social phenomena, such as the "Barnum effect" (in which people are likely to believe comments made about them, no matter how bogus, if they are presented as scientifically based), rather than

with individual differences (Layne, 1979).

Julian Rutter is one of the few who have studied individual differences in gullibility and pointed out its heavy cognitive component. His interest in gullibility stemmed from his research on interpersonal trust and his disagreement with the view that highly intelligent people are likely to be low on trust. Rotter (1980) believed trust, and the related construct of locus of control, to be largely independent of intelligence. To test this, he conducted an experiment in which subjects who varied in level of interpersonal trust were confronted by an experimenter who put them in a situation (having to handle equipment that threw off sparks and, despite the assurances of the experimenter, did not seem to be fixed) in which being trusting (i.e., to go along with the experiment) could be perceived to be risky. Under these circumstances highly intelligent people who rated high on trust (i.e., who in most circumstances might give someone the benefit of the doubt) were likely to say "no way." Thus, to Rotter, what was seen as distrust in bright people could be understood in terms of low gullibility and their ability to see through situations in which they are being conned or manipulated. For Rotter gullibility was evidence not of trust per se but of what might be considered "foolish" or "naive" trust. And *foolishness* and *naiveté* are terms used in folk psychology to connote low social intelligence and to describe people with mental retardation.

How might one assess credulity (the cognitive underpinnings of gullibility)? Answers to this question germinated as I engaged in the favorite activity of American male academics: lying on the couch watching a sports event on TV. An ad for a new sports news network gave a number of incredible sports headlines (e.g., "Indy 500 to add 23 miles"; "Jack Nicklaus wins professional beach volley ball tournament") with a laughing background voice saying, "Mr. Gullible," followed by the announcement: "If you watched ESPN-News, you would know if these headlines were true or not." It occurred to me that such an approach might be extremely useful in tapping credulity in people with mental retardation.

A measure of credulity could easily be constructed, which contained various forms of false news stories, with the task of having to decide which stories are probably phony. Preliminary piloting of such an instrument (with normally developing children) suggests that there is a strong age trend, with credulity declining in middle childhood, but with social credulity (the kind most relevant to vulnerability to interpersonal exploitation) persisting for many individuals much later than physical incredulity. I strongly suspect that people with mental retardation will be found as a group to be quite high on credulity, and that those considered to be particularly vulnerable to exploitation (even with IQ over 70) will be especially credulous. This belief is speculative, however, as there is as yet virtually no research on credulity in people with mental retardation.

Direct measures of credulity and gullibility, using both verbal and videotaped stimuli, could be combined with rating instruments (such as direct measures, yet to be developed) filled out by knowledgeable informants. These would, one hopes, provide a multifaceted picture of a person's history of, and future susceptibility to, deception and manipulation. Discussions with caregivers have encouraged me to think that this may, indeed, be a quite promising avenue for research and instrument development. For example, the parents of a young man with Asperger disorder told me that in spite of relatively high IQ (he has done some college work), their son can be talked into almost anything. Thus, when they throw out some of his extensive newspaper collection when it threatens to take over the house, they make up a fantastic story (e.g., "they spontaneously combusted and were thrown out by firemen," or "they were eaten by paper mites"), and he always falls for the story, no matter how incredible. One can imagine that evidence of his credulity, combined with knowledge of his disorder (where retarded social intelligence, under the rubric of "theory

of mind," is now considered by some the core impairment), would be helpful if he ever were to find himself in the shoes of Richard Lapointe.

A Proposed Action Framework for Social Adaptation

Being susceptible to deceptive manipulation is, of course, not the exclusive purview of people with developmental disorders. Social effectiveness and ineffectiveness, like any behavioral outcome, is multiply determined; there are differing and complex pathways (what developmental contextualists call "the principle of equifinality") to the same endpoint. Attempting to understand the relationship between credulity (and other aspects of low social intelligence) as an input and gullibility and other failed or maladaptive outcomes, I made a preliminary effort to transform my model of personal competence from a static trait model (see Figure 4.1), useful in describing one's general characteristics, to an action model, useful in explaining or predicting one's behavior in specific circumstances.

This proposed action model (see Figure 4.2), much more fully described in Greenspan (in press), builds on the work of motivation theorists, particularly Bandura (1986) and Ford (1992). The model, very similar to Ford's—except that it substitutes social intelligence for his more general term "competence"—can be summarized in the following formula: relative social effectiveness in complex situations is a function of environment (severity of situational demands) times motivation (goals plus affect plus personal agency beliefs) times social intelligence (decoding plus insight) times biology (endurance plus sensory functioning).

Context Demands

Context demands refer to the difficulties posed in a particular microsituation. Thus, those who could survive a 10-hour ordeal such as Richard Lapointe's might crack under the pressure of a

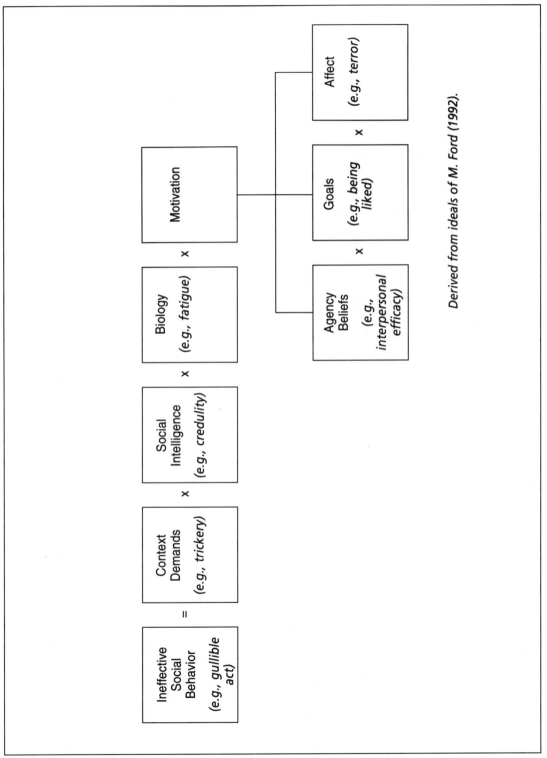

Figure 4.2. *Proposed action-outcome model of social effectiveness.*

4-day interrogation (as in the Mike Pardue case, summarized in Connery, 1995) or months of brainwashing and terrorization, as experienced by American POWs in Vietnam and Korea or political prisoners in the former Communist nations.

Motivation

The term *motivation* refers to the patterning of needs and self-regulatory mechanisms that give direction and force to one's behavior. Motivation comprises three interacting components: (a) goals, (b) affect, and (c) personal agency beliefs.

Goals (which can be considered an aspect of "character" in the earlier static model) are the intentional purpose(s) that one brings to a particular situation. In a manipulative situation (e.g., an interrogation) one may prioritize a seemingly important short-term goal (e.g., winning the approval of police officers) in a situation where another goal (e.g., avoiding self-incrimination) may have much greater long-term importance. Social intelligence obviously affects goal selection and coordination, as people with low social intelligence are less able to evaluate which goal is most relevant to the situation, especially when others make it appear that safety (as well as harmony) is will be attained through cooperation rather than through resistance (Greenspan, in press).

Affect is of obvious importance, as a panic state (e.g., brought about by fear that one's child will be taken away) could impel anyone to cave in. Social intelligence, again, comes into play, as less naive people would be better able to see through such threats and, thus, be less easily terrified. Independent of their ability to evaluate threats, however, people who are generally able to maintain calm in highly stressful situations undoubtedly will be better able to resist fear-inducing tactics than are those who tend to become highly anxious when stressed. Affect can be considered an aspect of "temperament" in the earlier static mode (see Figure 4:1).

The term *personal agency beliefs* refers essentially to personal efficacy, the key component of Bandura's theory, except that Ford divides it into "competence beliefs" (confidence in one's ability to carry out a task) and "context beliefs" (the sense that a particular setting is amenable to one's efforts). Belief in one's anticipated effectiveness is an aspect of motivation in which people with mental retardation or related disorders are known to be lacking. Their history of failure in dealing with complex and challenging situations makes them, as a group, more likely to give up when faced with ambiguity or complexity and to take their lead from others, particularly others in authority positions. Such a strategy, quite functional in many situations, might have tragic consequences in the context of a situation like a police interrogation.

Social Intelligence

The important role of social intelligence in mediating both goal selection and affect has already been discussed. Social intelligence has primary relevance, however, for one's degree of credulity, as people with normal social intelligence are presumably better equipped to see through deception and manipulation. Two aspects of social intelligence come into play here: (a) ability to decode social cues (i.e., to pick up on subtle nonverbal indicators of deceit) and (b) insight into and wisdom about relevant institutions and phenomena. In the case of the interrogation example, this could include things such as knowledge of one's rights under the criminal justice system, ability to reflect on the possible motives of the interrogating officers, understanding that police officers do not always tell the truth, and knowledge of relevant content areas (such as forensic techniques).

Biology

Biology comes into play in the same sense that all behavior is affected by organic capabilities and states. Exhaustion is often a factor contributing to false confession (Lapointe's ordeal occurred late at night, which is commonly the case), and people with high endurance and ability to tolerate physical discomfort have an advantage over those who do not. Sensory impairments contribute to one's vulnerability as well (e.g., Lapointe has hearing aids in both ears and often agrees with statements as a way of covering up his hearing and comprehension deficits). This source of vulnerability to manipulation is, interestingly, recognized in Texas, where interrogations of deaf people must be captured on video or audiotape. However, such a safeguard, which provides the only reliable way of judging after the fact if a confession was freely and fairly given, is mandated in only two states: Alaska and Minnesota.

Such protections applied without regard to one's formal disability status are considered advisable for the simple reason that a significant minority of people are vulnerable to moderate forms of psychological persuasion, while perhaps a majority are vulnerable to extreme forms of persuasion. The proposed action model could help explain why any person could prove gullible or otherwise ineffective in a stressful and complex interpersonal situation such as a police interrogation. Social naiveté (as reflected, e.g., in not understanding why legal representation is advisable in such a situation) is not limited to people with mental retardation; even one who is socially sophisticated could prove ineffective if the other factors (situational demands, affect, efficacy beliefs, biological state, etc.) were sufficiently impelling. Having mental retardation places one at particularly high risk for exploitation, however, because people with mental retardation typically manifest several of the personal risk factors in this model, especially low social intelligence and low interpersonal efficacy beliefs.

Summary

This proposed action model, although not yet validated by research on gullibility, may have heuristic value in explaining why social exploitation of some individuals is as easy as "taking candy from a baby." Such a model may

also have some value in helping adaptive behavior researchers, who tend to adhere to a mechanistic metamodel, understand the most important message of contextualism: that human behavior is complex and not perfectly predictable.

Conclusion

This chapter differs from most others in this volume in that it suggests that the development of valid adaptive behavior instruments requires a different metamodel, one that conceptualizes human effectiveness in terms of ability to actively cope with cognitively complex social situations. This volume is intended to celebrate, to some extent, the substantial progress that has been made in the area of adaptive behavior research and measurement. It may be, however, that such a celebration is premature.

Although the field has made some significant strides, as reflected in the shift from measuring deficits to measuring support needs and in the development of some consensus regarding the meaning of adaptive behavior, the contextualist perspective needs to be better integrated into both research and assessment practices. In particular, there needs to be: (a) more attention to the role of a person with mental retardation as an active problem solver attempting to make sense of specific minicontexts; (b) greater recognition that social intelligence (as opposed to lack of psychopathology) is critical for people with mental retardation to survive in a world where the most difficult challenges typically involve other people; (c) an understanding that ability to cope with social ambiguity, particularly involving deceptive and manipulative exploitation, may be central both to successful community inclusion and to identifying the core deficits in people with mental retardation; and (d) greater commitment to using methods and explanatory paradigms that are more dynamic and that make use of methods (e.g., interactive video) and explanatory paradigms (e.g., action-outcome models) that have greater potential for tapping and conveying the ongoing complexity and ambiguity of real-world transactions and the quality of one's ability to adapt successfully to that complexity.

The "support revolution," that so-called paradigm shift that characterizes the way people with mental retardation are now viewed and served, may be attributed to the incorporation of quasicontextualist concepts into applied work in this area. Although aspects of contextualism have also begun to be incorporated into scholarly conceptualizations of mental retardation and adaptive behavior, much more can be done. For example, there is a tendency to overstate the extent to which fundamentally different approaches are equivalent, as reflected in the fuzzing of the distinction between social skills (the acting out behaviors that are likely to be valued) and social intelligence (the understanding of people and social situations).

Psychology in general and the study and measurement of adaptive behavior in particular are still operating largely within a mechanistic metamodel. A shift to a contextualist metamodel promises to bring to research and clinical assessment a more meaningful way of thinking about adaptive behavior, one that is more directly grounded in the natural prototype of mental retardation. Such a shift will require significant changes in the way psychologists and others approach the task of understanding and assessing people who may have mental retardation.

References

Baltes, P. B., Dittmann-Kohli, F., & Dixon, R. A. (1984). New perspectives on the development of intelligence in adulthood: Toward a dual-process conception and a model of selective optimization with compensation. In P. B. Baltes & O. G. Brim, Jr. (Eds.), *Life-span development and behavior* (Vol. 6, pp. 33-76). New York: Academic Press.

Bandura, A. (1986). *Social foundations of thought and action: A social cognitive theory*. Englewood Cliffs, NJ: Prentice-Hall.

Barnes, M. L., & Sternberg, R. J. (1989). Social intelligence and decoding of nonverbal cues. *Intelligence, 13*, 263-287.

Bradley, V., & Knoll, J. (1995). Shifting paradigms in services to people with disabilities. In O. C. Karan & S. Greenspan (Eds.), *Community rehabilitation services for people with disabilities*. Boston: Butterworth-Heinemann.

Brunswick, E. (1952). *The conceptual framework of psychology*. Chicago: University of Chicago Press.

Cantor, N., & Genero, N. (1986). Psychiatric diagnosis and natural categorization: A close analogy. In T. Millon & G. L. Klerman (Eds.), *Contemporary directions in child psychopathology: Toward the DSM-IV* (pp. 233-256). New York: Guilford Press.

Carroll, J. B. (1986). What is intelligence? In R. J. Sternberg & D. K. Detterman (Eds.), *What is intelligence?: Contemporary viewpoints on its nature and definition* (pp. 51-54). Norwood, NJ: Ablex.

Ceci, S. J. (1996). *On intelligence: A bioecological treatise on intellectual development* (Expanded ed.). Cambridge, MA: Harvard University Press.

Connery, D. C. (Ed.). (1995). *Convicting the innocent: The story of a murder, a false confession, and the struggle to free a "wrong man."* Cambridge, MA: Brookline Books.

Dennett, D. C. (1991). *Consciousness explained*. Boston: Little Brown.

Dennett, D. C. (1996). *Kinds of minds: Toward an understanding of consciousness*. New York: Basic Books.

Dennis, M., Jacennik, B., & Barnes, M. A. (1994). The content of narrative discourse in children and adolescents after early-onset hydrocephalus and in normally developing age peers. *Brain and Language, 46*, 129-165.

Dewey, J. (1939). Experience, knowledge, and value: A rejoinder. In P. A. Schilpp (Ed.), *The philosophy of John Dewey* (pp. 515-608). Evanston, IL: Northwestern University Press.

Dixon, R. A. (1986). Contextualism and life-span developmental psychology. In R. Rosnow & M. Georgoudi (Eds.), *Contextualism and understanding in behavioral research* (pp. 125-144). New York: Praeger.

Fodor, J. A. (1983). *The modularity of mind*. Cambridge, MA: MIT Press.

Ford, A., Schnorr, R., Meyer, L., Davern, L., Black, J., & Dempsey, P. (1989). *The Syracuse community-referenced curriculum guide*. Baltimore: Paul H. Brookes.

Ford, D. H. (1987). *Humans as self-constructing living systems: A developmental perspective on personality and behavior*. Hillsdale, NJ: Lawrence Erlbaum.

Ford, D. H., & Lerner, R. M. (1992). *Developmental systems theory: An integrative approach*. Newbury Park, CA: Sage.

Ford, M. E. (1986). A living systems conceptualization of social intelligence: Processes, outcomes and developmental change. In R. J. Sternberg (Ed.), *Advances in the psychology of human intelligence* (Vol. 3, pp. 119-171). Hillsdale, NJ: Lawrence Erlbaum.

Ford, M. E. (1992). *Motivating humans: Goals, emotions, and personal agency beliefs.* Newbury Park, CA: Sage.

Ford, M. E. (1994). Social intelligence. In R. J. Sternberg (Ed.), *Encyclopedia of human intelligence* (Vol. 2, pp. 974-978). New York: Macmillan.

Gillespie, D. (1992). *The mind's we: Contextualism in cognitive psychology.* Carbondale: Southern Illinois Press.

Gollin, E. S. (Ed.). (1981). *Developmental plasticity: Behavioral and biological aspects of variations in development.* New York: Academic Press.

Goodnow, J. J. (1986). A social view of intelligence. In R. J. Sternberg & D. K. Detterman (Eds.), *What is intelligence?* (pp. 85-90). Norwood, NJ: Ablex.

Greenspan, S. (1979). Social intelligence in the retarded. In N. R. Ellis (Ed.), *Handbook of mental deficiency: Psychological theory and research* (2nd ed). Hillsdale, NJ: Lawrence Erlbaum.

Greenspan, S. (1981). Defining childhood social competence: A proposed working model. In B. K. Keogh (Ed.), *Advances in special education* (Vol. 3, pp. 1-39). Greenwich, CT: JAI Press.

Greenspan, S. (1995). There is more to intelligence than IQ. In D. C. Connery (Ed.), *Convicting the innocent: The story of a murder, a false confession, and the struggle to free a "wrong man"* (pp. 136-151). Cambridge, MA: Brookline Books.

Greenspan, S. (1997). Dead manual walking? Why the AAMR manual needs redoing. *Education and Training in Mental Retardation and Developmental Disabilities, 32,* 179-190.

Greenspan, S. (in press). Motivation and social adaptation in people with developmental disorders. In H. Switzky (Ed.), *Motivation and mental retardation.* Mahwah, NJ: Lawrence Erlbaum.

Greenspan, S. (1998). Dandy-Walker syndrome. In L. A. Phelps (Ed.), *Practitioner's handbook of health-related disorders in children.* Washington, DC: American Psychological Association.

Greenspan, S., & Delaney, K. (1983). Personal competence of institutionalized adult males with and without Down syndrome. *American Journal of Mental Deficiency, 88,* 218-220.

Greenspan, S., & Driscoll, J. (1997). The role of intelligence in a broad model of personal competence. In D. P. Flanagan, J. Genshaft, & P. L. Harrison (Eds.), *Contemporary intellectual assessment: Theories, tests, and issues* (pp. 131-150). New York: Guilford Press.

Greenspan, S., & Love, P. F. (1997). Social intelligence and developmental disorder: Mental retardation, learning disabilities and autism. In W. F. MacLean, Jr. (Ed.), *Ellis' handbook of mental deficiency* (3rd ed., pp. 311-342). Mahwah, NJ: Lawrence Erlbaum.

Greenspan, S., & McGrew, K. S. (1996). Response to Mathias and Nettlebeck on the structure of competence: Need for theory-based methods to test theory-based questions. *Research in Developmental Disabilities, 17,* 145-152.

Greenspan, S., & Shoultz, B. (1981). Why mentally retarded adults lose their jobs: Social competence as a factor in work adjustment. *Applied Research in Mental Retardation, 2,* 23-38.

Greenspan, S., Switzky, H., & Granfield, J. (1996). Everyday intelligence and adaptive behavior: A theoretical framework. In J. Jacobson & J. Mulick (Eds.), *Manual on diagnosis and professional practice in mental retardation* (pp. 127-135). Washington, DC: American Psychological Association.

Grossman, H. J. (Ed.). (1983). *Classification in mental retardation* (3rd ed.). Washington. DC: American Association on Mental Deficiency.

Gudjonsson, G. (1992). *The psychology of interrogations, confessions, and testimony*. London: Wiley.

Guilford, J. P. (1967). *The nature of human intelligence*. New York: McGraw-Hill.

Horner, R. H. (1994). Functional assessment: Contributions and future directions. *Journal of Applied Behavior Analysis, 27*, 40-404.

Jacobson, J. W., & Mulick, J. A. (1996). *Manual of diagnosis and professional practice in mental retardation*. Washington, DC: American Psychological Association.

Keating, D. P. (1978). A *search for social intelligence, 70*, 218-223.

Keating, D. P. (1994). Contextualist theories of intelligence. In R. J. Sternberg (Ed.), *Encyclopedia of human intelligence* (Vol. 1, pp. 293-298). New York: Macmillan.

Kolb, B. (1989). Brain development, plasticity, and behavior. *American Psychologist, 44*, 1203-1212.

Layne, C. (1979). The Barnum effect: Rationality versus gullibility? *Journal of Consulting and Clinical Psychology, 47*, 219-221.

Leland, H. (1992, May). Adaptive behavior or adaptive skill? Dimensions in coping development. Paper presented at the annual meeting of the American Association on Mental Retardation. Boston, MA.

Lerner, R. M. (1984). *On the nature of human plasticity*. New York: Cambridge University Press.

Lerner, R. M., & Busch-Rossnagel, N. A. (Eds.). (1981). *Individuals as producers of their development: A life-span perspective*. New York: Academic Press.

Luckasson, R. (1992). People with mental retardation as victims of crime. In R. W. Conley, R. Luckasson, & G. N. Bouthilet (Eds.), *The criminal justice system and mental retardation: Defendants and victims* (pp. 209-220). Baltimore: Paul H. Brookes.

Luckasson, R., Coulter, D. L., Polloway, E. A., Reiss, S., Schalock, R. L., Snell, M. E., Spitalnik, D. M., & Stark, J. A. (1992). *Mental retardation: Definition, classification, and system of supports* (9th ed.). Washington, DC: American Association on Mental Retardation.

McGrew, K. S., Bruininks, R. H., & Johnson, D. R. (1996). A confirmatory factor analysis investigation of Greenspan's model of personal competence. *American Journal on Mental Retardation, 100*, 533-545.

Morrison, A. (1824). *Outlines of mental diseases*. Edinburgh: MacLachlan & Stewart.

Nihira, K., Foster, R., Shellhaas, M., & Leland (1968). Adaptive behavior checklist. Washington, DC: American Association on Mental Deficiency.

Ofshe, R. J., & Leo, R. A. (in press). The social psychology of police interrogation: The theory and classification of true and false confessions. *Studies in Law, Politics, and Society*.

Pepper, S. C. (1942). *World hypotheses*. Berkeley: University of California Press.

Perske, R. (1997). The world of Richard Lapointe: Observations and statements which help us see how he responds to the world around him. Darien, CT: Unpublished manuscript.

Piaget, J. (1969). *The child's conception of the world*. Totowa, NJ: Littlefield, Adams. (originally published 1929).

Rosch, E. H. (1988). Coherences and categorization: A historical view. In F. Kessel (Ed.), *The development of language and language researchers: Essays in honor of Roger Brown* (pp. 373-392). Hillsdale, NJ: Lawrence Erlbaum.

Rosnow, R., & Georgoudi, M. (Eds.). (1986a). *Contextualism and understanding in behavioral research*. New York: Praeger.

Rosnow, R., & Georgoudi, M. (1986b). The spirit of contextualism. In R. Rosnow & M. Georgoudi (Eds.), *Contextualism and understanding in behavioral research* (pp. 3-22). NY: Praeger.

Rotter, J. (1980). Interpersonal trust, trustworthiness, and gullibility. *American Psychologist*, 35, 1-7.

Rourke, B. P. (1995). *Syndrome of nonverbal learning disabilities: Neurodevelopmental manifestations*. New York: Guilford Press.

Sarason, S. (1981). *Psychology misdirected*. New York: Free Press.

Sarbin, T. R. (1977). Contextualism: A world view for modern psychology. In J. K. Cole & A. W. Lundfield (Eds.), *Nebraska symposium on motivation* (pp. 1-41). Lincoln: University of Nebraska Press.

Sarbin, T. R. (1991). The social construction of schizophrenia. In W. F. Flack, Jr., D. R. Miller, & M. Wiener (Eds.), *What is schizophrenia?* (pp. 173-198). New York: Springer-Verlag.

Sarbin, T. R., & Juhasz, J. B. (1982). The context of mental illness: A historical sketch. In I. Al-Issa (Ed.), *Culture and psychopathology*. Baltimore: University Park Press.

Semirud-Clikeman, M., & Hynd, G. W. (1990). Right hemisphere dysfunction in nonverbal learning disabilities: Social, academic, and adaptive functioning in adults and children. *Psychological Bulletin*, 107, 196-209.

Skultans, V. (1975). *Madness and morals: Ideas on insanity in the nineteenth century*. London: Routledge & Kegan Paul.

Spitz, H. H. (1988). Mental retardation as a thinking disorder: The rationalist alternative to empiricism. In N. Bray (Ed.), *International review of research in mental retardation* (Vol. 15, pp. 1-32). New York: Academic Press.

Sternberg, R. J. (1984). Macrocomponents and microcomponents of intelligence: Some proposed loci of mental retardation. In P. H. Brooks, R. Sperber, & C. McCauley (Eds.), *Learning and cognition in the mentally retarded* (pp. 89-114). Hillsdale, NJ: Lawrence Erlbaum.

Sternberg, R. J. (1988). *The triarchic mind: A new theory of intelligence*. New York: Viking.

Sternberg, R. J. (1990). *Wisdom: Its nature, origins, and development*. Cambridge: Cambridge University Press.

Switzky, H. (1997). Individual differences in personality and motivational systems in persons with mental retardation. In W. F. MacLean, Jr. (Ed.), *Ellis' handbook of mental deficiency* (3rd ed., pp. 343-378). Mahwah, NJ: Lawrence Erlbaum.

Thorndike, E. L. (1920). Intelligence and its uses. *Harper's*, 140, 227-235.

Vygotsky, L. S. (1978). *Mind in society: The development of higher psychological processes*. Cambridge, MA: Harvard University Press.

Walker, R. E., & Foley, J. M. (1973). Social intelligence: Its history and measurement. *Psychological Reports*, 33, 839-864.

Warren, S. F. (1977). A useful ecobehavioral perspective for applied behavioral analysis. In A. K. Rogers-Warren & S. F. Warren (Eds.), *Ecological perspectives in behavioral analysis* (pp. 173-196). Baltimore: University Park Press.

Wertsch, J. (1985). *Vygotsky and the social formation of mind*. Cambridge, MA: Harvard University Press.

Widaman, K. F., & McGrew, K. S. (1996). The structure of adaptive behavior. In J. W. Jacobson & J. A. Mulick (Eds.), *Manual of diagnosis and professional practice in mental retardation* (pp. 97-110). Washington, DC: American Psychological Association.

CHAPTER 5

Assistive Technology and Adaptive Behavior

BRIAN R. BRYANT

PENNY CREWS SEAY

DIANE PEDROTTY BRYANT

The University of Texas at Austin

Introduction

With the passage of the Americans With Disabilities Act in 1990, the people of the United States recognized formally that disabilities are a natural part of the human experience. People with disabilities have a right to live independently, enjoy self-determination, contribute to society, pursue meaningful careers, and enjoy full inclusion and integration in the economic, political, social, cultural, and educational mainstream of society. Of these rights, the ability to live independently is fundamental to the human existence. Many of the skills associated with independent living can be found in the adaptive areas identified in the newest definition of mental retardation offered by the American Association on Mental Retardation (AAMR) (Luckasson et al., 1992). For instance, the abilities to care for oneself, maintain a home, compete in the job market, and engage in social activities reflect independent living skills that minimize overreliance on others in everyday decision-making activities.

Of critical importance to independent living is the ability to maintain control over and have choices in one's life. The ability to make decisions based on availability of choices and options is an indicator of quality of life for people with mental retardation and developmental disabilities. All too often people with disabilities have had limited opportunity to exercise control over their lives. Recently service providers have recognized the importance of people's right to freedom of choice and decision making. The increased availability of assistive technology devices and services has opened up options for individuals whose disabilities may limit communication, mobility, self-sufficiency, and vocational opportunities.

For people with mental retardation and developmental disabilities, assistive technology is providing heretofore unavailable opportunities for independent living (Bryant, 1995). Formerly perceived to be used solely by individuals with sensory or motor impairments, assistive technology devices are increasingly being used by people with all types of disabilities (e.g., learning disabilities, psychiatric disorders, mental retardation) to compensate for a variety of disability-related functional limitations that inhibit successful adaptation and may serve as a barrier to independent functioning (Bryant, Rivera, & Moore, 1996; Parette, 1991). The purpose of this chapter is to (a) provide a brief introduction to the independent living movement and its relationship to adaptive behavior, (b) identify the relationship between personal choice and successful community integration, and (c) discuss how assistive technology devices and services can be used by individuals with disabilities to live independently.

Introduction to Independent Living

Independent living has been defined by Frieden, Richards, Cole, and Bailey as "control over one's life based on the choice of acceptable options that minimize reliance on others in making decisions and in performing everyday activities" (as cited in Nosek, 1992, p. 103). The concept involves being able to take advantage of opportunities in areas such as education and employment, home and family, leisure, community involvement, emotional and physical health, and personal responsibility and relations (Cronin & Patton, 1993). Nosek has identified the following factors as contributing fundamentally to independent living: mobility (in the home and within the community, including use of public transportation); activities of daily living; use of personal assistants (i.e., attendants); communication; source and amount of income; living arrangement (including housing and housemates); employment status; education level; use of leisure time; health status (including fulfilling health maintenance requirements); marital status; social life; and self-concept.

When examining the factors associated with independent living, it becomes apparent that they are interdependent to a great extent; that is, the factors of independent living are interrelated and affect one another in such a way that the status of one (e.g., education) may directly affect the status of another (e.g., employment, source and amount of income).

It is also evident that independent living factors are closely related to constructs associated with adaptive behavior. The 1992 AAMR definition of mental retardation (Luckasson, et al.) identifies 10 adaptive areas that must be examined prior to diagnosing someone as having mental retardation: communication (i.e., understanding and expressing messages through either symbolic or nonsymbolic behaviors); self-care (i.e., toileting, eating, dressing, and grooming skills); home living (i.e., home-environment skills relating to housekeeping, property maintenance, cooking, budgeting, home safety, and scheduling); social (i.e., skills related to social exchanges, including the initiation, interaction, and termination of the interaction with others); community use (i.e., the use of appropriate community resources, such as traveling in the community, shopping, purchasing services, and using public transportation); self-direction (i.e., skills related to making choices, completing tasks, seeking

assistance, and resolving); health and safety (i.e., first aid, physical fitness, illness identification, and safety skills); functional academics (i.e., skills related to learning in school, such as basic reading, writing, and practical mathematics); leisure (i.e., recreational interests and activities that may involve social interaction, mobility skills, taking turns, and playing appropriately); and work (i.e., job skills, such as task completion and money management) (Bryant, Taylor, & Rivera, 1996).

Skills associated with these adaptive areas clearly parallel the independent living factors presented by Nosek (1992). Such an observation is further supported by the work of Dever (1989), who created a taxonomy of community skills necessary for independent functioning. These skills include maintaining home safety, following employer rules, interacting with family and friends, maintaining personal cleanliness, following accident procedures, and demonstrating numerous abilities associated with adaptive behavior. In a similar fashion, Aveno (1989) listed a variety of community involvement skills (e.g., using a laundromat, riding in a car, banking, accessing health care) associated with adaptive behavior. Thus, adaptive behaviors could well be subsumed under the independent living skills rubric.

The focus on adaptive behavior and related independent living skill development is critical, because more people with mental retardation and developmental disabilities have moved from institutional to community settings as advocates have pushed for community placement (Beirne-Smith, Ittenbach, & Patton, 1998). In the United States, there are an increasing number of supervised group homes with 15 or fewer residents with mental retardation (Braddock, 1991). Braddock reported that in 1977, 86% of the individuals with mental retardation in the United States were living in large (16 beds or more) congregate care institutional settings; this percentage dropped to 60% in 1988, and it continues to decline. In 1990, the number fell below 90,000, and it is expected that there will be fewer than 55,000 residents in state schools by the year 2000. Yet living "in the community" does not necessarily guarantee that a person with a disability will be included in that community (Lord & Pedlar, 1991; Nirje, 1980; O'Brien, 1987, 1991). Most adults with disabilities live with family members or in homes established to offer treatment and supervision (O'Brien, 1991). People living in treatment facilities of any size typically have limited control of their homes, with limited choices available to them. Their daily schedules, activities, meals, and bedtimes are frequently regulated by professionally approved individual programs. Additionally, choice is not offered regarding housemates or control of necessary personal assistance (O'Brien). Living in community group homes often offers physical, functional, and organizational integration but not necessarily social, personal, and societal integration (Nirje, 1980).

Adaptive behaviors reflect a person's ability to cope with the natural and social demands of his or her environment (Leland, 1996). Thus, attainment of skills related to adaptive behavior permits an individual to cope better with those environmental demands and, consequently, participate to a greater extent in societal activities. The remainder of this chapter examines two factors that relate to attainment of skills related to adaptive behavior: personal choice and assistive technology.

Choice and Consumer Direction

The freedom to choose and express personal preferences is highly valued in our society. Persons without disabilities are confronted daily with a multitude of decisions and choices. Some choices may be relatively insignificant; others may have great personal importance.

All too often, people with mental retardation and other disabilities are denied opportunities to exercise choice and control over many aspects of their lives; such denial may lead to learned helplessness and dependence.

Discussing the difficulty for some people with severe disabilities to exercise their freedom to choose, Newton, Horner, and Lund (1991) noted that choice making is problematic when "one has few communication skills, no history of sampling available options, minimal funds, inadequate social support, or little control over daily events and schedules" (p. 207).

The opportunity to make choices and decisions in one's life is an important aspect in living independently and achieving an enhanced quality of life for people with disabilities (Gardner, 1990; Gardner & Chapman, 1985; O'Brien, 1987; Schalock & Kiernan, 1990). O'Brien, Gardner, and Chapman, and Gardner and O'Brien (1990) described five service dimensions—each involving an element of choice—that promote a high quality of life for people with disabilities. These five elements of normalization—community presence, community participation, skill enhancement, image enhancement, and autonomy and empowerment—indicate a person's level of community integration.

Community presence refers to physical integration into the community, which makes way for community participation. Tourists and other visitors may participate superficially in community activities, whereas residents may become involved in their communities' affairs.

Community participation is a measure of the social integration into the community. Such integration is not ensured simply by residing in the community. Successful integration results from a combination of meaningful social interactions with friends, family, coworkers, and/or fellow students.

Skill enhancement is promoted by programs that do not physically and socially overprotect community residents. Programs promote acquisition of skills by allowing citizens to experience normative dangers, risks, and growth and learning challenges. It is also important to teach skills or shape behaviors that produce valued consequences.

Image enhancement is a byproduct of programs that help people with disabilities project a positive image. Unfortunately, people with disabilities who project negative images tend to be treated poorly, which may cause them to behave according to the negative expectations.

Gardner and O'Brien's (1990) final dimension, *autonomy and empowerment*, involves transferring power and control to people with disabilities and encouraging their participation in the development of program plans, meetings, and reviews. West and Parent (1992) define empowerment as: "the transfer of power and control over the values, decisions, choices, and directions of human services from external entities to the consumers of services, resulting in increased motivation to participate and succeed and a greater degree of dignity for the consumer" (pp. 47-48).

Choice and preference are fundamental elements of empowerment, as is the notion that individuals with disabilities must be given opportunity to engage in a range of familiar activities on a regular basis. Additionally, information regarding services, programs, funding, and other options must be shared with individuals to enable them to make choices.

Several critical issues surround choice for individuals with severe disabilities. Their choices must be identified accurately and opportunities to choose among preferred options must be created and supported (Newton et al., 1991). Because individuals with severe disabilities may communicate their preferences and choices in nonconventional ways (Campbell, 1989), understanding those choices presents challenges for family members, friends, service providers, and professionals. Additionally, a limited repertoire of activities and little control over their own lives confounds the choice-making difficulties experienced by people with disabilities. An active effort is required of others to enhance the opportunities for choice.

Unfortunately, service providers have traditionally exercised considerable control over the individuals in their care and have not allowed them to make choices and decisions regarding their lives (Guess, Benson, & Siegel-Causey, 1985; Kishi, Teelucksingh, Zollers, Park-Lee, & Meyer, 1988; Turnbull & Turnbull, 1985; Turnbull, Turnbull, Bronicki, Summers, & Roeder-Gordon, 1989; Veach, 1977; Wolfensberger, 1972). Mithaug and Hanawalt (1978) summarized the importance of choice to independent living when they stated, "If an ultimate goal for the severely handicapped is independent functioning, we must specify the procedures that promote the ability, as well as the opportunity, to make selections" (p. 154).

Clearly, then, people who exhibit adaptive behaviors and have independent living skills have more control over their lives than those who lack these abilities. Therefore, a reasonable goal of any educational program for people with mental retardation should be the acquisition of adaptive behaviors, allowing them to be in a better position to make choices and act on those choices appropriately. The next section discusses one method that can be used to attain adaptive behavior competence: the use of assistive technology.

Assistive Technology and Independence

Recognizing the significant abilities and contributions that people with disabilities have to offer society, national policy makers have fundamentally changed the meaning of disability. Traditional models have focused solely on a person's functional weaknesses (i.e., what the person cannot do). Public policy now examines disability with respect to the external barriers that limit a person's access to educational, economic, social, and many other opportunities (Elrod, 1997) and the supports that are needed to improve access. Assistive technology can help remove barriers, allowing people with disabilities to be full participants in everyday experiences (Texas Assistive Technology Partnership, 1995). Assistive technology is an integral part of an effective support system used by people with disabilities (Enders, 1995). While assistive technology

Setting-Specific Demands		Individual-Specific Characteristics		Adaptations
Task	Requisite Abilities	Functional Capabilities	Functional Limitations	Simple-to-Complex
• Brush Teeth	• Locate Materials • Grasp Utensils • Apply Paste • Brush • Rinse • Put Materials Away	• Sight • Gross Motor • Hearing	• Fine Motor • Memory • Attention	• Other Person to Brush Teeth • Checklist • Adapted Handle on Brush • Electronic Dispenser • Electronic Toothbrush

Figure 5.1. *Considerations for selecting assistive technology adaptations.*

is rarely the only support needed, it could be argued that, ultimately, availability of assistive technology (and its proper use) can help people with disabilities function more independently.

Bryant (1995), Bryant and Rivera (1995), and Rivera and Bryant (in press) present considerations when examining the tasks that people do: What assistive technology adaptations can be selected and identified to make such tasks easier or, in many instances, possible? These considerations examine setting-specific demands and individual-specific characteristics to identify how well the setting and the individual match (i.e., how well the person's skills and abilities match the task

demanded by the person's setting). Based on this examination, when the setting-individual match is not good (i.e., when the person's abilities are insufficient to meet the demands of the setting), a person uses adaptations that allow him or her to perform the task at hand. Such adaptations may include the use of assistive technology. The considerations for selecting assistive technology adaptations are shown in Figure 5.1, with each element described below.

Setting-Specific Demands

More than a decade of research (e.g., Deshler & Schumaker, 1986; Riegel, 1988; Rieth & Evertson, 1988; Schumaker & Deshler, 1984) has documented the importance of examining the setting-specific demands (setting-demands) of learning environments. Although such research deals mostly with classroom applications, these findings generalize to all settings in which activities take place, including the home, work place, and leisure settings.

Setting-demands are tasks that people are expected to accomplish in a particular setting. Such tasks might be cleaning one's room or work area, cooking breakfast, eating lunch, playing volleyball on the beach, riding the bus to work, or engaging in conversation. These and many other tasks are associated with adaptive behavior. According to Widaman and McGrew (1996), adaptive behaviors involve skills that people exhibit or tasks they complete in response to demands of their environment (or setting).

According to Rivera and Bryant (in press),

the first step in considering the setting-individual match is to look at the required tasks and the abilities that must be present in order to meet those demands successfully. Task demands and requisite abilities are described here, along with specific examples of adaptive behaviors.

Tasks

The literature is replete with studies analyzing the required tasks of individuals with mental retardation. Sample tasks for the 10 adaptive areas cited in the 1992 AAMR definition of mental retardation (Luckasson, et al.) are found in Table 5.1. These tasks are associated with social skills or behavior (Forness & Nihira, 1984; McMahon, Wacker, Sasso, Berg, & Newton, 1996; Rosen & Burchard, 1990), supported employment or work skills (Nietupski, Hamre-Nietupski, Vanderhart, & Fishback, 1996), communication (Bufkin &

Table 5.1
Sample Tasks for 10 Adaptive Areas

Adaptive Area	Tasks
Communication	Listen during a conversation. Speak to make needs known.
Self-Care	Apply toileting skills. Brush teeth.
Home Living	Do laundry. Cook food.
Social	Participate in group activities. Know people's names.
Community Use	Order meals in restaurants. Use the local bus system.
Self-Direction	Save money for a purpose. Maintain own bank accounts.
Health and Safety	Recognize danger signs. Know where to seek medical help.
Functional Academics	Make correct change. Write notes or memos.
Leisure	Know location of local theater. Understand board game rules.
Work	Arrive to work on time. Seek or accept help.

Altman, 1995; Kuder & Bryen, 1991; Owen, McDonald, & Baine, 1994); school work or functional academics (Frederick-Dugan, Test, & Varn, 1991; Podell, Tournaki-Rein, & Lin, 1992); self-direction (Briggs, et al., 1990; Davis, Williams, Brady, & Burta, 1992; Ellis, Cress, & Spellman, 1992), recreation and play or leisure (Dattilo, 1987; Demchak, 1989; Rettig, Kallam, & McCarthy-Salm, 1993), self-care (Reese & Snell, 1991), health and safety (Collins, Wolery, & Gast, 1991; Fletcher & Abood, 1988; Spooner, Stem, & Test, 1989; Tymchuk, Hamada, Andron, & Anderson, 1990), and home living (Collins, Branson, & Hall, 1995; Schuster, 1988).

Requisite Abilities

Requisite abilities are skills that must be possessed to accomplish the tasks of the setting-demands (Bryant & Rivera, 1995). For instance, the task of reading a book requires visual acuity, decoding, reading comprehension, and fluency skills. Listening to someone speak requires the ability to hear, attend, and identify important points. For the vast majority of people, these requisite abilities are present, but for some with mental retardation and developmental disabilities the requisite skills for meeting specific tasks may be lacking unless adaptations are implemented.

To illustrate, examine the sample task, "brush teeth," associated with self-care in Table 5.1. and illustrated in Figure 5.1. Typically, the requisite abilities to brush one's teeth are: (a) the ability to find the toothpaste and toothbrush, (b) the ability to grasp the tube of toothpaste, (c) the ability to apply the paste to the bristles of the brush, (d) the ability to maneuver the brush to the teeth and to brush properly, (e) the ability to rinse, and (f) the ability to put the utensil away. Thus, identifying requisite abilities involves task analysis and asking what abilities are needed to accomplish each step.

The point is this: Setting-demands require discrete and interrelated abilities. As will be seen in the next section, the presence or absence of these abilities determines the extent to which people meet the natural and social demands of their environment (i.e., exhibit adaptive behaviors).

Individual-Specific Characteristics

Once setting-demands have been examined, the focus shifts from the task to the individual. Specifically, what are the person's functional strengths and limitations? By identifying factors that facilitate and inhibit performance, one paves the way for making adaptations that allow people to participate more fully in their surroundings.

Functional Capabilities

Whereas traditional models for interventions focus on deficits, the assistive technology problem-solving and evaluation considerations examine first a person's functional strengths. Raskind and Bryant (1996) have identified a series of behaviors that can occur across areas (i.e., listening, speaking, reading, writing, mathematics, memory, organization, physical or motor, and behavior). Functional strengths can also occur within and across the 10 adaptive behaviors identified by the AAMR (Luckasson et al.). Functional strengths play a crucial role in the selection of adaptations, including assistive technology adaptations, that may help people perform specific tasks demanded by specific settings.

All people have relative strengths, because all people can do some things better than other things. For people with mental retardation or other developmental disabilities, these strengths may be more limited than those of people without such disabilities, but they remain relative strengths nonetheless. For instance, Tim's listening skills may not be as good as Jose's. In fact, when compared to Jose, Tim demonstrates poor listening skills; yet Tim's listening skills far surpass his abilities to use spoken language expressively. So, for Tim, listening is a relative strength and should be considered when exploring potential adaptations.

Functional Limitations

Functional limitations are disability-related barriers that may impede the ability to meet the demands of the setting (Rivera & Bryant, in press). Functional limitations can be manifested in many areas, including the 10 adaptive areas and the areas (e.g., difficulties with academic skills, motor skills, sensory abilities, memory, and organizational skills) noted by Raskind and Bryant (1996).

Functional dissonance occurs when a person's limitations are at odds with the abilities required to meet the demands of a setting. The challenge is to identify adaptations that can be made to alleviate the dissonance and accomplish the task.

Rivera and Bryant (in press) provide questions that can help identify appropriate assistive adaptations to meet individual needs (see Figure 5.2).

Adaptations

When the setting-specific demands and individual-specific characteristics do not match (i.e., the individual is unable to perform tasks because of disability-related limitations), it becomes necessary to examine a series of adaptations that might allow the person to perform those tasks. Bryant (1997) noted that adaptations may involve technology or assistive technology and may range from simple to complex. The selection of adaptations requires careful scrutiny of the person's specific needs. When appropriate, the user must be trained to access the adaptation. Also, assistive technology adaptations must be evaluated, to determine the degree to which they are successful.

Nontechnological Adaptations

Numerous adaptations may be made that do not involve assistive technology. For instance, if a sixth grader has adequate listening skills yet cannot read, an assigned reader (i.e., someone who reads the material to the student) might be an effective adaptation, providing access to material in a textbook or storybook. In the same way, a person with motor impairments who cannot write can benefit from a scribe (i.e., someone who transcribes information for the person). Yet another example of a nontechnological adaption would be a checklist that reminds a person of the steps necessary to complete a particular task.

Assistive Technology adaptations. According to the Technology-Related Assistance for Individuals With Disabilities Act of 1988, an assistive technology device refers to "any item, piece of equipment, or product system, whether acquired commercially off-the-shelf, modified, or customized, that is used to increase, maintain or improve the functional capabilities of individuals with disabilities" (p. 102). Bryant and Rivera (1995) noted that assistive technology, in most instances, is simply technology that becomes assistive when its use satisfies the criteria found in the definition cited above. Consider a standard remote control unit for a television set. When that device is used by most people, it is helpful technology because it saves them from having to get up, walk across the room, change the channel manually, and return to the chair. For a person with a motor limitation that inhibits such movement, the remote control unit makes changing the channel possible from the distant location; thus, it improves his or her functional capabilities thereby making the same device assistive technology. Similar analogies exist across environments.

Simple-to-Complex Continuum. Many simple nontechnological adaptations might allow an individual to participate in activities from which he or she would otherwise be excluded. For instance, a student who experiences difficulty hearing the teacher's directions can sit closer to the teacher. In the same way, furniture in a room can be arranged to facilitate easier mobility by a person who uses a wheeled unit.

For the most part, adaptations that are simple are the easiest to implement and may well be sufficient to allow an individual to

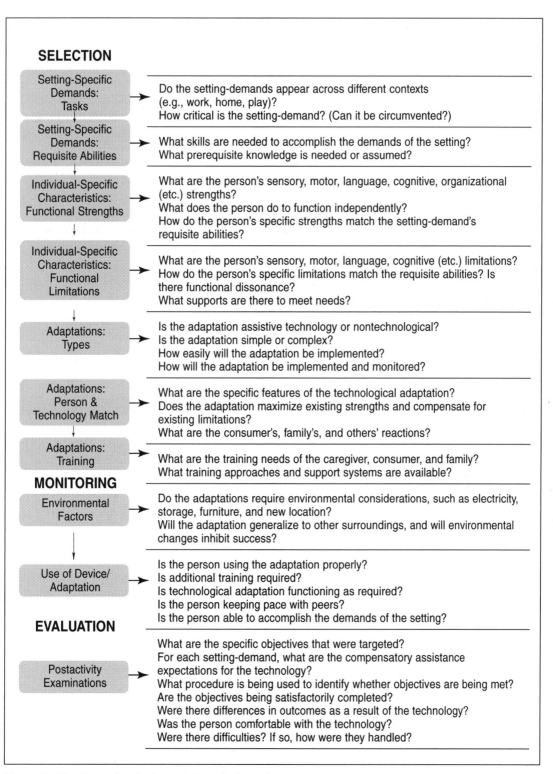

Figure 5.2. *Identifing and evaluating assistive technology adaptations.*

participate in a number of activities that would otherwise be impossible. More complex nontechnological adaptations might assist some individuals with mental retardation. For example, a person may have social limitations that create functional dissonance when matched with the abilities requisite for working in small groups (e.g., in a classroom or in an office pool). Complex nontechnological adaptations might include setting up a token economy system for modifying the intrusive social behaviors or perhaps a behavior management plan. Such adaptations are far more complex than furniture arrangement or classroom placement.

Assistive technology adaptations also range on a continuum from simple to complex (McGregor & Pachuski, 1996), depending on factors such as ease of implementation; technological features (e.g., hardware platform specifications, electronic capabilities); client, family, and teacher or caregiver training requirements; and maintenance. A tape recorder might be considered a relatively simple device, because it requires pressing a button or a switch to activate; the technology features auditory output and recording capabilities; most people know how to use a tape recorder or can learn to operate one easily; and tape recorders are fairly durable, low maintenance devices. An example of a complex assistive technology adaptation would be an electronic augmentative communication device. Such a device might include complex instructions and programming, might be expensive to purchase, and might require considerable training to use. A brief sampling of assistive technology devices for specific adaptive areas is presented in Table 5.2.

Selecting Devices

When deciding to use assistive technology adaptations, people must ask a basic question: What types of adaptations would enhance task performance? (Bowser & Reed, 1995). During the process of matching the adaptation to the person's needs, certain

evaluation criteria should be considered: (a) ease of use (set-up, operation, maintenance); (b) amount of training required for the user (person with the disability) and provider (teacher, caregiver, family member); (c) cost (to purchase, to maintain, to repair); (d) technological features (e.g., computer modifications, specialized software programs, compatibility with other devices); (e) functional assistance (e.g., pencil grip enables some people with motor problems to grasp and hold a pencil more readily; speech synthesizer [with appropriate software] reads text shown on the monitor, thus enabling people with reading difficulties to access the written material); (f) performance (reliable, durable, safe); (g) use across environments and tasks; (h) promotion of personal independence; and (i) user's knowledge level of how to use the device (Raskind & Bryant, 1996).

Selection and Training

The features of assistive technology devices must be examined to determine an appropriate match with the setting-specific demands (i.e., tasks and requisite abilities) and the individual-specific characteristics (i.e., strengths and limitations).

Selection of an assistive technology device should be guided by the setting-specific demands, the capabilities a person must possess to use the device, and the individual's functional limitations for which compensation will occur by using the device. Specifically, an individual's strengths must be examined to ensure that he or she has the skills required to use a particular device. For instance, software adaptations require the individual to be able to access a computer and perhaps read or listen. If these requisite abilities are not present, the adaptation is unlikely to be beneficial.

Whenever possible, family members should be active members of any decision-making process (Bryant & Kemp, 1995; Raskind & Bryant, 1995, 1996). Richards (1995) discussed family-related guidelines to be considered when making appropriate person-

Table 5.2
Sample Assistive Technology Adaptations for Setting-Specific Demands

Setting-Specific Demands	Assistive Technology Adaptations
Listen.	Assistive listening device
Speak.	Augmentative communication board
Wash self.	Bath or shower safety bench
Brush teeth.	Large handled brush or electric brush
Do laundry.	Laundry sorter
Cook food.	Long-ring timer
Participate in recreational activities.	Adaptive recreational equipment
Know people's names.	Pocket organizer
Order meals in restaurants.	Digital voice pad
Use the local bus system.	Audio schedule
Write checks.	Check-writing guide
Maintain own bank accounts.	Big-number desktop calculator
Take body temperature.	Thermometer pads
Know where to seek medical help.	Preset telephone numbers
Make correct change.	Big-number compact calculator
Write notes or memos.	Voice recorder or speech recognition
Read for pleasure.	Books on tape
Play board game.	Adaptive games
Arrive to work on time.	Appointment reminder
Follow instructions.	Hand-held tape recorder

Reprinted with permission from "Using Assistive Technology Adaptations To Include Students With Learning Disabilities in Cooperative Learning Acitivites" by D. P. Bryant and B. R. Bryant, 1998, *Journal of Learning Disabilities*, 31 (1), pp.41-54, Copyright 1998 by Pro-Ed, Inc.

technology matches. Families should be aware of the expected outcomes of assistive technology adaptations; these outcomes should reflect the needs of the technology consumers and of their families in promoting independence (Parette & Brotherson, 1996). Assistive technology devices should enhance the abilities of the family to help meet the consumer's needs. Assistive technology services, such as training and funding options, must be provided to families and/or caregivers as they work with the technology consumer. The diversity of family values and viewpoints about technology adaptations should be considered. This includes family experience and comfort level with technology and their views toward adaptations in general. Any resources necessary to help families accommodate assistive technology adaptations in their home and other locales must be addressed.

When selecting assistive technology adaptations, the viewpoint and motivational level of the consumer are also critical (Carney & Dix, 1992; Raskind & Bryant, 1996). Consider the consumer's opinions about adaptation options and the sometimes intrusive nature of adaptations, attitude about using adaptations, and interest in trying available options. The consumer has absolute veto power over the use of an assistive technology device. No adaptation will work if the consumer is against it, because the device simply will not be used.

Training

Once an assistive technology device has been obtained, the consumer and others in his or her surroundings must be trained on the device and its capabilities and intent. Consumer training should include components of effective instruction: (a) providing a rationale for the device's use; (b) teaching the vocabulary related to the device and its use; (c) giving explicit instructions (e.g., modeling, examples, feedback) in how to use the device; and (d) monitoring the device's use to ensure proper implementation (Anderson-Inman, Knox-Quinn, & Horney, 1996; Church & Glennen, 1992; Rivera & Bryant, in press).

Day and Edwards (1996) suggested several training methods that can be used, including the use of visual, oral, and written instructions where consumers review videotapes and diagrams on correct implementation; further, the use of adaptations could be modeled and then imitated by the consumer. Guided practice opportunities can ensure that consumers are learning to use adaptations correctly, and frequent comprehension checks are necessary to determine that the consumer understands the adaptation.

If a computer is provided, the consumer's computer literacy and key-boarding skills must be assessed and developed (Anderson-Inman et al., 1996; MacArthur, 1988; Raskind & Bryant, 1996). Exercises that time and evaluate the person's key-boarding skills could be a part of the instructional process (Rivera & Bryant, in press). Training needs to include use of the input device (e.g., touch sensitive mouse, track ball mouse, touch screen). It takes time to develop the motor dexterity needed to use various input devices.

Evaluating the Effectiveness of Assistive Technology Adaptations

Someone must be identified to work with the consumer and monitor the overall use of assistive technology adaptations (Bowser & Reed, 1995). Evaluations should note environmental factors and observe the person's use of devices.

Environmental Factors

The sound, bulk, or electrical specifications of a device may require one to manipulate the environment to foster effective device integration (Church & Glennen, 1992; Raskind & Shaw, 1996).

The effects of device noise must be considered relative to others' ability to work without distractions (Carney & Dix, 1992). Voice output devices (e.g., talking calculators, speech synthesizers, tape recorders, speaking spelling programs) may need to be used in locations with minimal sound distractions and where devices will be unobtrusive.

Some large devices require environmental space considerations. Any space configurations should maintain opportunities for face-to-face interactions and allow the consumer to work collaboratively and interdependently with others (Rivera & Bryant, in press).

Many assistive technology devices (e.g., computers, tape recorders) require electricity; to use them the consumer must be close to electrical outlets and situated in an area where electrical cords do not impede traffic patterns. The location of electrical outlets often dictates environmental configurations of group activities and furniture placement (Rivera & Smith, 1997). Thus, as people monitor activities, they can address environmental considerations that may impede the successful integration of assistive technology adaptations.

Observation of Assistive Technology Use

Through careful monitoring and intervention, consumers and others can determine the successful implementation of the adaptation by examining and evaluating several factors (Rivera & Bryant, in press). First, one must monitor the ease with which the technology adaptation is being implemented and whether the consumer is using the device as instructed. In some cases, it may be necessary to use corrective feedback, cue cards, modeling, or further training to ensure that the device is being used properly.

Second, the reliability and durability of technological adaptations should be monitored carefully (Bowser & Reed, 1995; Raskind & Bryant, 1996). If the device or adaptation requires intrusive interventions (e.g., to correct "error messages," replace parts, decipher speech output, correct speech recognition problems), consumer performance will be deleteriously affected; the device may not meet expectations or be so frustrating to the user that it is set aside.

Third, the use of the assistive technology device should be monitored in terms of the validity of the adaptations. Simply put, is the adaptation working? One should pay particular attention to whether the person's identified strengths are indeed facilitating the use of the device to compensate for the person's limitations.

Conclusion

Earlier, we stated that disability is now being defined in the context of barriers that impede one's access to areas such as education, social activities, and economic endeavors, and the supports needed to enhance access. The extent to which supports are provided determines largely the degree to which a person becomes involved in community activities.

Adaptive behaviors are associated with independent living skills, which in turn are associated with community integration. By definition, people with mental retardation and developmental disabilities struggle with these skills and subsequently struggle with the natural and social demands of their environments. By examining carefully the task-demands of their environments, by identifying the tasks and the requisite abilities to accomplish those demands, and by surveying a person's strengths and limitations, one can identify adaptations that may help a person better meet the social and natural demands. A method for accomplishing this task was presented in this chapter.

Using the method described and helping a person make assistive technology and non-technological adaptations, adaptive behaviors may be improved. The person then is afforded more choices, because the repertoire of abilities increases, in turn offering more opportunities for community involvement. The potential of technology to enhance one's independent living skills will continue to influence the public's perception of disabilities. Further, a person's ability to use assistive technology and make other adaptations to increase adaptive behaviors may have a dramatic effect on subsequent adaptive behavior assessments.

References

Americans with Disabilities Act of 1990. P. L. 101-336, 42 U.S.C.A. 12, 101-12, 213 (West Supp. 1991).

Anderson-Inman, L., Knox-Quinn, C., & Horney, M. A. (1996). Computer-based study strategies for students with learning disabilities: Individual differences associated with adoption level. *Journal of Learning Disabilities, 29*(5), 461-484.

Aveno, A. (1989). Community involvement of persons with severe retardation living in community residences. *Exceptional Children, 55*(4), 309-314.

Beirne-Smith, M., Ittenbach, R. F. & Patton, J. R. (1998). *Mental Retardation* (5th ed.). Columbus, OH: Merrill.

Bowser, G., & Reed, P. (1995). Education TECH points for assistive technology planning. *Journal of Special Education Technology, 12*(4), 325-338.

Braddock, D. (1991). *Issues in the closure of state schools in Texas: A briefing paper.* Unpublished manuscript. Austin: Texas Planning Council for Developmental Disabilities.

Briggs, A., Alberto, P., Berlin, K., McKinley, C., Sharpton, W., & Ritts, C. (1990). Generalized use of a self-operated audio prompt system. *Education and Training in Mental Retardation, 25*(4), 381-389.

Bryant, B. R. (1995, May). *Assistive technology: Specific applications for independent living.* Proceedings at the 3er. Curso Internacional de Postgrado en Excepcionalidad Humana, Arequipa, Peru.

Bryant, B. R. (1997, February). *LD and AT: A lifetime partnership.* Workshop presented at Region 10 Educational Service Center, Arlington, TX.

Bryant, B. R., & Kemp, C. (1995, June). *Assistive technology and the individualized education program.* Paper presented at the Texas Federation CEC Annual Conference, Fort Worth.

Bryant, B. R., & Rivera, D. P. (1995, March). *Using assistive technology to facilitate cooperative learning.* Paper presented at the Annual Conference on Special Education and Technology, CEC Technology and Media Division, Orlando, FL.

Bryant, B. R., Rivera, D., & Moore, J. (October, 1996). *Cooperative learning: Teaching in the age of technology.* Preconference workshop presented, Learning Disability Association of Texas Annual Conference, Austin.

Bryant, B. R., Taylor, R., & Rivera, D. P. (1996). *Assessment of adaptive areas.* Austin, TX: Pro-Ed.

Bufkin, L. J., & Altman, R. (1995). A developmental study of nonverbal pragmatic communications in students with and without mild mental retardation. *Education and Training in Mental Retardation and Developmental Disabilities, 30*(3), 199-207.

Campbell, P. H. (1989). Dysfunction in posture and movement in individuals with profound disabilities. In F. Brown and D. H. Lehr (Eds.), *Persons with profound disabilities* (pp. 163-189). Baltimore: Paul H. Brookes.

Carney, J., & Dix, C. (1992). Integrating assistive technology in the classroom and community. In G. Church and S. Glennen (Eds.), *The handbook of assistive technology* (pp. 207-240). San Diego, CA: Singular Publishing.

Church, G., & Glennen, S. (1992). *The handbook of assistive technology.* San Diego, CA: Singular Publishing.

Collins, B. C., Branson, T. A., & Hall, M. (1995). Teaching generalized reading of cooking product labels to adolescents with mental disabilities through the use of key words taught by peer tutors. *Education and Training in Mental Retardation and Developmental Disabilities, 30*(1), 65-75.

Collins, B. C., Wolery, M., & Gast, D. L. (1991). A survey of safety concerns for students with special needs. *Education and Training in Mental Retardation, 26*(3), 305-318.

Cronin, M. E., & Patton, J. R. (1993). *Life skills for students with special needs: A practical guide for developing real-life programs.* Austin, TX: Pro-Ed.

Dattilo, J. (1987). Computerized assessment of leisure preferences: A replication. *Education and Training in Mental Retardation, 22*(2), 128-133.

Davis, C. A., Williams, R. E., Brady, M. P., & Burta, M. (1992). The effects of self-operated auditory prompting tapes on the performance fluency of persons with severe mental retardation. *Education and Training in Mental Retardation, 27*(1), 39-50.

Day, S. L., & Edwards, B. J. (1996). Assistive technology for postsecondary students with learning disabilities. *Journal of Learning Disabilities, 29*(5), 486-492, 503.

Demchak, M. (1989). A comparison of graduate guidance and increasing assistance in teaching adults with severe handicaps leisure skills. *Education and Training in Mental Retardation, 24*(1), 45-55.

Deshler, D. D., & Schumaker, J. B. (1986). Learning strategies: An instructional alternative for low-achieving adolescents. *Exceptional Children, 52,* 583-590.

Dever, R. B. (1989). A taxonomy of community living skills. *Exceptional Children, 55*(5), 395-404.

Ellis, D. N., Cress, P. J., & Spellman, C. R. (1992). Using timers and lap counters to promote self-management of independent exercise in adolescents with mental retardation. *Education and Training in Mental Retardation, 27*(1), 51-59.

Elrod, S. (1997). *Assistive technology as an element of individual support in public policies concerning people with disabilities.* Unpublished manuscript. Austin: Texas Assistive Technology Partnership.

Enders, A. (1995, June). *Personal assistance services and assistive technology: Allies or adversaries.* Paper presented at the RESNA '95 conference, Washington, DC.

Fletcher, D., & Abood, D. (1988). An analysis of the readability of product warning labels: Implications for curriculum development for persons with moderate and severe mental retardation. *Education and Training in Mental Retardation, 23*(3), 224-227.

Forness, S. R., & Nihira, K. (1984). Relationship between classroom behavior and adaptive behavior of institutionalized retarded children. *Education and Training of the Mentally Retarded, 19*(3), 222-227.

Frederick-Dugan A., Test, D. W., & Varn, L. (1991). Acquisition and generalization of purchasing skills using a calculator by students who are mentally retarded. *Education and Training of Mental Retardation, 26*(4) 381-387.

Gardner, J. F. (1990). Introduction: A decade of change. In J. F. Gardner and M. S. Chapman (Eds.), *Program issues in developmental disabilities* (2nd ed., pp. 3-17). Baltimore: Paul H. Brookes.

Gardner, J. F., & Chapman, M. S. (1985). *Staff development in mental retardation services: A practical handbook.* Baltimore: Paul H. Brookes.

Gardner, J. F., & O'Brien, J. (1990). The principle of normalization. In J. F. Gardner and M. S. Chapman (Eds.), *Program issues in developmental disabilities,* (2nd ed., pp. 39-57). Baltimore: Paul H. Brookes.

Guess, D., Benson, H. A., & Siegel-Causey, E. (1985). Concepts and issues related to choice making and autonomy among persons with severe disabilities. *Journal of The Association for Persons With Severe Handicaps*, 10, 79-86.

Kishi, G., Teelucksingh, B., Zollers, N., Park-Lee, S., & Meyer, L. (1988). Daily decision-making in community residences: A social comparison of adults with and without mental retardation. *American Journal on Mental Retardation*, 92, 430-435.

Kuder, S. J., & Bryen, D. N. (1991). Communicative performance of persons with mental retardation in an institutional setting. *Education and Training in Mental Retardation*, 26(3), 325-332.

Leland, H. (1996). *Adaptive behavior scale for young children: Field test manual.* Unpublished manuscript. Austin, TX: Pro-Ed.

Lord, J., & Pedlar, A. (1991). Life in the community: Four years after the closure of an institution. *Mental Retardation*, 4, 213-221.

Luckasson, R., Coulter, D. L., Polloway, E. A., Reiss, S., Schalock, R. L., Snell, M. E., Spitalnik, D. M., & Stark, J. A. (1992). *Mental retardation: Diagnosis, classification, and systems of support* (9th ed.). Washington, DC: American Association on Mental Retardation.

MacArthur, C. A. (1988). The impact of computers on the writing process. *Exceptional Children*, 54, 536-542.

McGregor, G., & Pachuski, P. (1996). Assistive technology in schools: Are teachers, ready, able, and supported? *Journal of Special Education Technology*, 13(1), 4-15.

McMahon, C. M., Wacker, D. P., Sasso, G. M., Berg, W. K., & Newton, S. M. (1996). Analysis of frequency and type of interactions in a peer-mediated social skills intervention: Instructional vs. social interactions. *Education and Training in Mental Retardation and Developmental Disabilities*, 31(4), 339-352.

Mithaug, D. E., & Hanawalt, D. A. (1978). The validation of procedures to assess prevocational task preferences in retarded adults. *Journal of Applied Behavior Analysis*, 11, 153-162.

Newton, J. S., Horner, R. H., & Lund, L. (1991). Honoring activity preferences in individualized plan development: A descriptive analysis. *The Association for Persons With Severe and Profound Handicaps*, 16, 207-212.

Nietupski, J., Hamre-Nietupski, S., Vanderhart, N. S., & Fishback, K. (1996). Employer perceptions of the benefits and concerns of supported employment. *Education and Training in Mental Retardation and Developmental Disabilities*, 31(4), 310-323.

Nirje, B. (1980). The normalization principle. In R. J. Flynn and K. E. Nitsch (Eds.), *Normalization, social integration, and community services* (pp. 31-49). Baltimore: University Park Press.

Nosek, M. A. (1992). Independent living. In R. M. Parker and E. M. Szymanski (Eds.), *Rehabilitation counseling* (2nd ed., pp. 103-134). Austin, TX: Pro-Ed.

O'Brien, J. (1987). A guide to life-style planning. In B. Wilcox & G. T. Bellamy (Eds.), *A comprehensive guide to the Activities Catalog* (pp. 175-189). Baltimore: Paul H. Brookes.

O'Brien, J. (1991). *Down stairs that are never your own: Supporting people with developmental disabilities in their own homes.* Paper prepared for the Center on Human Policy, Syracuse University, Syracuse, NY.

Owen, M. S., McDonald, L., & Baine, D. (1994). Direction observation of communicative interaction in a group home setting. *Education and Training in Mental Retardation and Developmental Disabilities*, 29(1), 34-42.

Parette, H. P. (1991). The importance of technology in the education and training of persons with mental retardation. *Education and Training in Mental Retardation*, 26(2), 165-178.

Parette, H. P., Jr., & Brotherson, M. J. (1996). Family participation in assistive technology assessment for young children with mental retardation and developmental disabilities. *Education and Training in Mental Retardation and Developmental Disabilities, 31*(1), 29-43.

Podell, D. M., Tournaki-Rein, N., & Lin, A. (1992). Automization of mathematics skills via computer-assisted instruction among students with mild mental handicaps. *Education and Training of Mental Retardation, 27*(3), 200-206.

Raskind, M., & Bryant, B. R. (1995, June). *Assessing students with learning disabilities for assistive technology needs.* Workshop at the Texas Assistive Technology Partnership's First Annual Conference on Assistive Technology, Austin, TX.

Raskind, M., & Bryant, B. R. (1996). *Examiner's manual: Functional evaluation for assistive technology—field test version.* Austin, TX: Pro-Ed.

Raskind, M., & Shaw, T. (1996, March). *An overview: Assistive technology for students with learning disabilities.* Presented at the Council for Learning Disabilities Assistive Technology Symposium, Las Vegas, NV.

Reese, G. M., & Snell, M. E. Putting on and removing coats and jackets: The acquisition and maintenance of skills by children with severe multiple disabilities. *Education and Training of Mental Retardation, 26*(4), 398-410.

Rettig, M., Kallam, M., & McCarthy-Salm, K. (1993). The effect of social and isolate toys on the social interactions of preschool-aged children. *Education and Training in Mental Retardation, 28*(5), 252-256.

Richards, D. (1995). *Assistive technology: Birth to five years.* Cromwell, CT: ConnSense.

Riegel, R. H. (1988). *A guide to cooperative consultation.* Jason Court, MI: RHR Consultation Services.

Rieth, H. J., & Evertson, C. (1988). Variables related to the effective instruction of difficult-to-teach children. *Focus on Exceptional Children, 20*(5), 1-8.

Rivera, D. P., & Bryant, B. R. (in press). Using assistive technology to include students with learning disabilities in cooperative learning activities. *Journal of Learning Disabilities.*

Rivera, D. P., & Smith, D. D. (1997). *Teaching students with learning and behavior problems* (3rd ed.). Boston: Allyn & Bacon.

Rosen, J. W., & Burchard, S. N. (1990). Community activities and social support networks: A social comparison of adults with and adults without mental retardation. *Education and Training in Mental Retardation, 25*(2), 193-204.

Schalock, R. L., & Kiernan, W. E. (1990). *Habilitation planning for adults with disabilities.* New York: Springer-Verlag.

Schumaker, J. B., & Deshler, D. D. (1984). Setting demand variables: A major factor in program planning for the LD adolescent. *Topics in Language Disorders, 4*(2), 22-40.

Schuster, J. W. (1988). Cooking instruction with persons labeled mentally retarded: A review of literature. *Education and Training in Mental Retardation, 23*(1), 43-50.

Spooner, F., Stem, B., & Test, D. W. (1989). Teaching first aid skills to adolescents who are moderately mentally handicapped. *Education and Training in Mental Retardation, 24*(4), 341-351.

Technology-Related Assistance for Individuals With Disabilities Act of 1988, P. L. 100-407, 29 U.S.C. §§ 2201, 2202. (1988)

Texas Assistive Technology Partnership. (1995). *Public forum: People with disabilities speak their mind about assistive technology service delivery in Texas.* Austin, TX: Author.

Turnbull, A. P., & Turnbull, H. R. (1985). Developing independence. *Journal of Adolescent Health Care, 6,* 108-119.

Turnbull, H. R., Turnbull, A. P., Bronicki, G. J., Summers, J. A., & Roeder-Gordon, C. (1989). *Disability and the family: A guide to decisions for adulthood*. Baltimore: Paul H. Brookes.

Tymchuk, A. J., Hamada, D., Andron, L., & Anderson, S. (1990). Home safety training with mothers who are mentally retarded. *Education and Training in Mental Retardation*, 25(2), 142-149.

Veach, D. M. (1977). Choice with responsibility. *Young Children*, 32, 22-25.

West, M. D., & Parent, W. S. (1992). Consumer choice and empowerment in supported employment services: Issues and strategies. *Journal of The Association for Persons With Severe Handicaps*, 17, 47-52.

Widaman, K. F., & McGrew, K. S. (1996). The structure of adaptive behavior. In J. W. Jacobson & J. A. Mulick (Eds.), *Manual of diagnosis and professional practice in mental retardation* (pp. 97-110). Washington, DC: American Psychological Association.

Wolfensberger, W. (1972). *The principle of normalization in human services*. Toronto: National Institute on Mental Retardation.

PART 2

The Measurement of Adaptive Behavior

Introduction

Demographers tell us that the United States will not have any racial or ethnic majority at some point between 2050 and 2100. Even today, five school districts in the United States serve children from more than 100 racial and ethnic groups. For a number of years, the consideration of ethnic and sociocultural factors in the assessment of adaptive behavior has been recommended as part of the various diagnostic and classification systems. Exactly what should be considered and what adjustments made have not been clear. This is the major purpose of the five chapters composing this second part of this monograph.

To date, there have been some 200 adaptive behavior instruments developed and marketed. Because of the increasing need for good measures of adaptive behavior, it is essential for any bookon adaptive behavior to include a chapter on basic measurement theory and standards. Scott Spreat's chapter does that well. In chapter 6, Dr. Spreat: (a) discusses what a test is ("an empirical sampling procedure"); (b) defines the specifications that will measure the 1992 AAMR (Luckasson et al.) 10-part construct of adaptive behavior; (c) discusses both the demand characteristics of an adaptive behavior instrument and the psychometric standards to which the test must adhere; (d) summarizes the uses of adaptive behavior instruments, including identifying strengths and weaknesses, diagnosis, documenting progress, and research; and (e) suggests that the primary focus of adaptive behavior measures should be for classification decisions.

In chapter 7, Pat Craig and Marc Tassé review the literature in assessed adaptive behavior regarding cultural and demographic differences across five ethnic groups. The authors report that although differences in adaptive behavior functioning are found, these differences are not always large and there are multiple confounding variables. In the second section of their chapter, Drs. Craig and Tassé identify the specific variables that may be operating when cross-cultural differences are found. Chief among these variables are age, gender, socio-economic status, language, acculturation, geographic region, family structure, family training and disciplinary practices, and attitudes toward disability.

The focus on the differences in assessed adaptive behavior continues in chapter 8, where Brian Bryant, Diane Pedrotty Bryant, and Steve Chamberlain summarize the results of a large national study that compared adaptive behavior scores on the 10 adaptive skills areas found in the 1992 AAMR definition (Luckasson et al.), using the recently published *Assessment of Adaptive Behavior Areas*, (Bryant, Taylor, & Rivera, 1996). Prior to describing that study, the authors discuss: (a) adaptive behavior and its assessment as it relates to test bias, (b) the nature of test bias, (c) test bias in adaptive behavior assessment among races and genders, (d) how researchers typically examine scales for bias, and (e) how researchers typically control for test bias.

In chapter 9, Marc Tassé and Pat Craig discuss a number of critical procedures and standards in the cross-cultural assessment of adaptive behaviors. They also point out that deficits in adaptive behavior have strong societal or cultural bases. This points out how important it is for evaluators and practitioners to understand the critical procedures and standards for the cross-cultural assessment of adaptive behavior discussed by the authors. In this chapter, Drs. Tassé and Craig: (a) present a historical perspective on the role that cultural factors (and differences) have had on the diagnosis of mental retardation, (b) examine the current methods surrounding the cross-cultural assessment of adaptive behavior, (c) examine the current methods used for cross-cultural translation and adaptation of adaptive behavior scales, (d) outline the necessary steps involved in validating adaptive behavior measures that are used cross-culturally, and (e) summarize recent guidelines for recommended practices of adapting educational and psychological tests that have direct implications for the cross-cultural adaptations and testing.

In chapter 10 Laird Heal and Marc Tassé discuss the development and initial evaluation of a culturally sensitive individualized assessment of adaptive behavior. This presents logical merging of the concepts of adaptive skills, cultural sensitivity, and person-referenced assessment. The authors place their work within the following framework: (a) The taxonomy of adaptive skills reflects a comprehensive curriculum of skills to assess; (b) the four types of proposed supports clarify the meaning of support; (c) the five levels of support define the standards for quantifying support and drawing a correspondence between one's level of support and one's degree of mental retardation; and (d) the individualization of the assessment maximizes its cultural fairness.

In their proposed individualized, criterion-referenced system of adaptive behavior, the authors: (a) discuss the assessment challenges posed by the 1992 AAMR (Luckasson et al.) definition of mental retardation and the classification of adaptive behavior areas and levels of support; (b) propose a culturally sensitive, individualized system to address these challenges; and (c) present the results of an initial study that illustrates the feasibility of applying the proposed system to adults with mental retardation in community settings.

Throughout part 2, the reader will appreciate the complexity of assessing adaptive behavior with individuals from nonmainstreamed cultural or ethnic groups. You will be challenged to consider what role deficits in adaptive behavior should play in the definition of mental retardation in an increasingly multicultural environment.

Key points to keep in mind as you read part 2 include:

- Which makes better sense: a criterion-referenced or norm-referenced approach to cross-cultural adaptive behavior assessment?

- What standards and procedures should one use in assessing adaptive behavior cross-culturally?

- What role do cultural factors play in the assessment of adaptive behavior, and what is the significance of any found cultural or demographic group differences?

References

Bryant, B.R., Taylor, R.L., & Rivera, D.P. (1996). *Assessment of adaptive areas.* Austin, TX: Pro Ed.

Luckasson, R., Coulter, D.L., Polloway, E.A., Reiss, S., Schalock, R.L., Snell, M.E., Spitalnick, D.M., & Stark, J.A. (1992). *Mental retardation: Diagnosis, classification, and systems of support* (9th ed.) Washington, D.C.: American Association on Mental Retardation.

CHAPTER 6

Psychometric Standards for Adaptive Behavior Assessment[1]

SCOTT SPREAT
Wood's Services Incorporated

Introduction

Adaptive behavior formally became part of the definition of mental retardation in 1959, when the American Association on Mental Deficiency (AAMD) published its first manual on terminology and classification in mental retardation (Heber, 1959). Under the terms set forth in this manual, mental retardation was to be diagnosed on the basis of concurrent deficits in intellectual functioning and adaptive behavior, both of which were to be evident prior to the age of 18 years. This three-part definition of mental retardation composed of adaptive behavior, intelligence, and age of onset has been retained through several revisions to the AAMD terminology and classification manual (Grossman, 1973, 1983). It has also been incorporated into other recognized classification schemes, most notably the *Diagnostic and Statistical Manual* series published by the American Psychiatric Association (1994).

The widespread popularity of the adaptive behavior construct has spawned the development of well over 200 scales, each purporting to measure adaptive behavior (Spreat, Roszkowski, & Isett, 1983). It is curious that, while these many scales have shared a number of common elements, there have been marked differences in terms of content, depth, and scope. A report on 69 adaptive behavior instruments (Mayeda, Pelzer, & Van Zuylen, 1978) revealed at least 19 distinct topic areas being measured under the construct of adaptive behavior. Self-help, communication, motor development, socialization, and prevocational/vocational were the most frequently included constructs within these 69 scales.

This diversity suggests a lack of clarity regarding the conceptual definition of adaptive behavior. Early critics described the construct as "vague" (Baumeister & Muma, 1975; Clausen, 1972; Zigler), "ill-defined" (Baumeister & Muma, 1975; Clausen, 1972), "value laden" (Maloney & Ward, 1979; Zigler), "arbitrary" (Clarke & Clarke, 1974), and "loose" (Meyers, Nihira, & Zetlin, 1979). Coulter and Morrow (1978) noted that adaptive behavior could encompass almost anything that qualified as human behavior. Meyers et al. (1979) suggested that it might be better to define the construct of adaptive behavior in terms of specific scales, rather than attempt to define it abstractly to everyone's satisfaction.

Compounding the difficulties regarding the construct of adaptive behavior and its measurement, clinicians have had little guidance with respect to how information obtained from an adaptive behavior scale is to be used to make diagnoses and classifications. Grossman (1977) advised clinicians simply to use judgment in integrating the multidimensional adaptive behavior information with information obtained from intelligence tests. Early evidence suggested that the intelligence component of the definition received far greater emphasis than the adaptive behavior dimension (Adams, 1973; Junkala, 1977; Smith & Polloway, 1975). Similarly, Roszkowski, Spreat, and Isett (1983) concluded that adaptive behavior was, in practice, a relatively minor component in the classification of levels of mental retardation.

In 1992, the American Association for Mental Retardation (AAMR; the new name for

[1] Many thanks to Laird Heal for his helpful comments on an earlier version of this chapter.

AAMD) put forth a new definition of mental retardation (Luckasson et al.). The three basic components of the 1959 definition were retained (adaptive behavior, intelligence, and age), but the adaptive behavior component was more specifically described. AAMR defined 10 relevant dimensions of adaptive behavior: communication, self-care, home living, social skills, community use, self-direction, health and safety, functional academics, leisure, and work. In addition to providing an operational definition for adaptive behavior, the new manual offered guidance to clinicians for determining whether an individual had deficits in adaptive behavior. A person was considered to have deficits in adaptive behavior if he or she had limitations in at least 2 of the 10 domains of adaptive behavior. The 1992 classification manual (Luckasson et al.) also indicated that limitations in adaptive behavior must be related to the significantly subaverage intellectual functioning, and they must be documented within the context of a community environment, typical of the individual's age peers and indexed to the individual's need for support; valid determination of adaptive behavior skill levels requires the use of an appropriately normed and standardized instrument.

The task of the clinician was made a little easier by this definition, at least conceptually. It provided guidelines regarding the integration of adaptive behavior findings with intelligence test scores. There were also general guidelines for the use of information obtained from adaptive behavior scales. The only real problem was that no test existed to measure each of the 10 specific domains in a way that supported decision making as required by the new AAMR definition (Luckasson et al.). It should be noted that it is beyond the scope of this chapter to discuss whether the underlying structure of adaptive behavior is best described by 10 domains. Factor analytic studies have yielded a variety of ways to summarize the structure of adaptive behavior, but no factor analytic study has identified the 10 specific domains proposed by

the AAMR. This does not preclude the development of a valid and reliable instrument that employs 10 subscales, even if there might be a more parsimonious or congruent summary of adaptive behavior items. It does, however, beg a basic question regarding the necessity for the complexity that 10 separate domains add to the AAMR definition of mental retardation. If a number of domains are sufficiently intercorrelated to justify reducing the number of domains, are 10 domains really needed in the definition of mental retardation? Perhaps this is an issue best addressed by the AAMR Terminology and Classification Committee in the next revision of the classification manual.

The purpose of this chapter is to discuss appropriate psychometric standards for such a 10-domain test and, in conjunction with the 1992 definition of mental retardation, to define the specifications that will measure the AAMR 10-part construct of adaptive behavior. To do this, the chapter will discuss both the demand characteristics of an adaptive behavior instrument and the psychometric standards to which the test must adhere.

What Is a Test?

Cronbach (1970) wrote that a test was a systematic procedure for observing a person's behavior and describing it with the aid of a numerical scale or category system. Implicit within this definition are several basic assumptions. First, it must be recognized that a test merely samples the behavior of an individual. The behavior of that individual within the testing situation must be assumed to represent the behavior of the individual in other situations. That is, it is assumed that the test is measuring a trait of the person, a consistency of behavior or performance that will transcend the immediate testing situation. This implies, of course, that a traditional psychometric approach is unlikely to measure successfully behaviors or performances that are environmentally specific or sensitive to minor environmental changes. The recognition of this is implicit in the rejection of tests and psychometric devices by most behavior analysts, who typically believe that behavior is a state that reflects the unique environmental contingencies in place at a specific time (Rimm & Masters, 1974).

Second, the test itself must be considered a sample of the infinite number of items that might be constructed about any given topic. For example, to assess the toileting skills of an individual, the test developer selects a finite number of items from the infinite number of possible items about that skill.

Tests are typically administered at one point in time. They measure performance at that time and under the existing conditions. If measurements collected under such "snapshot" conditions are to be valid, it is necessary to assume that they would be repeated under similar conditions on other occasions. One must assume that if a second "snapshot" were taken the next day, similar results would be obtained. There's an underlying assumption that the test is measuring a trait, a behavior or pattern of behaviors that is likely to be repeated. If a behavior varies considerably, the use of a test is probably not the ideal way to measure it.

A test also samples the universe of questions about a given topic. Consider the national psychology licensing exam. It contains 300 questions. This does not constitute the entirety of knowledge about psychology; it is a sample of the knowledge within the field, and from the individual's performance on the test, licensing boards make inferences about the person's knowledge of psychology.

Perhaps a stronger definition than that given above is that a test is an empirical sampling procedure. It is a sample of items from a given content area, and it is a sample of human performance on these items. In doing this in a structured and consistent manner, a test yields some sort of numeric score or classification.

Many Expectations for Adaptive Behavior Measures

Adaptive behavior instruments have been marketed and used for many purposes in addition to the diagnosis and classification of mental retardation. The current version of the AAMR *Adaptive Behavior Scale* is reported to have four uses (Nihira, Leland, & Lambert, 1993). These uses are (a) identifying strengths and weaknesses, (b) diagnosis, (c) documenting progress, and (d) research. While these seem appropriately conservative, it should be noted that various adaptive behavior scales have been proposed for a relatively wide spectrum of uses, including diagnosis (Grossman, 1977), individual goal setting (Berdine, Murphy, & Roller, 1977; Bogen & Aanes, 1975), communication (Fogelman, 1975), administration of programs (Fogelman, 1975), and program evaluation (Conroy, Efthimou, & Lemanowicz, 1982; Schwartz & Allen, 1974). In other words, adaptive behavior scales have been suggested as tools for clinical use with individuals and administrative use with groups.

A major problem for any instrument proposed for such a wide range of uses is this: To obtain sufficient information to support individualized programming, the test must be quite detailed and, in the case of a multifaceted construct like adaptive behavior, quite lengthy. An instrument of sufficient length to permit individual programming is simply unwieldy for the clinician conducting a diagnostic classification. This dilemma is sometimes called the bandwidth-fidelity problem (Cronbach, 1970). The test developer must simultaneously address the issues of depth and breadth to arrive with a test of useful proportions.

Otto, McMenemy, and Smith (1973) proposed various levels of assessment that more clearly link the purpose of assessment to the nature of assessment. With respect to adaptive behavior, it must be recognized that the instrument useful for program evaluation (like the Conroy et al. [1982] use of the *Behavior Development Survey*) will not be the best instrument for diagnosis, nor will it be the best instrument for use in individual programming. With a broad construct like adaptive behavior, it is unrealistic to think that the same test can be used for program evaluation, diagnosis, classification, and individual programming. In anticipation of the development of new adaptive behavior measures, it seems appropriate to suggest here that the primary focus of such instrumentation should be on the classification decision. Program evaluators have used multiple regression techniques to produce shorter indexes that are adequate for research purposes (Roszkowski & Bean, 1980). Individual programming should always be supplemented by direct observation and other assessment methods; the psychometric demands to create sufficient reliability at the item level preclude the application of a classification scale to microscopic programming decisions. The *Behavior Characteristics Progression* (Fickel, 1972) provides sufficient detail for individual programming, but it is too time consuming for reasonable use as a classification tool. It seems unlikely that any instrument can adequately serve every potential measurement purpose. A screening tool won't support individual programming, and a tool for individual programming will not be a satisfactory screening device. The test developer must identify a priori the purposes of its instrument so an appropriate balance of bandwidth and fidelity can be achieved.

It is difficult to suggest how many items would be necessary to adequately sample each of the 10 domains of adaptive behavior. A balance must be struck—having enough items to thoroughly sample the domain relative to the purpose of the scale and not so many items that practitioners avoid use of the scale. It is certainly an area in which psychometric and marketing issues must be considered simultaneously.

Psychometric Standards for Adaptive Behavior Measures

An adaptive behavior scale can be used in a rational and informed manner only if the test user is aware of the information regarding the technical characteristics of the test (American Psychological Association, 1985). Minimally, these technical characteristics should include reliability and validity coefficients for each of the skill areas, as well as any other relevant research data such as norms. This information should be presented in a manual that accompanies the test. The American Psychological Association (1985) has defined the basic standards that are to be expected of any test used with individuals. These standards are reviewed below.

Reliability

Reliability refers to the repeatability of measurement (Thorndike, 1971; Thorndike & Hagen, 1961) or perhaps more specifically to the extent to which test scores are a function of systematic sources of variance. A test is reliable to the extent that an individual gets the same score or retains the same general ranking within a population on repeated applications of a test. It is important to note that reliability indexes should be reported for each level of measurement to be used. Thus, if decision making is based only on scale scores (e.g., the 10 adaptive skill area scores), one is compelled to report reliability indexes for scale scores. If, however, one proposes to use items with which to identify specific problem areas, the test manual must provide information on the reliability of items. Three basic types of reliability are pertinent to adaptive behavior measures: test-retest reliability, interobserver reliability, and internal consistency.

Test-Retest

Test-retest reliability, conceptually the most simple of the various reliability measures, refers to the consistency of test scores on separate testing occasions. To establish test-retest reliability, a scale is administered to a group of individuals at Time 1, and then readministered to the same group a few days later. The correlation of scores from Time 1 and from Time 2 constitute this index of reliability. The time span between administrations must be relatively brief to prevent scores from fluctuating as a result of actual development trends or environmental events that affect individuals differently.

A measure of test-retest reliability is considered an essential part of the technical information with respect to any adaptive behavior measure, and it should be included in the technical manual that accompanies the test.

It is interesting that the nature of adaptive behavior assessment, in which a third party completes the questionnaire rather than relying on direct assessment of the individual, actually eliminates some of the potential threats to test-retest reliability. Normally, one worries that memory for past items and learning from the first test administration may be significant threats to test-retest reliability. These are not threats in the typical third-party administration mode used for adaptive behavior instruments.

Interobserver Reliability

Interobserver reliability (or interobserver agreement) refers to the extent to which two or more independent observers agree on the rating for a given individual. Leland (1972, 1978) has argued that differences between two raters may reflect true behavioral variation under different environmental conditions, or at least real differences in the perceptions of the raters. With this line of thought, poor interobserver reliability might not necessarily reflect diminished psychometric properties of the instrument, but rather legitimate variation. There is certainly some validity to this argument, but it raises certain interpretive challenges. It should be clear that the design of an instrument and its mode of administration make implicit assumptions about the nature of the behavior being measured (Spreat et al., 1983). If one is attempting to measure an enduring trait of an individual, to obtain an accurate assessment of that trait, one need administer a test only once. If, on the other hand, behavior varies significantly as a function of various properties of the environment (including the rater), a measurement approach that assumes an underlying trait will not be likely to yield an accurate measure. Instead, one would need to adopt repeated measurement strategies such as those employed by behavior analysts and such as those outlined by Hersen and Barlow (1976). If behavior is state dependent, measurement strategies must address the various states. Because virtually all adaptive behavior scales are designed to be used in the former manner, it would appear that the test developers have implicitly assumed that adaptive behavior is a trait or an enduring quality that generally persists across most conditions. If this is the case, differences among raters should generally be considered error, and consistency across raters becomes an essential component of the psychometric quality of the instrument. The implicit assumption regarding whether adaptive behavior is best considered a trait or a temporary state is important with respect to the approach to measurement. If adaptive behavior is a broad, general trait, perhaps only one administration on an instrument is necessary to assess that trait. On the other hand, if adaptive behavior is environmentally variable, multiple administrations using multiple informants would be necessary to describe even partially the individual's typical adaptive behavior. Perhaps the notion that adaptive behavior instruments seek to describe and measure typical behavior lends itself more to a trait definition, with the ever-apparent consideration that different environments and different informants may invite different behavior.

Nevertheless, there are obvious situations in which a person exhibits a skill for one observer but not for another. One must not dismiss differences as error, but should, rather, treat them as indicators of the need for more intensive assessment.

The intraclass correlation coefficient is the preferred index of interobserver reliability for interval and ordinal scales. In contrast with the commonly reported Pearson correlation coefficient, the intraclass correlation treats differences in rater leniency as a source of error. A simple Pearson correlation could be as high as 1.0 if two observers always disagreed by a constant. If Rater A always rated performance one point higher than Rater B, the correlation would be perfect, even though the two raters never actually agreed. The intraclass correlation corrects for this problem, offering a more conservative estimate of reliability. Various percentage agreement indexes are often reported for nominal scales and for quantifying rater agreement on specific items (cf. Zarcone, Rodgers, Iwata, Rourke, & Dorsey, 1991). However, the results of percentage agreement indexes must be interpreted with caution (cf. Hartmann, 1977). The use of Cohen's Kappa is recommended (Heal & Fujiura, 1984).

As with test-retest reliability, measures of interobserver reliability should be included in the technical manual that accompanies any adaptive behavior scale. This statistic is considered absolutely essential because most measures of adaptive behavior rely on third-party observers to complete the scales. These observers then become significant sources of potential error variance, and their impact must be assessed and reported in the test manual.

Internal Consistency Reliability

Internal consistency reliability was developed in response to some of the inherent threats to test-retest reliability. It was reasoned that if one were to develop two parallel forms of a given instrument from a single test content outline and then correlate performance on the two parallel forms, the resulting reliability indexes would be free of the threats of maturation and learning (mentioned above).

Developing alternate forms of an instrument would be difficult and time consuming. What about shorter alternatives? One example, split-half reliability, compares the scores from one half of the instrument with scores from the other half of the instrument. This approach is viewed as a variation of parallel forms reliability. The most common split-half approach is to administer the test to a group and divide the resulting test scores into two batches—answers from the odd-numbered items and answers from the even-numbered items. The scores from the odd-numbered items are correlated with the scores from the even-numbered items. The resulting correlation is then corrected for the length of the test, because reliability is a function of test length in addition to other factors.

Cronbach and Furby (1970) introduced a more sophisticated variant of spit-half reliability. Cronbach's "alpha" is the average correlation for all possible split halves of a given test, corrected for scale length. This approach, and the simpler split-half reliability, measures the extent to which items on the scale are measuring the same basic construct. The term *internal consistency* derives from this.

Some theorists (e.g., Cattell, 1986) have argued that internal consistency approaches to reliability assessment can be inappropriate and not entirely useful. They note that it is possible to obtain excellent test-retest and interobserver reliabilities from a scale that yields much weaker internal consistency estimates. This is true, of course, but it is curious that anyone would propose to develop or define a scale based on uncorrelated items. Uncorrelated items can certainly have substantial validity. Bean and Roszkowski (1982) noted that the fire-setting item of the original *Adaptive Behavior Scale* (Nihira, Foster, Shellhaas & Leland, 1974) did not correlate well with the total score of the domain of which it was a part. As an administrator and as a practitioner, I certainly want to know who has a propensity for setting fires, but importance alone is not a criterion for defining an item as part of a scale.

Perhaps such items are best left to the realm of checklists, where no effort is made to obtain a total score, but where test-retest and interobserver reliabilities remain a concern.

A vital question has to do with determining an acceptable level of reliability. All three indexes discussed above (test-retest, interobserver, and internal consistency) are essentially correlation coefficients, with possible values ranging -1.00 to +1.00. Nunnally (1967) advised that reliability coefficients in excess of .90 are desirable for an instrument to be used to make clinical decisions about individuals. Others (cf. Batjelsmit, 1977) have been more tolerant, suggesting that reliability coefficients in the .80s are acceptable. It should be noted that the highest standard of reliability must pertain to instruments that are used to make decisions about individuals. One could argue that lower reliability is more tolerable in group research, where the primary risk of lower reliability would be the increased probability of Type 2 error. Significant differences would be harder to detect with a less reliable instrument.

Most published adaptive behavior instruments that purport to measure constructs similar to the 10 listed by AAMR have acceptable levels of reliability. For example, each of the 10 Part-I domains of the current version of the AAMR *Adaptive Behavior Scale* (Nihira et al., 1993) have test-retest reliability estimates of at least .88. Six achieve the .90 standard. Similar indexes are reported with respect to interobserver reliability. Given the increased importance of adaptive behavior in the most recent AAMR definition of mental retardation (Luckasson et al., 1992), it would seem prudent to strive for reliability coefficients over .90 for all adaptive behavior scales and subscales. If the risks associated with labeling an individual as having mental retardation are thought to exceed the risk of denying services because of not having mental retardation, perhaps even greater caution is needed.

It must be remembered that reliability is at least partially a function of the number of items within a scale (Stanley, 1971). The Spearman-Brown prophecy formula shows that reliability can be increased in a predictable manner by simply adding items of equal or similar reliabilities. The logic underlying the Spearman-Brown prophecy is similar to, but somewhat more complicated than, the logic that underlies sampling. By increasing the sample of items used to measure a given construct, one increases the likelihood of getting an accurate measure of that construct. To ensure sufficient reliability, it is evident that each scale must contain a sufficient number of similar items. Similarly, it has been suggested that reliability can be increased by employing multiple third-party raters and averaging their scores (Strahan, 1980); however, such an approach would tend to obscure true differences in performance that occur in response to different informants. The approach also risks assigning or creating an "average" score that suggests a performance level never actually emitted by the individual being assessed.

It can be argued that an individual's performance on a test is a function of his or her luck as well as skill. Good luck inflates a score beyond a person's true score, while bad luck depresses the score below the true score. Luck, of course, must be recognized as measurement error or unreliability. The extent to which individual scores on a given test might be expected to fluctuate as a function of unreliability is quantifiable through the *standard error of measurement*, which is a mathematical function of the test's standard deviation and the test's reliability. It can be used to estimate a confidence level around a test score (or, more precisely, to estimate the confidence with which one can state that a person's true score falls within certain boundaries). An estimate of the standard error of measurement for each of the three reliability coefficients must appear in the test manual supporting the use of any adaptive behavior measure.

Validity

The validation of an instrument is based on a determination of the types of inferences that can be drawn from the test scores. Entry-level measurement courses typically teach that no test is ever described as valid, but rather described as valid for a number of specific purposes. There are as many possible validation approaches as there are potential uses of an instrument, but there are two basic approaches (American Psychological Association, 1985). These two approaches assess what is being measured by the test and what the test scores enable the user to infer about other behavior.

Test Validity

Content validity. Content validity refers to the determination of whether the test adequately samples the domain of interest. At face value, this would appear to be a relatively simple task; but there can be difficulties in this process. The first involves defining the domain to be measured. It should be noted that the 1992 AAMR classification manual (Luckasson et al.) does in fact define the construct of adaptive behavior as consisting of 10 specific skill areas. This significantly simplifies the content validation task. One must next determine that all relevant domains within each of the 10 areas are adequately sampled. For example, it would be important to note whether toileting skills are included in a test that purports to measure self-care. The second concern has to do with the proposed uses of the test. A test proposed for the development of individual program plans needs to measure items with sufficient detail to support that process, while a test for research or program evaluation purposes can be less detailed.

Content validity is essentially a mechanical process, in which technicians determine whether the universe of possible items is adequately sampled. A more empirical approach has been suggested. The test developer would first specify the domain of the universe to be measured. Then two teams of competent item writers would develop independent tests from the same set of test specifications. The entire test development process would be completed by two independent teams, and resultant scores would be correlated. If the scores of the subjects on the two tests differed by no more than errors of measurement, one would have a valid test.

Construct validity. Construct validity, the second aspect of determining what is being measured, refers to the determination of the broad, general aspects of behavior being measured. There are three broad approaches to construct validity.

The first is factor analysis, a statistical technique used to isolate the broad and ideally uncorrelated dimensions being measured. With respect to both the old and the new versions of the AAMD/AAMR *Adaptive Behavior Scale* (Nihira et al., 1974; Lambert, Nihira & Leland, 1993), considerable factor analytic work has been done to help establish construct validity (Nihira, 1969a; Nihira, 1969b; Nihira, Leland, & Lambert, 1993).

The second approach to construct validity involves the regression of adaptive behavior scale scores on age. This approach, which was used in the development of the old *Vineland Social Maturity Scale* (Doll, 1937), assumes that the development of adaptive behavior follows the pattern of chronological maturation. This may not necessarily be a valid assumption to make with respect to people who have developmental disabilities, although perhaps one could collect data on intellectually normal children and adolescents and use this approach.

Third, construct validity can also be supported by item analytic techniques used to determine the extent to which items within a given scale reflect the construct that is being measured by the scale. Anastasi (1988) suggested that corrected item-total correlations in the .2 to .3 range could be considered acceptable. An item that does not positively correlate at least this high with the corrected scale total score (minus the contribution of that item) may detract from construct validity. Of course, any item that has a negative correlation with the corrected scale score detracts from the scale; it must be omitted or assigned to a different scale. Summaries of item analyses such as those described above should be presented in the test manual.

Concurrent validity. The third approach to determining what a test measures is concurrent validity, which is a kind of empirical validity. The logic underlying concurrent validation is that if Test A correlates highly with Test B, the tests are concurrently valid. Thus, if Test A is already an accepted measure of adaptive behavior, the high correlation of Test B with Test A suggests that Test B is also a measure of adaptive behavior. Although it has been suggested (Meyers et al., 1979) that this approach begs the question in that it is based on circular logic, it is a commonly reported strategy for test validation. An example of this approach was evident in Roszkowski's (1980) study of the AAMD *Adaptive Behavior Scale* and the *Vineland Social Maturity Scale* (Doll, 1953). Similar evidence appears in the current manual of the revised AAMR *Adaptive Behavior Scale* (Nihira et al., 1993). It would be incumbent upon the developer of any new measure of adaptive behavior to establish concurrent validity by correlating scores from the new measure with scores from other scales purporting to measure the same construct. Subscale-by-subscale correlation would be recommended.

Criterion and Predictive Validity

The second broad approach to validation addresses the issue of what types of inferences can be drawn from test scores. This determination of predictive (or criterion) validity cannot be made in terms of a single study. Instead, it must be demonstrated in terms of the ability of an instrument to discriminate among individuals in various categories assumed to possess different behavioral characteristics. In predictive validity, scores from a test are used to predict some subsequent performance; in criterion validity, scores from the test are used to predict some current measure of performance.

Several possible validity studies would be useful to support any new adaptive behavior measure. Ideally, a new adaptive behavior instrument should lead to classification decisions that are similar to those reached with another adaptive behavior instrument(s). One might correlate the classification results yielded by the new instrument with those from the established instrument(s). Such a study probably could not be done because the AAMR has changed the classification guidelines, so that no acceptable single criterion measure exists. One would probably have to use multiple comparison measures.

It might be reasonable to expect that performance on an adaptive behavior measure would correlate with need for support (or some similar index of independence), with individuals who have lower adaptive behavior scores having greater need for supports. Such an analysis would be useful evidence of criterion-related validity. One might reasonably argue that this is the only standard for validity of an adaptive behavior scale that meets the demands of the new AAMR definition of mental retardation (Luckasson et al.).

One might also conduct a study in which change in adaptive behavior scale scores was examined in relationship with progress on Individual Habilitation Plan (IHP) goals, or one might monitor the impact of a significant life event (e.g., moving from an institution to a community-based program) using two different adaptive behavior measures. Such an analysis, of course, would be complicated by the troublesome properties of change scores (Cronbach & Furby, 1970), and the actual study might require design changes to avoid the use of actual change scores.

Conclusion

Measurement reliability will limit the extent to which two variables can correlate with each other (Stanley, 1971). A validity coefficient, the correlation of a scale with some criterion, is mathematically limited by the reliabilities of the scale and the criterion variable. Any validity coefficient will be limited by the reliability of the measure being validated, such that a marginally reliable instrument will have, at best, marginal validity coefficients. One way to increase the validity coefficients of an instrument is to increase the reliability of that instrument, typically by increasing its length, apparent from the logic of the Spearman-Brown prophecy (Stanley).

A perfectly reliable instrument would yield the highest possible validity coefficients. It is mathematically possible to determine what a validity coefficient would be if both measures were perfectly reliable. This is called correcting for attenuation, and while it affords a conceptual perspective on validity, it makes a test appear more acceptable than it really is. On the other hand, one might argue that uncorrected validity coefficients are actually underestimates of true validities. There is debate regarding whether a test manual should report corrected or uncorrected validity coefficients. There is no clear consensus on the matter, but it is clear that any corrected values reported in the test manual should be identified as corrected values.

Interpreting Tests

Test Fairness

President Johnson's War on Poverty during the 1960s focused substantial attention on people with limited economic assets. With this general attention grew a specific concern that various psychological tests, most notably intelligence tests, yielded different types of results for people with different backgrounds. It was recognized that test performance was a product of the interaction between a person and his or her environments.

Concerns about differential test performance generated interest in what came to be called culture-free testing or the development of tests that performed similarly across different cultures (Tyler & Walsh, 1979). The development of useful, culture-free tests is

perhaps an admirable goal but one not likely to be met. Because of this, it is essential to evaluate the fairness of tests with different cultural groups. Tyler and Walsh recommended that tests be evaluated on several different cultures, with specific interest in the issues of mean differences and predictive differences. Spreat et al. (1983) suggested that the primary issue is not mean diffrences but rather the relationship between predictor and criterion measures. The interactive relationship between predictor and criterion variables must be studied in terms of the mean, the slope, the intercept, the standard error of estimate, and the correlation among the variables. The situation is too complex to analyze simply on the basis of mean differences across cultural groups; all relevant indices need to be considered.

Consider the matter of single-group validity. This is said to occur when the predictor-criterion correlation is statistically significantly different from zero for one cultural group but not for another cultural group. Such a finding could be the result of differences in sample sizes alone, a factor that often occurs when majority cultural groups are compared with minority cultural groups. Theoretically, a correlation of any given magnitude could be statistically significant for a large group but not significant for a small group. This is because the determination of statistical significance (but not correlation magnitude) is at least partially a function of sample size. Evidence of predictor-criterion correlations are insufficient to describe the extent to which a test is culturally fair.

Differential group validity occurs when the predictor-criterion correlations for two cultural groups are both significantly different from zero, but also significantly different from each other. This, however, does not necessarily mean differential prediction. Other factors that describe the relationship between predictor and criterion must be compared.

The preferable way to present data on test fairness is to present information on all traditional regression parameters that link the predictor with the criterion. These would include slope, intercept, and standard error of estimate. These data should be provided for a variety of cultural groups.

Role of Norms

Nihira (1973) noted that a person is adaptive or maladaptive only in context of the demands of his or her environment. This would seem to imply that the evaluation of an individual's adaptive behavior status can be undertaken only with reference to some sort of standard. Indeed, this expectation would seem to be the case with respect to the 1992 AAMR definition of mental retardation. The 1992 AAMR manual (Luckasson et al.) is quite specific in requiring reference to the use of an adaptive skill assessment to evaluate the person's adaptive skill profile on an appropriately normed and standardized instrument.

Selecting the Norm Group

The use of norming is not without controversy or difficulty. The first question must deal with the composition of any norm group. Because any norm group is simply a measuring stick to which an individual is compared, one might argue that the only real requirement for a norm group is that it be large enough to accommodate variation. Yet the AAMR definition of mental retardation stipulates that an individual must exhibit limitations in at least 2 of 10 adaptive behavior skill areas. Limitation must be recognized as a relative term that applies to some sort of standard of "normal." Thus, a convenient-norm group of people living in residential facilities might be a suitable general yardstick, but this reference group would not really enable the test user to address the issue of limitation relative to "normal." One is tempted to suggest that the appropriate norm group for an adaptive behavior instrument would be composed of members of the general public. Such a norm group, however, would prove to be a daunting statistical challenge, given the nonnormal distribution of adaptive behavior (Spreat et al., 1983) among people without mental retardation. Most adults without mental retardation

possess and display most if not all adaptive behaviors listed on typical adaptive behavior scales. There is minimal variance, and variance is essential to the construction of a norm group.

One might be tempted to suggest that a norm group be constructed from people with mental retardation who live in community homes. Such an approach would be as valid as constructing a norm group from individuals who live in institutions. It would be an adequate yardstick. It would not, however, be useful in helping a clinician make a classification of mental retardation. One cannot define significant deficits in terms of a group that, by its very definition, has significant deficits. There is also the very real concern that any such norm group might sometime be construed as some sort of criterion group with regard to community placement.

Developmental Age Norms

Perhaps one alternative to traditional norming approaches would be to incorporate the concept of developmental expectations. Within this framework, an adaptive behavior "deficit" would be defined in terms of a performance that is incongruent with typical age-based expectations. Thus, if toilet training is typically achieved within a culture between the ages of 2 and 4 years, the 6-year-old who is not toilet trained would be identified as having a marked deficit. A norm group under this model would be composed of a random (ideally) sample of individuals through the age of 18 years. This would enable a clinician to set a developmental age in each of the 10 adaptive behavior areas, and some guideline could be given for identifying a significant deficit. The advantages of this approach are that it would probably yield normally distributed data at each age level, and it would focus the identification of developmental delays on the typical development within a culture.

Criterion-Referenced Approach

Some critics of norm-referenced measurement (e. g.,Heal, 1995) have argued that group statistical norms are inherently inappropriate to scale the level of support needed for individuals to function in specified settings. They in turn argue that a criterion-referenced approach (see Tassé & Craig, this volume) would be preferable. In this approach, some absolute standard of performance would be specified with respect to the culture of the individual to which the assessment is being applied. It should be noted that these standards of performance would have to be specified prior to the development of the test to ensure that the test adequately addressed each one.

One might argue that most existing measures of adaptive behavior are, in part, criterion-referenced measurement, in which mastery is indicated when an individual achieves all possible points in a given area of adaptive behavior. An argument can be made that the AAMR should delete its requirement that adaptive behavior instruments be norm referenced, because adaptive behavior deficits are more appropriately described in terms of absolute, rather than relativistic, terms. An adult who is not toilet trained has a significant challenge whether living in the community or among equally challenged individuals. The deficit, it can be argued, is not simply a matter of falling in a low-percentile group. The important issue for adaptive skill assessment is the level of support required for the assessed individual to use a public or private rest room.

Summary

It is clear that the new definition of mental retardation that was put forth by AAMR (Luckasson et al., 1992) will require the development of a new adaptive behavior instrument. Any such instrument will require evidence of psychometric support. Such evidence should include minimally: test-retest reliability, interobserver agreement, internal consistency reliability, construct validity, concurrent validity, predictive validity, and cultural fairness. Consideration should be given to identifying the absolute standards required to survive or flourish in an examinee's personal setting, rather than applying the norms of the larger population, of which less than 2 or 3% are challenged by the tasks included on adaptive behavior scales.

References

Adams, J. (1973). Adaptive behavior and measured intelligence in the classification of mental retardation. *American Journal of Mental Deficiency*, 78, 77-81.

American Psychiatric Association. (1994). *Diagnostic and statistical manual of mental disorders* (4th ed.). Washington, DC: American Psychiatric Association.

American Psychological Association. (1985). *Standards for educational and psychological testing.* Washington, DC: American Psychological Association.

Anastasi, A. (1988). Psychological testing (6th ed.). New York: Macmillan.

Batjelsmit, J. (1977). Reliability and validity of psychometric measures. In R. Andrulis (Ed.), *Adult assessment.* New York: Thomas.

Baumeister, A., & Muma, J. (1975). On defining mental retardation. *Journal of Special Education*, 9, 193-306.

Bean, A., & Roszkowski, M. (1982). Item-domain relationships in the Adaptive Behavior Scale (ABS). *Applied Research in Mental Retardation*, 3, 359-367.

Berdine, W., Murphy, M., & Roller, J. (1977). A criterion referenced training program based on the ABS: The Oakwood Resident Scale for training and evaluating programs. *Mental Retardation*, 15(6), 16-18.

Bogen, D., & Aanes, D. (1975). The ABS as a tool in comprehensive MR programming. *Mental Retardation*, 13(1), 38-41.

Cattell, R. B. (1986). The 16PF personality structure and Dr. Eysenck. *Journal of Social Behavior and Personality*, 1, 153-160.

Clarke, A. M., & Clarke, A. B. D. (1974). Criteria and classification of subnormality. In A. M. Clarke & A. D. B. Clarke (Eds.), *Mental deficiency: The changing outlook* (3rd ed.). New York: Free Press.

Clausen, J. (1972). Quo vadis, AAMD? *Journal of Special Education*, 6, 51-60.

Conroy, J., Efthimou, J., & Lemanowicz, J. (1982). A matched comparison in the developmental growth of institutionalized and deinstitutionalized mentally retarded clients. *American Journal of Mental Deficiency*, 86, 581-587.

Coulter, A., & Morrow, H. (1978). *Adaptive behavior: Concepts and measurements.* New York: Grune and Stratton.

Cronbach, L. (1970). *Essentials of psychological testing* (3rd ed.). New York: Harper & Row.

Cronbach, L., & Furby, L. (1970). How should we measure "change" or should we? *Psychological Bulletin*, 74(1), 68-80.

Doll, E. (1937). *The management of social competence: A manual for the Vineland Social Maturity Scale.* Minneapolis: Educational Publishers.

Doll, E. A. (1953). *Measurement of Social Competence: A manual for the Vineland Social Maturity Scale.* Minneapolis: Educational Test Bureau.

Fickel, R. (1972). *Behavioral Characteristics Progression.* Santa Cruz, CA: Santa Cruz County Office of Education.

Fogelman, C. (1975). AAMD *Adaptive Behavior Scale Manual.* Washington, DC: American Association on Mental Deficiency.

Grossman, H. (Ed.) (1973). *Manual on terminology and classification in mental retardation.* Washington, DC: American Association on Mental Deficiency.

Grossman, H. (Ed.) (1977). *Classification in mental retardation.* Washington, DC: American Association on Mental Deficiency.

Grossman, H. (Ed.) (1983). *Classification in Mental Retardation.* Washington, DC: American Association on Mental Deficiency.

Hartmann, D. (1977). Considerations in the choice of reliability estimates. *Journal of Applied Behavior Analysis*, 10, 103-116.

Heal, L. (1995). Criterion referenced assessment of adaptive behavior. Presentation at 119th annual meeting of the American Association on Mental Retardation.

Heal, L., & Fujiura, G. (1984). Methodological considerations in research on residential alternatives for developmentally disabled citizens. In N. R. Ellis & N. W. Bray (Eds.), *International Review of Research in Mental Retardation* (Vol. 12, pp. 205-244). New York: Academic Press.

Heber, R. (1959). A manual on terminology and classification on mental retardation.

American Journal on Mental Deficiency Monograph, 64.

Hersen, M., & Barlow, D. (1976). *Single case experimental designs*. New York: Pergamon Press.

Junkala, J. (1977). Teacher assessments and team decisions. *Exceptional Children*, 44, 31-32.

Lambert, N., Nihira, K., & Leland, H. (1993). AAMR *Adaptive Behavior Scale—School and Community*. Austin, Texas: Pro-Ed.

Leland, H. (1972). Mental retardation and adaptive behavior. *Journal of Special Education*, 6, 71-80.

Leland, H. (1978). Theoretical considerations of adaptive behavior. In W. A. Coulter & H. W. Morrow, (Eds.), *Adaptive behavior: Concepts and measurements*. New York: Grune and Stratton.

Luckasson, R., Coulter, D., Polloway, E., Reiss, S., Schalock, R., Snell, M., Spitalnik, D., & Stark, J. (1992). *Mental retardation: Definition, classification, and system of supports*. Washington, DC: American Association on Mental Retardation.

Maloney, M., & Ward, M. (1979). *Mental retardation and modern society*. New York: Oxford University Press.

Mayeda, T., Pelzer, I., & Van Zuylen, J. (1978). *Performance measures of skill and adaptive competencies in the developmentally disabled*. Pomona, CA: UCLA; Neuropsychiatric Institute Research Group at Pacific State Hospital.

Meyers, C., Nihira, K., and Zetlin, A. (1979). The measurement of adaptive behavior. In N. Ellis (Ed.), *Handbook of mental deficiency: Psychological theory and research* (2nd ed.). Hillsdale, NJ: Lawrence Erlbaum.

Nihira, K. (1969a). Factorial dimensions of adaptive behavior in adult retardates. *American Journal of Mental Deficiency*, 73(6), 868-878.

Nihira, K. (1969b). Factorial dimensions of adaptive behavior in mentally retarded children and adults. American Journal of Mental Deficiency, 74(1), 130-141.

Nihira, K. (1973). Importance of environmental demands in the measurement of adaptive behavior. In R. K. Eyman, C. E. Meyers, & G. Tarjan (Eds.), *Sociobehavioral studies in mental retardation* (pp. 127-142). Washington, DC: American Association on Mental Deficiency.

Nihira, K., Foster, R., Shellhaas, M., & Leland, H. (1974). AAMD *Adaptive Behavior Scale*. Washington, DC: American Association on Mental Deficiency.

Nihira, K., Leland, H., & Lambert, N. (1993). AAMR *Adaptive Behavior Scale—Residential and Community Examiner's Manual*. Austin, TX: Pro-Ed.

Nunnally, J. (1967). *Psychometric theory*. New York: McGraw Hill.

Otto, W., McMenemy, R., & Smith, R. (1973). *Corrective and Remedial Teaching*. Boston: Houghton Mifflin.

Rimm, D., & Masters, J. (1974). *Behavior therapy: Techniques and empirical findings*. New York: Academic Press.

Roszkowski, M. (1980). Concurrent validity of the Adaptive Behavior Scale as assessed by the Vineland Social Maturity Scale. *American Journal of Mental Deficiency*, 85, 86-89.

Roszkowski, M., & Bean, A. (1980). The Adaptive Behavior Scale (ABS) and IQ: How much unshared variance is there? *Psychology in the Schools*, 17, 452-459.

Roszkowski, M., & Bean, A. (1982). Abbreviated procedure for obtaining sums scores on the Adaptive Behavior Scale. *Exceptional Children*, 48, 265-267.

Roszkowski, M., Spreat, S., & Isett, R. (1983). A paramorphic representation of psychologists' clinical impressions of degree of mental retardation. *Journal of Psychoeducational Assessment*, 1, 243-251.

Schwartz, B., & Allen, R. (1974). Measuring adaptive behavior: The dynamics of a longitudinal approach. *American Journal of Mental Deficiency*, 79, 424-433.

Smith, J., & Polloway, E. (1979). The dimension of adaptive behavior in mental retardation research: An analysis of recent practices. *American Journal of Mental Deficiency*, 84, 203-206.

Spreat, S., Roszkowski, M., & Isett, R. (1983). Adaptive behavior. In S. Breuning, J. Matson, & R. Barrett (Eds.), *Advances in mental retardation and developmental disabilities* (Vol. 1). Greenwich, CT: JAI Press.

Stanley, J. (1971). Reliability. In R. L. Thorndike (Ed.), *Educational measurement* (2nd ed.). Washington, DC: American Council on Education.

Strahan, R. (1980). More on averaging judges' ratings: Determining the most reliable composite. *Journal of Consulting and Clinical Psychology*, 48, 587-589.

Thorndike, R. (Ed.). (1971). *Educational measurement* (2nd ed.). Washington, DC: American Council on Education.

Thorndike, R., & Hagen, E. (1961). *Measurement and evaluation in psychology and education*. New York: John Wiley and Sons.

Tyler, L., & Walsh, W. (1979). *Tests and measurements* (3rd ed.). Englewood Cliffs, NJ: Prentice-Hall.

Zarcone, J., Rodgers, T., Iwata, B., Rourke, D., & Dorsey, M. (1991). Reliability analysis of the Motivation Assessment Scale: A failure to replicate. *Research in Developmental Disabilities*, 12, 349-360.

Zigler, E. (1968). Mental retardation. In P. London & D. Rosenhan (Eds.), *Foundations of abnormal psychology*. New York: Holt, Rinehart, & Winston.

CHAPTER 7

Cultural and Demographic Group Comparisons of Adaptive Behavior

ELLIS M. CRAIG
Texas Department of Mental Health and Mental Retardation

MARC J. TASSÉ
Université du Québec à Montréal

Introduction

People live in a variety of systems that influence the development of their values, beliefs, attitudes, and behavior. The current ecological focus in the field of mental retardation, with its emphasis on describing the many contexts of development and behavior, underscores the importance that one's culture plays in defining the role of adaptive behavior and evaluating the importance placed on specific behaviors either exhibited or not exhibited by the person. Within this context, this chapter has two major purposes: (a) to review the literature regarding the differences in assessed adaptive behavior based on ethnic group membership and (b) to identify the specific variables that may be operating when cross-cultural differences are observed.

Throughout the chapter, we repeatedly use two terms: *culture* and *ethnic groups*. Culture has been defined as the set of values and beliefs that is learned and adopted as a result of living with a group of people. Major influences are religion, language, traditions, and laws of the group. The term *ethnicity* is used to categorize a unique ancestral, religious, or linguistic group, and is often associated with nationality or national origin (Peterson & Ishii-Jordan, 1994b).

Cohen (1969) described the distinctions among cultural deprivation, cultural difference, and cultural conflict. Deprivation involves a relative lack of concepts and experiences upon which to draw. Difference implies a different set of concepts and history of experiences but not necessarily any deficit. Conflict arises when one is unprepared to adapt to a new environment because of vastly different concepts or experiences.

Culturally related assessments can be characterized as emic or etic. An emic measure is culture-specific and employs criteria consistent with the values and practices of that culture. Etic measures are presumed to be culture-general or universal. A related term, *moderator variable*, refers to a correction or adjustment of assessment results to account for identified cultural differences. Level of acculturation (degree to which an individual has adopted the values and beliefs of a new culture) can be used as a moderator variable (Dana, 1993).

The names used for the various cultural or ethnic groups in this chapter are those that have been generally accepted. The terms refer more to broad geographic areas from which one's primary ancestors migrated to the United States than to any racial or specific ethnic group. The terms used here include: Anglo American, African American, Latino, Asian American, and Native American. There is also some discussion of individuals of Middle Eastern descent. Although other terms might be more common regionally (e.g., Hispanic as opposed to Latino) or in the published literature (e.g., Whites & Blacks), the current national conventions are used throughout the chapter.

Table 7.1

Adaptive Behavior Scales and Their Characteristics

Scale	Description
ABIC *Adaptive Behavior Inventory for Children* (Mercer & Lewis, 1978)	A component of the SOMPA, this adaptive behavior scale was designed for use in classification and placement decisions regarding children with mild retardation. It measures the child's performance in a variety of nonschool social roles and settings, including family, community, peer relations, nonacademic school roles, earner/consumer, and self-maintenance. Parents serve as the informants.
ABS *Adaptive Behavior Scale* (Nihira, Leland, & Lambert, 1993)	This scale was initially developed in 1969 by Nihira, Foster, Shellhaas, and Leland and revised in 1975. Part 1 focuses on personal independence, while Part 2 measures social maladaption. The normative group comprised individuals with mental retardation living in residential facilities. Subsequent editions include the ABS-S:2 (Lambert, Nihira, & Leland, 1993) and the ABS-RC:2 (Nihira, Leland, & Lambert, 1993). The ABS-S:2, (School Version) includes students both with and without developmental disabilities in the normative population. The ABS-RC:2 (Residential and Community Version) includes individuals with developmental disabilities living in the community or residential settings.
BRP *Behavior Rating Profile* (Brown & Hammill, 1978)	This scale has versions for completion by a parent (BRP-P), teacher (BRP-T), or child (BRP-C). It consists of descriptive phrases of problem behaviors regarding home, school, and peers.
CABS *Children's Adaptive Behavior Scale* (Richmond & Kicklighter, 1980)	This scale, normed on children ages 5 to 11, uses the child as a self-informant. It covers the domains of language development, independent functioning, family role performance, economic vocational activity, and socialization.
SIB-R *Scales of Independent Behavior—Revised* (Bruininks, Woodcock, Weatherman, & Hill, 1996)	This scale provides a comprehensive measure of problem behaviors and adaptive skills in motor, social and communication, personal living, and community living areas. The normative sample comprises nondisabled individuals from birth to age 40+. A short form of the scale is called *Inventory for Client and Agency Planning* (ICAP) (Bruininks et al., 1996).
SOMPA System of Multicultural Pluralistic Assessment (Mercer & Lewis, 1978)	This system was designed as comprehensive assessment system for children ages 5 to 11.

Continued on following page

Scale	Description
SSSQ	
Street Survival Skills Questionnaire (Linkenhoker & McCarron, 1993)	This scale, originally published in 1983, is administered by having the person respond to questions by pointing to the appropriate picture. Nine areas are assessed: basic concepts, functional signs, tools, domestic management, health and safety, public services, time, money, and measurement. Norms are available for children, adults, and disabled individuals.
VABS	
Vineland Adaptive Behavior Scales (Sparrow, Balla, & Cicchetti, 1984)	This scale, now probably the most frequently used, features separate sections for adaptive skills and maladaptive behavior. The major domains for adaptive skills are communication, daily living skills, socialization, and motor skills. Standard scores for each of these, as well as a composite score, are derived. The primary normative sample was composed of nondisabled individuals from birth to age 19. Supplementary norms were developed with disabled individuals. A classroom edition was normed on children between ages 3 and 13.
VSMS	
Vineland Social Maturity Scale (Doll, 1953)	This is probably the earliest adaptive behavior scale, being introduced in 1936. The normative sample was composed of nondisabled individuals from birth to 30 years of age. It focuses on adaptive skills, not maladaptive behaviors. Both social age (SA) and social quotient (SQ) measures are obtained.

In addition, a number of adaptive behavior scales are referenced throughout the chapter. The acronyms and names of these scales and their major characteristics are summarized in Table 7.1.

Cultural Group Comparisons

Anglo Americans

One of the largest migrations of all time was the movement of more than 36 million Europeans to the United States from 1820 to 1970 (Hanson, 1992b). The first wave primarily included settlers from England, Ireland, and Germany. The second wave in the 1860s to 1890s was dominated by Scandinavians. The third wave, post-1890, included immigrants from Italy, Russia, and the Austrian-Hungarian empire. The immigrants in the last wave were more likely to be unskilled than earlier ones and, in fact, were victims of cultural bias.

Selective immigration restrictions began in the 1920s. Immigration in recent decades has been primarily to the western United States and has mainly involved Latinos and Asians. Peterson and Ishii-Jordan (1994a) discussed the broad influence of the Anglo European culture on the United States today. They suggested that the major values and practices, such as the legal, health, and education systems, religion, industrialization, and even our social values, originated primarily in Europe. Further, our approach to medicine and psychology, especially for the treatment of mental retardation and behavior disorders, is strongly European. The approaches are often quite different in other cultures.

According to Lynch (1992b), values such as competitiveness and punctuality are highly emphasized in the Anglo culture, but often are not in others. In another paper, Lynch (1992a) discussed the key values of the dominant,

Anglo American culture, such as individualism, informality in interactions, a future orientation, and high achievement motivation. Hanson (1992b) pointed out that self-reliance is emphasized even at early ages, leading to a focus on self-help skill development. In an analysis of multicultural applications of cognitive-behavior therapy, Hays (1995) noted that the dominant Anglo European culture highly values assertiveness and perceives a lack of it to be a mental health problem. Hays pointed out that several ethnic groups, including Native American, Latino, Asian, and Middle Eastern, place greater value on respect and perceive many forms of assertiveness to be offensive.

Nevertheless, even differences between Anglo Americans and Europeans in adaptive behavior have been demonstrated. Fombonne and Achard (1993) analyzed the VABS scores of a group of normal French children and compared them to the American normative sample. The results indicated consistently lower scores (on the order of 1 standard deviation) in the daily living skills domain among the French children older than age 6. In their discussion of the results, the authors suggested that some of the VABS items might not be valid measures for the French culture. Six items related to telephone use and nine in money management were particularly suspicious, because these skills are not emphasized for children or adolescents in France. In fact, it was noted that autonomy and independence in general may be delayed relative to the American peer group.

In part due to its majority status in size (about 75% of the population in the 1990 census), the Anglo American group has been the primary source for normative data regarding adaptive behavior development. Thus, most of the discussions of the other cultural groups involve a comparison with this group. However, because of migration patterns and differential reproductive rates, it is becoming increasingly important to examine these cultural differences. Hanson (1992a) estimated that by the year 2000 38% of children in the United States will be non-Anglo. In some states, particularly in the southwest, non-Anglo children already represent a majority.

African Americans

Lynch (1992a) described the evolution of the terms used to name this group, ranging from Negro (the word meaning black for Portuguese slave traders) to Colored (a term adopted by many slaves) to Black (associated with the Black pride movement of the 1960s) and now to African American (a more recent self-chosen descriptor). According to Willis (1992), about 40 million Africans were taken from their homelands and sold into slavery between the 16th and 19th centuries. About 4 million of them were taken to North America. They are the primary ancestors of today's African Americans. In 1990, they represented about 12% (more than 30 million) of the United States population.

Some of the earliest studies of adaptive behavior involved comparisons of Anglo and African American adolescents on the VSMS (Doll & Fitch, 1939; Gambaro, 1944; Springer, 1941). These studies found negligible differences between the two groups. However, higher adaptive functioning by African Americans than Anglos has been reported in some studies. Mercer (1979) reported that African American children as a group scored three scaled score points above Anglo Americans on all the ABIC scales. Bailey and Richmond (1979) examined the ABS performance of a group of children referred for assessment for possible special-education placement. The only significant difference between Anglo American and African American students in the Part I domain scores was for vocational activity, with the African American students showing more proficiency. However, the authors suggested that this is one of the more suspect domains, especially for a younger age group. Reschly and Ward (1991) studied a random sample of special-education students in Iowa, looking for possible differences between African and Anglo American students in the reasons for the placements. In the teacher ratings of adaptive behavior, the African American students had significantly higher functioning than the Anglo students in three of eight adaptive skill areas (communication, self-direction, and motor skills). No significant differences in maladaptive behavior were observed.

A common finding is of no significant differences between Anglo and African Americans. In a study comparing African and Anglo American children, Adams, McIntosh, and Weade (1973) reported that, while the African American sample scored 11.5 points lower on an intellectual measure (Stanford-Binet; Terman & Merrill, 1973), there was no significant difference on the VSMS measures. Heflinger, Cook, and Thackrey (1987) analyzed the effects of applying the dual criterion classification system (deficits in both IQ & adaptive behavior), using Mercer's SOMPA standardization sample as subjects. Cutoff scores were those falling below the third percentile on each measure. On the intellectual measure (WISC-R), the typical discrepancy was observed, with 8.9% of the African American and only 1.5% of the Anglo American children falling below the cutoff. However, when low scores on both the ABIC and the WISC-R (Wechsler, 1991) became the criterion, only one child in each of the two ethnic groups was identified (out of more than 600 of each). In contrast to the California-based normative data on the ABIC, Kazimour and Reschly (1981) found only chance differences in the ABIC composite scores of Anglo, African American, and Latino children living in Arizona.

However, there have been indications of higher rates of maladaptive behavior in African than in Anglo American samples. Lambert and Hartsough (1981) reported that, in the development of the school version of the ABS, no systematic bias with regard to gender or ethnicity was found on Part I (adaptive skills), but differences were observed, particularly with African American males, on Part II (maladaptive behaviors). Related to this observation is that reported by Nelson and Pearson (1994) that, of all the major ethnic groups, only African Americans were over-represented in special-education classes for the seriously emotionally disturbed (or behaviorally disordered). In 1986, the group represented 16.1% of all students but 26.8% of the group in special education.

Informant issues have also come under study. In research comparing different adaptive behavior scales, informants, and ethnic groups, Keller (1988) reported mixed results. On the ABIC, African American parents gave higher ratings than Anglo Americans, with Latino parents giving the lowest ratings. However, there were no significant differences between the ethnic-parent ratings on the BRP-P. With teachers as informants (BRP-T), the African American children were given the lowest ratings of the three ethnic groups. With self-ratings (CABS & BRP-C), the ethnic ordering on the scales was inconsistent. Also, in a 1970 review, Sattler concluded that African American respondents were more likely to give inhibited or socially conforming responses to an Anglo American interviewer than to one of their own ethnicity.

Koegel and Edgerton (1982) conducted an anthropological follow-up study of the status of African American individuals who had received special-education services (EMR classes) while in school. Interviews were conducted with the individuals themselves, family members, and caretakers. Although very few of the individuals used the term *mental retardation* to describe themselves, about 60% did use a similar term (e.g., "slow learner" or "handicapped"). The remainder either rejected such labels or actively avoided discussion of the subject. The highest number (81%) acknowledged problems related to reading and writing, followed by mathematical skills (56%), job-related skills (41%), and domestic and self-maintenance skills (37%). Although the authors did not consider the limitations of these individuals to be significantly different from their Anglo American counterparts with a special-education background, they did suggest that African American adults with mild mental retardation are more fully integrated into the African American community than in the case of Anglos. A wider variety of social roles (e.g., having children) is expected and even encouraged. The authors also noted a reluctance within the African American community to use the label of mental retardation except for those individuals who are functioning at the more severe levels.

In analyzing the reasons underlying the underutilization of mental retardation services by African Americans, Kernan and Walker (1981) identified several important factors, including a cultural tradition of relying on extended family rather than strangers for assistance and resentment and rejection of labels (especially those associated with intelligence) applied by the broader society. There was also a belief, expressed even by African American professionals, that Anglo American professionals have poor understanding of the African American culture and are likely to label children as retarded simply on the basis of behavior problems and even to perceive culturally normal behavior as "behavior problems."

Latinos

Latinos are among the fastest growing ethnic groups in the United States (Plata, 1993). They are also a quite diverse group in terms of national origin, with about 63% having ties to Mexico, 14% to Central or South America, 12% to Puerto Rico, 5% to Cuba, and 8% more directly from Spain. They represent about 8% of the United States population (more than 19 million), although there may be as many as 2 million undocumented (Zuniga, 1992).

Language is usually an issue with this group. Chandler and Plakos (1970) described a study in which Spanish and English versions of the WISC (Wechsler, 1991) were compared for a group of Latino children who were primarily Spanish speaking and were enrolled in special-education classes. The children scored an average of 13 points higher on the Spanish version (average IQ of 82 vs. 69 on the English

test). Some of the items on the Spanish version (which had been normed in Puerto Rico) had to be modified for a California population. An in-depth analysis of general psychological testing issues in the Latino population can be found in a book edited by Geisinger (1992).

In contrast to the California-based ABIC norms, Kazimour and Reschly (1981) found only chance differences in the composite scores for Anglo and African American and Latino children in an Arizona sample. However, Heflinger, Cook, and Thackrey (1987) reported a different result. They analyzed the effects of applying the dual criterion classification system (i.e., significant deficits in IQ and adaptive behavior), using the SOMPA standardization sample as subjects. Children whose scores were below the third percentile on each of the SOMPA components were identified. The Latino group had a higher rate of identification on all the SOMPA components than the Anglo American and higher than the African American group on all but the WISC-R measure (6.0% vs. 8.9% for African Americans and 1.8% for Anglo Americans). On the ABIC, scores below the third percentile were found in 3.2% of the Latinos, as compared to 1.8% of the Anglo Americans and 1.0% of the African American children. When the dual criterion measure was applied, almost all the Anglo and African American children were declassified, while 1.5% of the Latinos met the criteria for a diagnosis of mental retardation.

In a discussion of behavior disorders among Latino students, Hoernicke, Kallam, and Tablada (1994) reported an underrepresentation of this group in special-education classes for the seriously emotionally disturbed in 1984 (13.2% of the students, but only 7.6% classified). In a similar finding, Vega, Khoury, Zimmerman, Gil, and Warheit (1995) compared the prevalence of behavior problems among Latino and African and Anglo American adolescents. The rates among Latinos were similar to or even lower than that of the Anglos, while African Americans had the highest reported rate. McCloskey, Southwick, Fernandez-Esquer, and Locke (1995) examined the adjustment of immigrant mothers and their children from Mexico and Central America. Most of the Central Americans had escaped from political violence. Within this group, both mothers and children showed a higher rate of symptoms of posttraumatic stress disorder than did the Mexican group. Aggression and hyperactivity were more prevalent among the Central American than the Mexican children.

Asian Americans

Asian Americans are the fastest growing ethnic group in the United States. They numbered more than 7 million (about 3% of the United States population) at the beginning of the decade and are expected to reach 10 million by the year 2000. Asia itself has more than half of the world's population and is also the largest source for immigrants worldwide. The Asian designation applies not only to countries such as China, Japan, and Vietnam, but also to the Philippines and India. Despite their numbers, Asian Americans are one of the most poorly understood minority groups (Chan, 1992).

According to Ishii-Jordan and Peterson (1994), Asian Americans are often identified as the "model minority," because their achievements often exceed that of other groups. In fact, they are overrepresented in classes for the gifted and underrepresented in most special-education disability categories (speech impairment being one exception).

However, there has been relatively little research on the adaptive behavior functioning of this group. One notable exception is a study by Nihira, Webster, Tomiyasu, and Oshio (1988). They researched environmental influences on the social competency and emotional adjustment of children in Japan and the United States. It was noted that the two countries have some strong similarities as well as differences. For example, the two countries have similar standards of living and emphasis on education. However, the nature of interpersonal relations and social expectations of children differ markedly. Little difference was seen in the ABS factor scores for the domains of personal self-sufficiency and community self-sufficiency, but American children scored significantly higher than Japanese on personal-social responsibility. This was interpreted as indicating that the American children were more independent and socially outgoing, while the Japanese children were more passive and socially withdrawn. Further, the American children had higher factor scores on the ABS social and personal maladaption scales, indicating more behavior problems in the American children. However, behavior problems in the American children appeared to be closely associated with lower socioeconomic status. In those families whose children have mental retardation, the Japanese appeared to feel more stigma toward the condition.

Native Americans

Joe and Malach (1992) noted that there were about 5 million natives in North America at the time European settlement began. The estimated population in what is now the United States was between 2 and 3 million (Hanson, 1992b). Although warfare decimated some of this population, communicable diseases were the most deadly factor. The North American native population was down to about 600,000 by the 1800s. By the beginning of the 20th century, it had dropped further to 250,000. But by 1990, about 1.9 million people in the United States identified themselves as members of the group. This represents about 0.75% of the total United States population. According to Lynch (1992a), many members of this group prefer the specific tribal affiliation name rather than the general term Native American or Indian. Over the years, there have been federal efforts to force assimilation into the larger culture, primarily by educating the young away from their families or by relocating individuals to the cities. Even today, over a quarter of the children are removed from their families and placed in foster or adoptive homes or institutions. As a result, there is an almost universal distrust of federal and other agencies.

By several indicators, Native Americans are a vulnerable population. About 28% are below the poverty level, and their median annual income is over 30% below the national average. About half of the students (twice the national average) fail to complete high school. Also, the group has some of the highest substance abuse and suicide rates in the United States (Kallam, Hoernicke, & Coser, 1994).

As in the case of Asian Americans, there has been relatively little research of the adaptive behavior functioning of Native Americans. In one of the few studies, Kazimour and Reschly (1981) found only chance differences in the ABIC performance of Anglo and African American and Latino children; a Native American group (Papagos) had significantly lower performance than the other three groups.

However, a case might be made for the development of alternate or compensatory skills with this group. Kleinfeld (1973), for example, provided an interesting analysis of the multiability model of intelligence and how it might reflect differential development of specific skills in different cultural groups. His demonstration of this approach involved Eskimos (a group typically included with Native Americans) in the Alaskan arctic. The environment of this group is characterized by extreme visual uniformity. Both anecdotal and research evidence summarized by Kleinfeld suggests highly developed visual memory and spatial and mechanical abilities in the Eskimo. It is suggested that this is in part an adaptation to a special environment, but it may also reflect particular child-rearing practices (e.g., encouragement of independence and exploration in contrast to strictness and expectations of conformity).

DeVault and Long (1988) provided a summary of research on the intelligence test performance of Native American individuals as compared to other ethnic groups. They concluded that Native Americans typically score higher than African Americans, but lower than Anglo Americans.

Connors and Donnellan (1993) reported the results of an anthropological study of the Navajo culture, with special emphasis on child-rearing practices and attitudes toward people with disabilities. Their major finding was that the Navajo do not necessarily equate disabling conditions with incompetence. That is, there is a broader acceptance of individuality and autonomy than what is considered normal and appropriate in the Anglo-European culture. The Navajo child-rearing practices are particularly illustrative. Up to about the age of 6, there is broad permissiveness, such that the child is rarely disciplined and is allowed great freedom in exploring the environment. Then after this age very high expectations are placed on the child in terms of assuming various duties and responsibilities and conforming to Navajo social conventions. However, in contrast to Anglo American child-rearing practices, there is little emphasis on developing skills related to future employment in the Anglo culture (e.g., learning to tell time and being prompt, handling money, or being competitive).

Attitudes toward and expectations of individuals with significant disabilities are especially unique within the Navajo culture. While such individuals are not considered "perpetual children" in terms of the permissiveness usually allowed young children; neither are they necessarily subject to the high expectations of older children and adults. Any contributions the person can make (e.g., governmental financial support which helps the family) are expected as a matter of course. However, there is a marked absence of the typical labeling of individuals in terms of their disability. Further, unusual behaviors are generally tolerated as simply a unique characteristic of the individual.

In summary, differences in adaptive behavior functioning of the major ethnic groups have been reported frequently in the professional literature. The differences are not always large, and there are multiple confounding variables, the most important of which will be discussed in the following section.

Factors Involved in Cross-Cultural Differences

This section of the chapter attempts to identify the specific variables that may be operating when cross-cultural differences are observed. Such variables, rather than ethnic group membership per se, may be the ultimate subject of interest in subsequent research.

Age

The definitions of mental retardation have traditionally made references to deficits in relation to age peers. Further, it has been noted that different types of adaptive skills attain precedence at different ages. For example, sensorimotor, communication, self-help, and socialization skill development are most important during infancy and early childhood. Cognitive and group social skills become important during the school-age years. During late adolescence and adulthood, vocational skills and community social adjustment become most important.

In a series of studies on the ABS, Lambert (1979, 1986) identified a number of significant age relationships. In a 1986 study of ABS factor scores, Lambert found larger ethnic differences for young children (ages 3-6) than for older children. In 1979, Lambert observed that the difference in scores between regular and special-education students became smaller with age for ABS Part I (adaptive skills) but larger for Part II (maladaptive behaviors). Finally, Lambert and Hartsough (1981) suggested that the ABS personal self-sufficiency factor would become less important with age, and the community self-sufficiency factor increasingly important.

A number of culture-specific age relationships have also been described. For example, Zuniga (1992) noted that Latino parents are often very permissive with young children and do not push them to reach developmental milestones in ways that are characteristic of Anglo American parents. Further, there is usually much physical contact between parents and children, even into the teens. For another group, Middle Easterners, Sharifzadeh (1992) noted that initial self-help skill development may be delayed in the children, but that very high expectations for doing chores are made by age 4 or 5.

Native American groups often emphasize developmental milestones different from those of the typical Anglo American (e.g., age at "first laugh" rather than walking). However, Joe and Malach (1992) noted that Native American children are encouraged to be self-sufficient at earlier ages than other ethnic groups. For example, they may dress themselves and do regular chores a year earlier than Anglo or African American children, and be as much as 5 years advanced with regard to being left alone. However, when Native American children enter school, it is often an environment alien in terms of language, values, and even method of learning. Their repertoire of skills may not be adaptive in this new environment.

Chan (1992) observed that Asian American parents are extremely solicitous of very young children, responding immediately to their needs and maintaining close physical contact. They may have later age expectations for developmental milestones. An unusual deviation here, however, is the practice of introducing toilet training at very young ages (3 - 4 months). As the child approaches school age, expectations increase dramatically. The father also assumes a more active teaching role at this time, especially for appropriate public behavior. As younger siblings come along, the elder children are expected to take on some of the child-rearing responsibilities and set a good example.

Gender

Lambert and Hartsough (1981) reported that in the development of the school version of the ABS, no systematic difference with regard to gender was found on Part I (adaptive skills), but that such differences did appear on Part II (maladaptive behaviors), with males exhibiting more maladaptive behaviors. Kehrberg (1994) reported a similar disproportion in special-education classes for the seriously emotionally disturbed (behavior disordered). In fact, the rate for males to females was over 3:1. It was suggested that this may be due, in part, to males being socialized to be more aggressive and may reflect a conflict of values between low-socioeconomic-status minority males and their middle-class, Anglo, female teachers.

In a study comparing different adaptive behavior scales, informants, and ethnic groups, Keller (1988) found significant gender differences only on the ABIC, which emphasizes functioning at home or in the community rather than at school and uses the parent as the informant. Females had higher scores on all the ABIC subscales. Instruments using the teacher or a self-informant yielded no significant gender effects.

In a study of older deinstitutionalized individuals with mental retardation, Fine, Tangeman, and Woodward (1990) reported significantly higher adaptive functioning among females than males, with level of retardation controlled. Significantly higher scores for the females were found on the ABS domains of independent functioning, language development, and domestic activity.

Overprotectiveness of females appears to be a factor in some cultural groups. Zuniga (1992) noted that female Latino children are highly protected and given few freedoms. However, they are expected to assist in caring for younger siblings. Boys, on the other hand, are taught to be dominant and independent. Sharifzadeh (1992) observed that in Middle Eastern cultures, girls are expected to do household work while boys are exempted, though other types of chores are expected at a relatively young age. Although boys may not be allowed to engage in independent activities in the community until after puberty, these activities are even more delayed for girls. In fact, there is extreme protectiveness of females in comparison to the Anglo American culture.

Socioeconomic Status

Reschly (1988) noted that low socioeconomic status is strongly associated with mild mental retardation. The vast majority of people living in poverty are never identified as having retardation; nevertheless, Reschly referenced the long-standing interaction among poverty, familial factors, and mild mental retardation. Reschly and Ward (1991) concluded that the most parsimonious explanation for the overrepresentation (percentage, not absolute number) of African American students in special-education placements is the high degree of poverty in this ethnic group. Willis (1992) noted that about 28% of African Americans live in poverty (about the same proportion as Native Americans) as contrasted with 24% of Latinos and only 8% of Anglo Americans.

Adams et al. (1973) observed that low-socioeconomic-status children who perform poorly on intellectual measures may do quite well in nonacademic areas, while high-socioeconomic-status children with lower IQ scores generally exhibit pervasive adaptive behavior deficits. However, Mercer (1979) reported a very low correlation between ABIC scores and socioeconomic status. This conclusion was supported in a study by Kazimour and Reschly (1981), who found no significant socioeconomic effects on the ABIC scores of Anglo, African, and Native American, or Latino children. Scott, Mastenbrook, Fisher, and Gridley (1982) found no significant differences on the ABIC between low- and middle-socioeconomic-status Anglos, low- and middle-socioeconomic-status African Americans, and middle-socioeconomic-status Latinos. Low-socioeconomic-status Latinos, however, scored significantly lower than the other five groups.

Nihira et al. (1988) found a higher rate of behavior problems in American children with mental retardation than Japanese, but the behavior problems were closely associated with lower socioeconomic status. Tombokan-Runtukahu and Nitko (1992) reported little correlation between socioeconomic status and scores on the VABS for an Indonesian population in contrast to typically high correlations in United States samples. However, Kamphaus (1987) had noted that the otherwise extensive normative sample of the VABS included an underrepresentation of low-socioeconomic status children.

Socioeconomic status may be an important factor in the validity of informant observations. Wolfensberger and Kurtz (1971) compared parental estimates of the developmental age of their children with independent professional assessments. The estimates of higher-socioeconomic-status parents tended to be similar to the professional findings, while the lower-socioeconomic-status parents overestimated the skills of their children. In a follow-up study of African American special-education students, Koegel and Edgerton (1982) found a general reluctance for the students and their parents to apply the label of mental retardation. However, higher-socioeconomic-status parents were more likely to apply the label.

Cohen (1969) described low-income populations, regardless of ethnicity, as usually being "shared-function" groups; that is, essential functions such as leadership and childcare are alternately filled by various members. Various types of evidence were presented to support the position that this type of social environment results in different cognitive (e.g., relational vs. analytical) and behavioral (e.g., impulsive vs. methodical) styles in low-income versus middle-class individuals.

Language

The 1990 population of the United States with a non-English language background was estimated to be more than 34 million and will rise to nearly 40 million by the year 2000 (Lasky, 1994). There is a danger of some of these individuals being labeled as mentally retarded or behaviorally disordered, when the primary problem may simply be language. According to Lynch and Hanson (1992), more than 50 different languages may be spoken by the families in a given local school district, especially where immigration has been heavy. Harry (1994) noted the problems associated with assessments by psychologists when many of them have little training on the issues related to bilingualism and second-language development.

The importance of language in assessments of children from minority groups was emphasized by Gonzalez (1974), who noted that all languages are equally capable of expressing any experiences of the group using it. Where there is not a word for a given concept, it is usually because the group has not had a need to express the concept. When assessments are made of children whose primary language is not English, it is essential that any translation be in the dialect the child uses (see Tassé and Craig, this volume). For example, standard Spanish may be almost as much of a foreign language as English for some Latino children. In a discussion of language use by Latinos, Zuniga (1992) observed that the type of Spanish spoken varies greatly by region of the United States, and that a mixture of Spanish and English is not uncommon. Fluency in Spanish is often related to acculturation status, and some U.S.-born individuals may actually lose the use of the language or be able to speak but not read or write it. Plata (1993) noted that the relatively large population of Latinos places a heavy stress on schools, because of the students' varying English language skills and the lack of bilingual teachers. Clear communication with the parents can also be a problem and often necessitates the use of an interpreter. Plata discussed a number of key factors necessary for successful interpreting.

Willis (1992) noted the survival of some of the original African language, especially with the African Americans in southern states. In fact, it is a component of "Black English," which features a different grammatical structure than standard English. The appropriateness of treating Black English as a separate language has become a controversial topic, especially within the African American community itself (e.g., the ebonics debate).

Lynch (1992a) described the different communication styles in high-context and low-context cultures. In high-context cultures shared experience and physical cues may be more important than actual verbal communication. High-context cultures include Asian, Native American, Middle Eastern, Latino, and African American. Low-context cultures, such as the Anglo American, usually focus on direct and concrete verbal communication. Lynch also described some key cross-cultural body language differences. For example, direct eye contact is a strong value among Anglo Americans, but is considered disrespectful among African Americans, Asians, Latinos, and Native Americans. Personal space also varies widely, with Latinos, Middle Easterners, and African Americans maintaining much closer conversational distances than Anglo Americans, while Asian Americans tend to prefer even more space. Finally, the types of gestures used may vary significantly, such as Latinos and Middle Easterners using much more expansive arm movements. Specific gestures may even communicate quite different messages, with one being a sign of praise in one culture but obscene in another.

Acculturation

Acculturation refers to the efforts and abilities of minority and immigrant families and individuals to adapt to the dominant culture in which they now live, and the extent to which they attempt to maintain the values and traditions of their culture of origin (Park, Pullis, Reilly, & Townsend, 1994). Hanson (1992a) discussed four categories of cultural integration: (a) mainstreamers are individuals who have assimilated and adopted the values of the dominant culture, (b) bicultural individuals take on many of the values and practices of the dominant culture but maintain close ties with the culture of origin, (c) culturally different individuals remain apart from the dominant culture and maintain the values and practices of the culture of origin, and (d) the culturally marginal do not follow the practices

of any particular culture, partly due to loss of ties with the old culture and failure to adopt the practices of the dominant culture.

Another four-level categorization was proposed by Harry (1994): (a) traditionalism, in which there is a clinging to the traditional culture; (b) marginality, in which the person is beginning to experience the new culture; (c) biculturalism, in which the person has effectively integrated the two cultures; and (d) overacculturation, in which there is an extreme rejection of the original culture. An additional stage has even been identified: panrenaissance, in which a person seeks out an ancestral but never learned culture (i.e., finding one's roots).

The phenomenon of culture shock affects many new immigrants (Lynch, 1992b). This refers to feelings of frustration and disorientation when old cultural values and practices are not successful in the new culture. Another problem concerns intergenerational conflicts, which usually occur because the younger generations acculturate much more readily than the older ones. In fact, there may be role reversals in which the children are the primary intermediaries with the outside world, because they more quickly pick up the language and customs. Such children sometimes abandon the traditional customs and values more readily than other immigrant children (Morrow, 1994).

Some interesting research has been conducted on an acculturation scale developed specifically for the Mexican American group, the *Acculturation Scale for Mexican Americans* (ARSMA) (Cuellar, Harris, & Jasso, 1980). The major content areas are ethnic identification, language preference and use, peer relationships, food preferences, and immigration generation. Montgomery and Orozco (1984) conducted a cross-validation study of the ARSMA. The findings were consistent with the original normative group. Further, there was evidence that nonacculturated individuals occupy marginal positions in American society. In a 1989 study,

Arnold and Orozco examined the relationship between acculturation status (based on ARSMA) and adaptive behavior functioning (based on the SSSQ scale). There was a significant positive correlation between the two measures. Finally, Vega et al. (1995) compared the prevalence of behavior problems among Latino, Anglo, and African American adolescents, focusing special attention on immigrant Latinos. Among this group, a relatively high percentage of behavior problems was noted when the adolescent was having acculturation problems due to language ability and use. Thus, acculturation status should be considered in any adaptive behavior assessment of a person from an ethnic minority, especially if the family immigration has been recent.

Geographic Region

Although changes are occurring throughout, certain regions of the United States have a disproportionate number of minority group members. In 1970, the four states with the most foreign-born residents were California, New York, New Jersey, and Illinois (53% of the nation's total). By 1994, Florida and Texas had joined California and New York, with the four states having 64% of the immigrants. Similarly, Larson and Palmer (1994) reported that rural areas have a disproportionate number of poor families and problems accessing adequate specialized services for children with disabilities. On the other hand, poverty and other social problems occur at a higher rate in specific inner city areas than in rural or suburban areas (McIntyre, 1994). Urban environments often require an aggressive style for simple survival, which may lead in part to the high numbers of referrals for special-education. Such conditions sometimes lead to gang membership, with special-education students perhaps being particularly vulnerable (Kodluboy, 1994).

The findings with regard to geographic and ethnic differences in adaptive behavior have been mixed. Kazimour and Reschly (1981) compared the California-based normative data

on the ABIC with a sample of Arizona children. The scores for the Anglo and African American Arizona children were significantly lower (around 4 points) than the California normative group. However, in contrast to the California group, there were only chance differences in the ABIC composite scores for the Arizona Anglo, African American, and Latino children. Further, urban-rural comparisons were nonsignificant. In a comparison of a Texas sample with the California norm group on the ABIC, Scott et al. (1982) found overall lower scores in the Texas group. However, neither the Anglo nor the African Texans scored lower than their California counterparts; the Texas Latinos did score significantly lower than California Latinos. Finally, in a Florida study of the ABIC, Taylor, Ziegler, and Partenio (1985) found no significant differences among Anglo American, African American, and Latino children, but those living in urban areas scored significantly higher than the rural children. From a nationwide perspective, therefore, there do not appear to be strong differences among children of various ethnic groups on the ABIC. Possible differences on other adaptive behavior scales need further study.

Family Structure

There are some marked cultural differences in family structure that could have an influence on adaptive skill development. A study by Nihira et al. (1988) compared the effect of home environment on the adaptive skills of children with mental retardation in the United States and Japan. Scores on three home environment scales (Henderson Environment Learning and Process Scale (Henderson, Bergan & Hurt, 1972), Family Environment Scale (Moos, Insel & Humphrey, 1974), & Home Quality Environment Scale (Meyers, Mink, & Nihira, 1977)) were correlated with ABS factor scores. The results indicated that the Japanese families placed more emphasis on teaching social norms, conformity, and obedience than on teaching specific skills and academic knowledge; socialization with adults and relatives was emphasized over peer relations.

American families, on the other hand, were more likely to promote independence and were more tolerant of behavior problems.

In another analysis of Asian Americans, Chan (1992) discussed the family-centered orientation of this group in which each individual is an interdependent part of the family, the larger social structure, and even the ancestors. Within the immediate family there are traditional roles, with the father serving as the family representative in public and the mother raising and educating the children and taking care of financial matters. The parents assume unquestioning obedience from the children. In addition, children are surrounded from a young age by many caregivers and authority figures.

Willis (1992) noted that almost 43% of African American children live in homes where the father is absent. However, extended family arrangements are common. Zuniga (1992) has described the traditional Latino family as having a clearly dominant father, a submissive mother, and strict gender role expectations of the children. Child rearing is almost exclusively a female function. Joe and Malach (1992) noted that extended family involvement is quite common in Native American groups. Further, extended family members may have primary responsibility for raising the children rather than the biological parents. Thus, parental models may differ systematically among ethnic groups.

The extended family is among the most important institutions in Middle Eastern culture; it is common for three generations to live together in the same house. There is a strong emphasis on having children. The father has the role of providing the necessities and interacting with the outside world, while the mother does all the child rearing. Close parent-child bonding is emphasized over the development of independence. Thus, self-help skill development may be delayed in children of Middle Eastern immigrants relative to Anglo American norms (Sharifzadeh, 1992).

Family Training and Disciplinary Practices

Distinct cultural differences in family training and disciplinary practices have been observed. For example, in a discussion of disciplinary practices among Asian American families, Chan (1992) noted that strict obedience is expected from children by the time they reach school age. Any type of disobedience, aggression toward siblings, or failure to complete assigned responsibilities is dealt with by verbal reprimands, including shaming. Inappropriate behavior is considered a reflection on the parents' ability to provide proper guidance to the child. More serious behaviors result in threats or actual removal of the child from the home or from family social life. In terms of academic achievement, effort and success are expected. Rewards and praise are generally not given, as success and appropriate behavior are expected. Social interactions outside the family may be closely controlled. Thus, the development of independent social skills usually occurs at much later ages than the Anglo American norm.

According to Kallam et al. (1994), Native American parenting practices are significantly different from that of other cultures. There is a strong belief that children are individuals, who will do things on their own schedule and in their own way. The parenting approach is noninterfering, assuming the child has the ability and right to make important choices. This approach has sometimes been misperceived as reflecting neglect.

Willis (1992) indicated that the disciplinary setting of limits for children is an essential feature of African American culture, often extending to nonfamily members of the community. She suggests distinct differences in this area from the more permissive approach of many Anglo Americans.

Tucker and her associates have conducted some interesting research in this area with African American children. Dunn and Tucker (1993) examined the influence of quality of family support on adaptive functioning and maladaptive behavior. Quality of family support was assessed via the *Family Environment Scale* (Moos et al., 1974), while adaptive functioning was based on the VABS. There was a significant positive relationship between quality-of-family-support measures and adaptive skills and a significant negative relationship with maladaptive behaviors. Similar relationships were observed with presence or absence of a father figure in the home (i.e., higher adaptive skills and less maladaptive behavior with a father figure present). The best predictor of maladaptive behavior, however, was conflict among family members.

Tucker, Brady, Harris, Fraser, and Tribble (1993) studied the relationship between parental practices and the adaptive and maladaptive behaviors of Anglo and African American children. Whether the father resided in the home was not a significant factor for either group. However, for younger African American children, having a father who provided most of the discipline and a mother who gave frequent praise were both associated significantly with less maladaptive behavior. This effect was not observed in the young Anglo children or the older groups of either ethnic group. Nevertheless, such findings with regard to family training and disciplinary practices have implications for the differential diagnosis of mental retardation, especially if an unstable family structure is present.

Attitudes Toward Disability

Distinctive cultural differences in the attitude toward disabilities is apparent. Hanson (1992a) described the typical modern Anglo American attitude toward disability as being something that can be overcome or at least the effects mitigated. This is associated with strong values in the areas of education and a future-oriented adaptability. The disability rights movement has focused on legal protections and the goal of being integrated into society in a culturally normative way.

Joe and Malach (1992) noted that traditional Native American cultures may view disability as having supernatural or natural causes or both. Witchcraft or the breaking of cultural taboos might be cited. Both tribal healers and mainstream services might be accessed. In any event, there appears to be general acceptance of individuals with disabilities themselves.

Zuniga (1992) indicated that some traditional Latino groups also associate disability with evil spirits. Various folk beliefs about taboo maternal behavior during pregnancy may be invoked. Nevertheless, there is usually a fatalistic acceptance of the disability, and the person may even be overprotected.

Willis (1992) observed that African Americans generally incorporate individuals with mild disabilities into the full mainstream of life. Although they may not have any particular prejudice against people with more severe disabilities, some seem hesitant to acknowledge their presence. This is generally attributed to lack of experience and a belief that it is rude to stare at people with disabilities.

According to Chan (1992), traditional Asian cultures view most types of disability with considerable stigma. It is often assumed that the disability is the direct result of the mother's failure to follow accepted dietary or other health care practices, violations of social taboos, or even divine punishment for actions of the parents or ancestors. A resultant sense of guilt or shame frequently leads to the child being kept from public view.

Sharifzadeh (1992) reported a similar reaction of guilt and shame surrounding disability in Middle Eastern cultures, noting overprotection, denial, and even abandonment of disabled children. However, individuals with mild disabilities and no overt physical problems often lead relatively normal lives under the strong protection of the family.

Summary and Conclusions

Lynch (1992a) has suggested that cross-cultural competence is a prerequisite for conducting valid assessments of individuals from other cultures. Cross-cultural skills include understanding of one's own values, knowledge of the other culture(s), and the ability to interact and communicate in a sensitive fashion with members of other cultures.

Further, knowledge of the relevant literature is important (Dana, 1993). Unfortunately, firm conclusions are scarce. For many of the cultural groups discussed, it is obvious that additional research is needed. This research needs to identify the specific skills and maladaptive behaviors for which differences are found. Further research on specific cultural and developmental factors would also be a meaningful contribution.

Another necessary step is the development of a consensus regarding the appropriate adjustments (moderator variables) that should be made in adaptive behavior assessment findings when clear evidence exists of a strong cultural difference (e.g., lack of opportunity or reinforcement for a particular skill). The development of separate norms for different cultural groups has sometimes been advocated, and yet support has generally been weak (Clausen, 1972; Cleary, Humphreys, Kendrick, & Wesman, 1975). We need a more objective approach than "clinical judgment." Discounting suspect items and extrapolating the norms may be an approach worth pursuing. Alternatively, criterion assessment might be used in the place of norms (see Heal & Tassé, this volume). Finally, it is anticipated that culturally competent assessment procedures will result in determining behaviors that are simply culturally different, in contrast to pervasive and chronic limitations in skill development.

References

Adams, J., McIntosh, E. I., & Weade, B. L. (1973). Ethnic background, measured intelligence, and adaptive behavior scores in mentally retarded children. *American Journal of Mental Deficiency*, 78, 1-6.

Arnold, B. R., & Orozco, S. (1989). Acculturation and evaluation of Mexican Americans with disabilities. *Journal of Rehabilitation*, 55, 53-57.

Bailey, B. S., & Richmond, B. O. (1979). Adaptive behavior of retarded, slow learner, and average intelligence children. *Journal of School Psychology*, 17, 260-263.

Brown, L. L., & Hammill, D. D. (1978). *Behavior rating profile: An ecological approach to behavioral assessment*. Austin, TX: Pro-Ed.

Bruininks, R. H., Woodcock, R. W., Weatherman, R. F., & Hill, B. K. (1996). *Scales of independent behavior* (SIB-R) (Rev. ed.). Chicago: Riverside.

Chan, S. (1992). Families with Asian roots. In E. W. Lynch & M. J. Hanson (Eds.), *Developing cross-cultural competence* (pp. 181-257). Baltimore: Paul H. Brookes.

Chandler, J. T., & Plakos, J. (1970). An investigation of Spanish speaking pupils placed in classes for the educable mentally retarded. *Journal of Mexican American Studies*, 1, 58-61.

Clausen, J. (1972). The continuing problem of defining mental retardation. *Journal of Special Education*, 6, 97-106.

Cleary, T. A., Humphreys, L. G., Kendrick, S. A., & Wesman, A. (1975). Educational uses of tests with disadvantaged students. *American Psychologist*, 30, 15-41.

Cohen, R. A. (1969). Conceptual styles, culture conflict, and nonverbal tests of intelligence. *American Anthropologist*, 71, 828-856.

Connors, J. L., & Donnellan, A. M. (1993). Citizenship and culture: The role of disabled people in Navajo society. *Disability, Handicap, & Society*, 8, 265-280.

Cuellar, I., Harris. L. C., & Jasso, R. (1980). An acculturation scale for Mexican American normal and clinical populations. *Hispanic Journal of Behavioral Sciences*, 2, 199-217.

Dana, R. H. (1993). *Multicultural assessment perspectives for professional psychology*. Boston: Allyn & Bacon.

DeVault, S., & Long, D. (1988). Adaptive behavior, malingering and competence to waive rights: A case study. *American Journal of Forensic Psychology*, 6, 3-15.

Doll, E. A. (1953). *The measurement of social competence: A manual for the Vineland Social Maturity Scale*. Minneapolis: Educational Publishers.

Doll, E. A., & Fitch, K. A. (1939). Social competence of juvenile delinquents. *Journal of Criminal Law and Criminology*, 30, 52-67.

Dunn, C. W., & Tucker, C. M. (1993). Black children's adaptive functioning and maladaptive behavior associated with quality of family support. *Journal of Multicultural Counseling and Development*, 21, 79-87.

Fine, M. A., Tangeman, P. J., & Woodard, J. (1990). Changes in adaptive behavior of older adults with mental retardation following deinstitutionalization. *American Journal on Mental Retardation*, 94, 661-668.

Fombonne, E., & Achard, S. (1993). The Vineland Adaptive Behavior Scale in a sample of normal French children: A research note. *Journal of Child Psychology and Psychiatry*, 34, 1051-1058.

Gambaro, P. K. (1944). Analysis of Vineland Social Maturity Scale. *American Journal of Mental Deficiency, 48,* 359-363.

Geisinger, K. F. (Ed.). (1992). *Psychological testing of Hispanics.* Washington, DC: American Psychological Association.

Gonzalez, G. (1974). Language, culture, and exceptional children. *Exceptional Children, 40,* 565-570.

Hanson, M. J. (1992a). Ethnic, cultural, and language diversity in intervention settings. In E. W. Lynch & M. J. Hanson (Eds.), *Developing cross-cultural competence* (pp. 3-18). Baltimore: Paul H. Brookes.

Hanson, M. J. (1992b). Families with Anglo-European roots. In E. W. Lynch & M. J. Hanson (Eds.), *Developing cross-cultural competence* (pp. 63-87). Baltimore: Paul H. Brookes.

Harry, B. (1994). Behavioral disorders in the context of families. In R. L. Peterson & S. Ishii-Jordan (Eds.), *Multicultural issues in the education of students with behavioral disorders* (pp. 149-161). Cambridge, MA: Brookline.

Hays, P. A. (1995). Multicultural applications of cognitive-behavior therapy. *Professional Psychology: Research and Practice, 26,* 309-315.

Heflinger, C. A., Cook, V. J., & Thackrey, M. (1987). Identification of mental retardation by the System of Multicultural Pluralistic Assessment: Nondiscriminatory or nonexistent? *Journal of School Psychology, 25,* 177-183.

Henderson, R. W., Bergan, J. R., & Hurt, M. (1972). Development and validation of the Henderson Environmental Learning Process Scale. *Journal of Social Psychology, 88,* 185-196.

Hoernicke, P. A., Kallam, M., & Tablada, T. (1994). Behavioral disorders in Hispanic-American cultures. In R. L. Peterson & S. Ishii-Jordan (Eds.), *Multicultural issues in the education of students with behavioral disorders* (pp. 115-125). Cambridge, MA: Brookline.

Ishii-Jordan, S., & Peterson, R. L. (1994). Behavioral disorders in the context of Asian cultures. In R. L Peterson & S. Ishii-Jordan (Eds.), *Multicultural issues in the education of students with behavioral disorders* (pp. 105-114). Cambridge, MA: Brookline.

Joe, J. R., & Malach, R. S. (1992). Families with Native American roots. In E. W. Lynch & M. J. Hanson (Eds.), *Developing cross-cultural competence* (pp. 89-119). Baltimore: Paul H. Brookes.

Kallam, M., Hoernicke, P. A., & Coser, P. G. (1994). Native Americans and behavioral disorders. In R. L. Peterson & S. Ishii-Jordan (Eds.), *Multicultural issues in the education of students with behavioral disorders* (pp. 126-137). Cambridge, MA: Brookline.

Kamphaus, R. W. (1987). Defining the construct of adaptive behavior by the Vineland Adaptive Behavior Scales. *Journal of School Psychology, 25,* 97-100.

Kazimour, K. K., & Reschly, D. J. (1981). Investigation of the norms and concurrent validity for the Adaptive Behavior Inventory for Children (ABIC). *American Journal of Mental Deficiency, 85,* 512-520.

Kehrberg, R. S. (1994). Behavioral disorders and gender/sexual issues. In R. L. Peterson & S. Ishii-Jordan (Eds.), *Multicultural issues in the education of behaviorally disordered youth* (pp. 184-195). Cambridge, MA: Brookline.

Keller, H. R. (1988). Children's adaptive behaviors: Measure and source generalizability. *Journal of Psychoeducational Assessment, 6,* 371-389.

Kernan, K. T., & Walker, M. W. (1981). Use of services for the mentally retarded in the African-American community. *Journal of Community Psychology, 9,* 45-52.

Kleinfeld, J. S. (1973). Intellectual strengths in culturally different groups: An Eskimo illustration. *Review of Educational Research, 43,* 341-359.

Kodluboy, D. W. (1994). Behavioral disorders and the culture of street gangs. In R. L. Peterson & S. Ishii-Jordan (Eds.), *Multicultural issues in the education of students with behavioral disorders* (pp. 233-248). Cambridge, MA: Brookline.

Koegel, P., & Edgerton, R. B. (1982). Labeling and the perception of handicap among Black mildly mentally retarded adults. *American Journal of Mental Deficiency, 87,* 266-276.

Lambert, N. M. (1979). Contributions of school classification, sex, and ethnic status to adaptive behavior assessment. *Journal of School Psychology, 17,* 3-16.

Lambert, N. M. (1986). Evidence on age and ethnic status bias in factor scores and the comparison score for the AAMD Adaptive Behavior Scale—School Edition. *Journal of School Psychology, 24,* 143-153.

Lambert, N. M., & Hartsough, C. S. (1981). Development of a simplified diagnostic scoring method for the School Version of the Adaptive Behavior Scale. *American Journal of Mental Deficiency, 86,* 138-147.

Lambert, N., Nihira, K., & Leland, H. (1993). AAMR *adaptive behavior scales—school version* (2nd ed.). Washington, DC: American Association on Mental Retardation.

Larson, D., & Palmer, B. (1994). Behavioral disorders in rural and isolated communities. In R. L. Peterson & S. Ishii-Jordan (Eds.), *Multicultural issues in the education of students with behavioral disorders* (pp. 208-215). Cambridge, MA: Brookline.

Lasky, B. (1994). Language and behavioral disorders. In R.L. Peterson & S. Ishii-Jordan (Eds.), *Multicultural issues in the education of students with behavioral disorders* (pp. 178-183). Cambridge, MA: Brookline.

Linkenhoker, D., & McCarron, L. (1993). *Street survival skills questionnaire* (SSSQ). New York: Psychological Corp.

Lynch, E. W. (1992a). Developing cross-cultural competence. In E. W. Lynch & M. J. Hanson (Eds.), *Developing cross-cultural competence* (pp. 35-62). Baltimore: Paul H. Brookes.

Lynch, E. W. (1992b). From culture shock to cultural learning. In E. W. Lynch & M. J. Hanson (Eds.), *Developing cross-cultural competence* (pp. 19-34). Baltimore: Paul H. Brookes.

Lynch, E. W., & Hanson, M. J. (Eds.). (1992). *Developing cross-cultural competence.* Baltimore: Paul H. Brookes.

McCloskey, L. A., Southwick, K., Fernandez-Esquer, M. E., & Locke, C. (1995). The psychological effects of political and domestic violence on Central American and Mexican immigrant mothers and children. *Journal of Community Psychology, 23,* 95-116.

McIntyre, T. (1994). Teaching urban youth with behavioral disorders. In R. L. Peterson & S. Ishii-Jordan (Eds.), *Multicultural issues in the education of students with behavioral disorders* (pp. 216-232). Cambridge, MA: Brookline.

Mercer, J. (1979). In defense of racially and culturally nondiscriminatory assessment. *School Psychology Digest, 8,* 89-115.

Mercer, J. R., & Lewis, J. F. (1978). *System of Multicultural Pluralistic Assessment (SOMPA).* New York: Psychological Corp.

Meyers, C. E., Mink, I. T., & Nihira, K. (1977). Home Quality Rating Scale. Pomona, CA: UCLA/Neuropsychiatric Institute-Lanterman State Hospital Research Group.

Montgomery, G. T., & Orozco, S. (1984). Validation of a measure of acculturation for Mexican Americans. *Hispanic Journal of Behavioral Sciences, 6,* 53-63.

Moos, R. H., Insel, P. M., & Humphrey, B. (1974). *Family, work and group environment scales manual.* Palo Alto, CA: Consulting Psychologists Press.

Morrow, R. D. (1994). Immigration, refugee, and generational status as related to behavioral disorders. In R. L. Peterson & S. Ishii-Jordan (Eds.), *Multicultural issues in the education of students with behavioral disorders* (pp. 196-207). Cambridge, MA: Brookline.

Nelson, C. M., & Pearson, C. A. (1994). Juvenile delinquency in the context of culture and community. In R. L. Peterson & S. Ishii-Jordan (Eds.), *Multicultural issues in the education of students with behavioral disorders* (pp. 78-90). Cambridge, MA: Brookline.

Nihira, K., Leland, H., & Lambert, N. (1993). AAMR *adaptive behavior scales—Residential and community* Version (2nd Ed.). Austin; TX: Pro-Ed.

Nihira, K., Webster, R., Tomiyasu, Y., & Oshio, C. (1988). Child-environment relationships: A cross-cultural study of educable mentally retarded children and their families. *Journal of Autism and Developmental Disorders*, 18, 327-341.

Park, E. K., Pullis, M., Reilly, T., & Townsend, B. L. (1994). Cultural biases in the identification of students with behavioral disorders. In R. L. Peterson & S. Ishii-Jordan (Eds.), *Multicultural issues in the education of students with behavioral disorders* (pp. 14-26). Cambridge, MA: Brookline.

Peterson, R. L., & Ishii-Jordan, S. (1994a). Behavioral disorders in European-American cultures. In R. L. Peterson & S. Ishii-Jordan (Eds.), *Multicultural issues in the education of students with behavioral disorders* (pp. 138-145). Cambridge, MA: Brookline.

Peterson, R. L., & Ishii-Jordan, S. (Eds.). (1994b). *Multicultural issues in the education of students with behavioral disorders*. Cambridge, MA: Brookline.

Plata, M. (1993). Using Spanish-speaking interpreters in special education. RASE: *Remedial & Special Education*, 14, 19-24.

Reschly, D. J. (1988). Assessment issues, placement litigation, and the future of mild mental retardation classification and programming. [Special Issue: Emerging challenges.] *Education and Training in Mental Retardation*, 23, 285-301.

Reschly, D. J., & Ward, S. M. (1991). Use of adaptive behavior measures and overrepresentation of black students in programs for students with mild mental retardation. *American Journal on Mental Retardation*, 96, 257-268.

Richmond, B. O., & Kicklighter, R. H. (1980). *Children's adaptive behavior scale*. Atlanta: Humanics.

Sattler, J. M. (1970). Social "experimenter effects" in experimentation, testing, interviewing, and psychotherapy. *Psychological Bulletin*, 73, 137-160.

Scott, L. S., Mastenbrook, J. L., Fisher, A. T., & Gridley, G. C. (1982). Adaptive Behavior Inventory for Children: The need for local norms. *Journal of School Psychology*, 20, 39-44.

Sharifzadeh, V. (1992). Families with Middle Eastern roots. In E. W. Lynch & M. J. Hanson (Eds.), *Developing cross-cultural competence* (pp. 319-351). Baltimore: Paul H. Brookes.

Sparrow, S. S., Balla, D. A., & Cicchetti, D. V. (1984). *Vineland adaptive behavior scales—Interview edition: Survey form manual*. Circle Pines, MN: American Guidance Service.

Springer, N. M. (1941). The social competence of adolescent delinquents: A comparative study of white and Negro first offenders and recidivists. *Journal of Social Psychology*, 14, 337-348.

Taylor, R. L., Ziegler, E. W., & Partenio, I. (1985). An empirical investigation of the Adaptive Behavior Inventory for Children. *Psychological Reports*, 57, 640-642.

Terman, L. M., & Merrill, M. A. (1973). The Stanford-Binet Intelligence Scale (3rd rev.). Boston: Houghton Mifflin.

Tombokan-Runtukahu, J., & Nitko, A. J. (1992). Translation, cultural adjustment, and validation of a measure of adaptive behavior. *Research in Developmental Disabilities*, 13, 481-501.

Tucker, C. M., Brady, B. A., Harris, Y. R., Fraser, K., & Tribble, I. (1993). The association of selected parent behaviors with the adaptive and maladaptive functioning of black children and white children. *Child Study Journal*, 23, 39-55.

Vega, W. A., Khoury, E. L., Zimmerman, R. S., Gil, A. G., & Warheit, G. J. (1995). Cultural conflicts and problem behaviors of Latino adolescents in home and school environments. *Journal of Community Psychology*, 23, 167-179.

Wechsler, D. (1991). WISC-III Manual. San Antonio, TX: Psychological Corporation.

Willis, W. (1992). Families with African American roots. In E. W. Lynch & M. J. Hanson (Eds.), *Developing cross-cultural competence* (pp. 121-150). Baltimore: Paul H. Brookes.

Wolfensberger, W., & Kurtz, R. A. (1971). Measurement of parents' perceptions of their children's development. *Genetic Psychology Monographs*, 83, 3-92.

Zuniga, M. E. (1992). Families with Latino roots. In E. W. Lynch & M. J. Hanson (Eds.), *Developing cross-cultural competence* (pp. 151-179). Baltimore: Paul H. Brookes.

CHAPTER 8

Examination of Gender and Race Factors in the Assessment of Adaptive Behavior

BRIAN R. BRYANT

DIANE PEDROTTY BRYANT

STEVE CHAMBERLAIN

The University of Texas at Austin

Introduction

The latest definition of mental retardation requires an examination of both intelligence and adaptive behavior (Luckasson et al., 1992). The assessment of these constructs has engendered considerable debate among professionals in education and psychology. Much of the debate centers on issues associated with test bias. More specifically, because intelligence and adaptive behavior testing is designed to differentiate among people of varying abilities, it is important to examine the nature of test bias for certain groups (e.g., Whites and non-Whites; males and females). Kaplan (1985) summarized the controversy:

> A basic tenet of U.S. society is that all people are created equal. This cornerstone of political and social thought is clearly defended in the Constitution. Yet all individuals are not treated equally, and the history of social action is replete with attempts to remedy this situation. Psychological tests are among the many practices that counteract the idea that all people are the same. Tests are designed to measure differences between people, and often the differences tests measure are in desirable personal characteristics such as intelligence and aptitude. Test scores that demonstrate differences between people may suggest to some that people are not created with the same basic abilities. (p. 465)

The purpose of this chapter is to examine test bias as it relates to one aspect of mental retardation assessment: adaptive behavior assessment of different races and genders. Specifically, the chapter examines bias in terms of scores derived on the *Assessment of Adaptive Areas* (AAA; Bryant, Taylor, & Rivera, 1996), a scale that redistributes items of the *Adaptive Behavior Scale—School Version* (ABS-S:2; Lambert, Nihira, & Leland, 1993) and the *Adaptive Behavior Scale—Residential and Community Edition* (ABS-RC:2; Nihira, Leland, & Lambert, 1993) for the 10 adaptive areas outlined in the Luckasson et al. (1992) definition of mental retardation. In the following sections, we discuss (a) adaptive behavior assessment, (b) the nature of test bias, and (c) how researchers typically examine scales for bias. We then present the methodology and discuss the results of the current study.

Adaptive Behavior and Its Assessment

Adaptive behavior has played a valuable role in mental retardation identification for decades (Heber, 1961). In 1959, the American Association on Mental Deficiency (AAMD; now the American Association on Mental Retardation, AAMR) first acknowledged the importance of adaptive behavior, when its Committee on Nomenclature published a classification system that introduced the criterion of adaptive behavior deficiencies into the process for diagnosing mental retardation. We note with interest that this definition, and the ones succeeding it, provided "cutoff scores" for intelligence tests (i.e., scores that indicate intellectual abilities) but did not include similar cutoffs for adaptive behavior tests.

The most recent classification manual of the AAMR (Luckasson et al., 1992) included several significant alterations to the previous definitions. Of particular relevance to this chapter was the introduction of 10 adaptive areas to mental retardation assessment:

> Mental retardation refers to substantial limitations in present functioning. It is characterized by significant subaverage intellectual functioning, existing concurrently with related limitations in two or more of the following applicable adaptive skill areas: communication, self-care, home living, social skills, community use, self-direction, health and safety, functional academics, leisure, and work. Mental retardation manifests before age 18. (p. 5)

In an effort to validate the changes in the definition, Luckasson et al. (1992) provided the following justification: (a) It is an attempt to express the changing understanding of what mental retardation is; (b) It is a formulation of what ought to be classified as well as how to describe the systems of supports people with mental retardation require; (c) it represents a paradigm shift from a view of mental retardation as an absolute trait expressed solely by an individual to an expression of the interaction between the person with limited functioning and the environment; and (d) it attempts to extend the concept of adaptive behavior another step from a global description to specification of particular skill areas (p. ix-x).

Some (e.g., Artiles & Trent, 1994; Baca & Cervantes, 1989) have proffered test bias as a possible reason for the overrepresentation of some racial groups in classes for students with mental retardation. Some professionals (e.g., Reschly, 1987) have also questioned whether measures of adaptive behavior might by their nature be biased. In chapter 7 of this monograph, Craig and Tassé provide an extensive review of the literature on adaptive behavior functioning of various groups. In this chapter, we briefly summarize findings related to adaptive behavior and gender and race or ethnicity.

Relationship Between Adaptive Behavior and Gender

Several studies examined the effects of gender on adaptive behavior using the AAMD *Adaptive Behavior Scales*. In one study, Lambert (1979) found that gender failed to make a contribution to Part-1 scores of the public school version of the ABS (Lambert, Windmiller, & Cole, 1975). Lambert's findings were similar to those of Salagaras and Nettleback (1983) who also found no significant differences on Part 1 of the ABS. On the other hand, Fine, Tangeman, and Woodard (1990) found that females scored significantly higher than males on three Part-1 domains: independent functioning, language development, and domestic activity.

Significant differences based on gender were found in some studies, but some of these researchers were hesitant to attribute those differences to gender bias of the test. For example, Lambert (1979) found significant differences on 14 of 72 analyses of Part-2 scores on the ABS, but explained that the domains in which there were differences reflected behaviors that boys and girls acquire differentially as a result of different socialization standards. Contrary to Lambert's findings, Weber and Epstein (1980) found no significant differences based on gender on Part 2 of the ABS.

Lambert (1986), in a study using the school version of the *Adaptive Behavior Scale* (ABS-S; Lambert, 1981), found that for the 7- to 16-year-old sample, gender contributed significantly to all scores but explained no meaningful amount of variance. Thus, she concluded that gender did not contribute significantly to factor scores for this age group. For the 3- to 6-year-old age group, the variance explained by gender never exceeded 2%; Lambert concluded that the mean scores of boys and girls for this age range could be expected to be similar. Salagaras and Nettleback (1983) found on measures of Part 2 of the ABS (Lambert, Windmiller & Cole, 1974) that males scored significantly higher on antisocial behavior and hyperactive tendencies, and females scored significantly higher on self-abusive behavior.

In studies using other adaptive behavior scales, Oakland and Feigenbaum (1980) found limited evidence of gender bias with a significant difference on one of six subtests (peers) on the *Adaptive Behavior Instrument for Children* (ABIC; Mercer & Lewis, 1977). However, the authors point out that several factors other than gender also influenced this domain. Adams, McIntosh, and Weade (1973) found no significant effects for gender on measures of the *Vineland Social Maturity Scales* (VSMS; Doll, 1965).

Relationship Between Adaptive Behavior and Race or Ethnicity

Several studies have found no significant differences based on race or ethnicity. For instance, Springer (1941), using the term "social competence" to describe adaptive behavior as measured on the VSMS (Doll, 1965), found no significant difference between Whites and non-Whites. Adams et al. (1973) likewise found no significant effects based on race on measures of the VSMS (Doll, 1965). Boroskin and Giampiccolo (1971) found no significant difference among scores for Anglo Americans, African Americans, and Latinos on the *Fairview Self-Help Scale* (Ross, 1970). Finally, Slate (1983) found similar results when comparing mean scores for Black and White children with mental retardation on the VSMS (Doll, 1965) or ABIC (Mercer & Lewis, 1977).

Several studies have found significant differences based on race, but some of these researchers explained that these differences might have been caused by factors other than test bias. For example, Lambert (1979) found that 9 of 18 analyses covering three domains of Part 2 of the ABS indicated significant difference based on race. She explained that different cultural demands can be reflected in maladaptive interpersonal behavior and recommended that separate norms be reported for different racial groups.

Oakland and Feigenbaum (1980) found significant difference based on race for only one of six ABIC (Mercer & Lewis, 1977) subtests (peers). They explained that six other comparison groups also showed significant differences on that subtest, indicating that peer-related adaptive behaviors appear to be influenced by a variety of factors.

Scott, Mastenbrook, Fisher, and Gridley (1982), in an effort to see if local norms were needed for measures of adaptive behavior, found that Mexican American children from south Texas scored significantly lower than the California sample on which the ABIC (Mercer & Lewis, 1977) was normed. A race-by-socioeconomic-status interaction analysis revealed significant differences on 26 of 35 comparisons between the low-socioeconomic-status Mexican American group and the other five race-by-socioeconomic-status groups. The authors also found that this subgroup scored lower on a measure of urban acculturation than the other groups, and recommended local and/or separate racial or ethnic group norms for Corpus school children on the ABIC.

Although Slate (1983) found no significant difference based on race or ethnicity for children with mental retardation, she found that Black and Anglo children without retardation had significantly different mean scores on the VSMS (Doll, 1965). Finally, Lambert (1986) found that for a sample of 7- to 16-year-old children, ethnic status was significant for all scores of the ABS, (Lambert et al., 1974) but the explained variance was zero for all factor scores except social adjustment, where ethnic status explained 3% of the variance. Lambert concluded that ethnic status did not significantly contribute to factor scores. For a sample of 3- to 6-year-old children, ethnic status was significant for all factor scores and explained 1 to 5% of the variance, with the largest amount of variance explained in the community self-sufficiency factor. Lambert concluded that the effects of differences in home environments and cognitive stimulation on early success in school between families from different cultural groups is more likely the explanation of this variance than test bias.

Nature of Test Bias

There are numerous definitions of test bias, but most of the definitions are similar enough for Brown (1983) to have concluded the following:

> A test can be considered biased if it differentiates between members of various groups (for example, between men and women or between blacks and whites) on bases other than the characteristic being measured. That is, a test is biased if its content, procedures, or use result in a systematic advantage or disadvantage to members of certain groups over other groups and if the basis of this differentiation is irrelevant to the test purpose. (p. 224)

Bryant et al. (in press) provide an example of how intelligence tests can be biased against a particular group. These authors cite the common school practice of administering group tests of intelligence to students districtwide. These tests include measures of vocabulary, in which students typically read a stimulus word and several response choices. The task is to select from the response choices the one word that means the same as or opposite from the stimulus word. It is assumed that the students can read the words presented; thus, the results are valid measures of each student's vocabulary knowledge. Such an assumption is fallacious; not all students can read the words presented. Therefore, the test results are inherently biased against nonreaders and do not provide a valid measure of vocabulary.

In another example, consider the case of an intelligence test that in part requires the stacking of blocks in order to reproduce a figure presented in a stimulus picture. Test administration assumes a sufficient level of manual dexterity to stack the blocks. But when the test is administered to a child with cerebral palsy and resulting motor difficulties, the test results may well be biased. Note that in both instances it is the result of the testing that is biased and not necessarily the test itself.

Sattler (1988) wrote cogently on the topic when he noted that some people erroneously examine mean differences of test scores between racial or ethnic groups as an index of test bias. He presents his argument by quoting Flaugher (1978):

> Mean differences are not a legitimate standard for identifying test bias. Because of disparities among various groups in our nation with respect to socioeconomic status and other variables, it would be surprising if intelligence and achievement tests did *not* show mean differences in favor of some groups. (as cited in Sattler, p. 566)

Numerous researchers (e.g., Cohen, Swerdlik, & Smith, 1992; Jensen, 1980; Reynolds & Kaiser, 1990; Witt, Elliott, Gresham, & Kramer, 1988) support the assertion that group difference scores should not necessarily be used as evidence of test bias.

McGloughlin and Lewis (1991) identified several sources of test bias that are not necessarily tied to the tests themselves. These include the professional preparation of the examiner, tester attitudes about different cultural groups, the working relationship between the examiner and examinee, and the manner with which test results are interpreted. Oakland and Parmelee (1985) noted that the factors related to bias are found not only in tests, but in several other sources, including children, parents, educational personnel, and school-system policies. These researchers concluded that nonbiased assessment can occur only if several factors and conditions relating to bias are eliminated, minimized, or at least recognized.

Controlling for Test Bias

Hammill, Pearson, and Wiederholt (1996) reviewed the literature on test bias and identified four techniques that test authors and test examiners can use to control tests for bias: (a) describe the content of their tests in terms of potential bias, (b) include targeted demographic groups (i.e., identifiable groups that differ from the "mainstream" population in their normative samples) in the same proportion as the groups occur at each age level in the most recent census data, (c) provide separate reliability and validity information for the targeted groups, and (d) show that their test items are as appropriate for the targeted groups as for the mainstream population. Each of these techniques is discussed here.

Test Content

An obvious source of test bias in adaptive behavior scales used in the United States involves the inclusion of items that are culturally irrelevant. Leland (1996) made this point when he stated that adaptive behavior, as used in the area of mental retardation, refers to the effectiveness with which an individual copes with the natural and social demands of his or her environment. It could be argued that appropriate adaptive behavior is context-dependent in that it depends on the social demands of the particular setting in which the individual resides and the expectations that accompany that setting. In this way, it is incumbent for the adaptive behavior examiner to make an individual judgment concerning the appropriateness of the scale's content to the particular child's environment.

Normative Sample Demographic Characteristics

Good norm-referenced tests have normative samples that are representative of the nation as a whole in which the test is being used (Hammill, Brown, & Bryant, 1992). Important demographic variables include geographic region, gender, race, ethnicity, urban or rural residence, family income, and disability status (see U.S. Bureau of the Census, 1990). Test users should compare data reported in test manuals to the data reported by the Census Bureau or to data reported from another valid source.

Reliability and Validity Studies

Simply put, *reliability* means the consistency with which a test measures a particular construct, and *validity* refers to the extent to which a test measures what its author says it measures. Test authors conduct several studies to examine their scales with regards to these two important indexes of technical adequacy. Yet very often test authors do not provide separate analyses for subgroups (e.g., racial groups, disability groups). This means that a test may be reliable and yield valid results for people as a whole, but not necessarily for individuals who are the primary target for test administration (e.g., individuals with mental retardation or learning disabilities). Hammill and colleagues (1992, 1996) suggest the importance of providing evidence of reliability and validity for many subgroups to show that there is no test bias in these regards.

Examination of Test Items for Different Groups

Two statistical techniques can be used to examine test items for potential bias: item response theory and the Delta scores approach. Shepard, Camilli, and Williams (1985) noted that item response theory is "a preferred procedure for detecting biased items in that it least confounds real mean differences in group performance with bias" (p. 77). Hammill et al. (1996) noted that this technique generates item characteristic curves, which are assumed to be stable across groups and represent a strategy for detecting item bias. The item characteristic curve represents the probability of an examinee's answering an item correctly based on the ability being measured. Scores for each item are analyzed for significant differences for dichotomous groups (e.g., African American vs. non-African American; American Indian vs. non-American Indian; males vs. females). Although there are no guidelines for how many significantly different items are necessary for demonstrating bias, clearly the more items that are statistically different, the higher the potential for bias.

The second technique is the Delta score approach (Jensen, 1980). Delta scores are derived linear scales that relate to item difficulties and are linear transformations of the z scale. Jensen noted that the correlation between Delta scores of different groups "indicates the degree of group resemblance in relative item difficulties when the rank order of the items is eliminated" (p. 442). When test authors report Delta scores, larger correlation coefficients are inversely related to test bias (i.e., the larger the coefficient, the less likely the test is biased).

An Empirical Examination of Gender and Race Factors in Adaptive Behavior

In the study reported here, the performance of the normative samples from the AAMR *Adaptive Behavior Scales* (Lambert et al., 1993) and the *Assessment of Adaptive Areas* (AAA; Bryant et al., 1996) were examined using three analyses: (a) adaptive area reliability and validity, (b) item response theory, and (c) Delta scores. Before we examine the results of our analyses, we discuss the instrumentation used for the study and describe the study's sample.

Instrument

The AAA (Bryant et al., 1996) is a scoring system that recategorizes the items of the AAMR ABS-RC:2 (Nihira et al., 1993) and ABS-S:2 (Lambert et al., 1993) to generate scores for each of the 10 adaptive skill areas identified by the AAMR (Luckasson et al., 1992) as being critical in assessing mental retardation. It consists of a test protocol that scorers use to rescore the ABS-RC:2 and/or ABS-S:2, and a set of normative tables used to generate standard scores and percentiles for the 10 adaptive skill areas. In 1993, MacMillan et al. noted that no adaptive behavior instrument yielded data according to the 10 adaptive skill areas noted in the 1992 AAMR manual (Luckasson et al.). The AAA was developed to rectify this shortcoming by creating a system to recategorize the items of the ABS-RC:2 and the ABS-S:2 to generate scores for each of the 10 adaptive skill areas. A brief description of these 10 areas was provided by Bryant et al. (1996).

Communication—Understanding and expressing messages through either symbolic or nonsymbolic behaviors.

Self-Care—Toileting, eating, dressing, and grooming skills.

Home Living—Home environment skills relating to housekeeping, property maintenance, cooking, budgeting, home safety, and scheduling.

Social—Skills related to social exchanges, including interaction with others, as well as the interaction and termination of this interaction.

Community Use—Use of appropriate community resources, such as traveling in the community, shopping, purchasing services, and using public transportation.

Self-Direction—Skills related to making choices, completing tasks, seeking assistance, and resolving problems.

Health and Safety—First aid, physical fitness, illness identification, and safety skills.

Functional Academics—Skills related to learning in school, such as basic reading, writing, and practical mathematics.

Leisure—Recreational interests and activities that may involve social interaction, mobility skills, taking turns, and playing appropriately.

Work—Employment (job) skills, such as task completion and money management. (p. 2)

To distribute ABS-RC:2 (Nihira et al., 1993) and ABS-S:2 (Lambert et al., 1993) items among the 10 adaptive areas, Bryant et al. (1996) asked 12 experts in mental retardation and assessment to examine each ABS-RC:2 and ABS-S:2 behavioral statement and assign the statement to one or more adaptive area(s). Using the ratings as a guide, the AAA authors selected the items that would contribute to each adaptive area. Weighted values, based on the expert ratings, were then assigned to each item. Not surprisingly, some adaptive areas (e.g., self-care) contain many items, while other adaptive areas (e.g., work) contain relatively few. This distribution reflects the content of the ABS-S:2 and ABS-RC:2. Rather than reduce the numbers of items for the more lengthy scales, the AAA authors kept the scales intact, thereby maintaining the integrity of the ABS items and the determination of the experts as to their placement on the AAA.

It is beyond the scope of this chapter to describe the AAA in its entirety. The interested reader may reference the *Assessment of Adaptive Areas* manual (Bryant et al., 1996) for specific details. Item analyses for the AAA were conducted for three separate groups: individuals without mental retardation, individuals with mental retardation attending school, and adults with mental retardation. On the average, the scale items satisfied the requirements set forth by assessment experts (e.g., Anastasi & Urbina, 1997; Garrett, 1965) and provide evidence of item validity. Additional studies of validity and reliability are provided by the test authors: Taylor (1997) has reported that the technical characteristics of the scale are acceptable, with average internal consistency reliability coefficients exceeding .9 in most instances and validity data available for content, criterion-related, and construct validity.

Sample

The sample employed in our current study is from the mental retardation normative group for the ABS-S:2 and the AAA. The ABS-S:2 was normed on people with and without mental retardation, but our study examined only those with mental retardation. According to the tests' manuals, the ABS-S:2 was normed on 2,074 individuals with mental retardation residing in 40 states. The specific demographic characteristics showed 77% of the sample was White, 16% was Black, and 7% was other. For ethnicity, 71% was other, 16% was African American, 2% was Native American, 4% was Asian, and 7% was Hispanic; 60% and 40% were male and female, respectively; 40% had IQ scores in the 50 to 70 range, 48% scored in the 20 to 49 range, and 12% scored < 20. Sixty-two percent of the sample resided in urban settings whereas 38% were from rural settings, and geographic

representation was fairly equally distributed. For this study, we dropped the 3- and 4-year-olds and those older than 18, leaving our age range 5 to 18.

Procedure and Results

In all cases, data were run using item scores from the AAA. For the adaptive area reliability study, the AAA weighted scores were used for each item. For the Delta scores and the item response theory analyses, unweighted scores were used, because both analyses require a dichotomous scoring system (i.e., 1 or 0). Here we describe the procedures and results for each study.

Reliability and Validity

To examine the reliability and validity of the 10 adaptive area scores on the AAA, we conducted internal consistency reliability and item validity analyses. Error associated with internal consistency reflects the degree of homogeneity among items within each adaptive area. Because the purpose of each AAA adaptive area is to assess a certain characteristic, ability, or content, the more the items relate to each other, the smaller the error in each area. If the items are unrelated to each other, they are likely measuring different qualities, and the amount of inventory error due to a lack of internal consistency would be great.

The internal consistency reliability of the items on the adaptive areas was investigated using the coefficient alpha procedure. All cases from the normative sample served as subjects for this analysis, and analyses were conducted at each 2-year age interval. Separate analyses were run by gender (i.e., male and female) and race (i.e., White and non-White). Reliability coefficients for the 10 adaptive areas are presented in Tables 8.1 (gender) and 8.2 (race).

Guilford and Fruchter (1978) pointed out that information about an inventory's construct validity can be obtained by correlating performance on the items with the total

Table 8.1
Coefficients Alpha for Males and Females (Decimals Omitted)

Adaptive Area	Age 5-6 M	F	7-8 M	F	9-10 M	F	11-12 M	F	13-14 M	F	15-16 M	F	17-18 M	F	Average M	F
Communication	96	96	96	95	95	96	96	97	96	96	95	96	97	96	96	96
Self-Care	98	97	97	97	97	98	97	98	97	97	97	97	97	97	97	97
Home Living	77	72	78	79	84	84	81	88	86	72	83	88	86	85	82	82
Social	94	94	94	93	94	96	95	94	93	92	94	96	94	95	94	94
Community Use	91	89	91	90	94	95	94	94	96	94	95	94	94	95	94	93
Self-Direction	94	94	93	92	93	92	92	95	92	90	92	94	94	92	93	93
Health & Safety	91	92	90	90	92	92	94	92	91	90	92	90	91	87	92	91
Functional Academics	94	95	95	95	96	97	97	97	97	96	97	96	97	97	96	96
Leisure	73	83	87	82	87	88	89	87	87	82	88	87	88	88	86	86
Work	87	91	87	84	90	86	89	91	88	88	89	92	88	87	88	89

score made on its related inventories. Such information can be derived using the item differentiation statistic.

Item differentiation refers to "the degree to which an item differentiates correctly among test takers in the behavior that the test is designed to measure" (Anastasi & Urbina, 1997, p. 179). More than 50 different indexes of item discrimination have been developed for use in test construction. With regard to selecting an appropriate index, several researchers (e.g., Anastasi & Urbina; Guilford & Fruchter, 1978; Oosterhof, 1976) have observed that there is little concern as to which procedure is used, because the various indexes provide similar results.

Ebel (1972) and Pyrczak (1973) suggest that discrimination indexes of .35 or higher are acceptable. Anastasi and Urbina (1997) and Garrett (1965) point out that indexes as low as .20 are acceptable under some circumstances.

The value of using the discrimination index to select good items cannot be overemphasized. A test composed of too many items

Table 8.2
Coefficients Alpha for Whites and Non-Whites (Decimals Omitted)

Adaptive Area	Age															
	5-6		7-8		9-10		11-12		13-14		15-16		17-18		Average	
	W	N	W	N	W	N	W	N	W	N	W	N	W	N	W	N
Communication	96	96	96	94	96	95	97	96	96	96	96	95	97	92	96	95
Self-Care	98	98	97	96	98	98	98	97	97	97	97	97	97	93	97	97
Home Living	76	76	80	63	84	87	84	85	82	83	85	85	86	88	83	82
Social	95	90	94	87	95	93	95	90	93	92	94	96	95	81	94	91
Community Use	90	91	91	83	94	95	94	93	95	95	94	96	94	93	93	93
Self-Direction	93	94	93	93	93	93	93	91	93	91	93	92	93	94	93	93
Health & Safety	92	88	92	81	92	92	93	90	91	89	91	92	90	88	92	89
Functional Academics	94	95	95	93	96	97	97	95	97	96	97	96	97	95	96	95
Leisure	80	66	86	82	86	89	88	80	85	86	88	88	88	87	86	84
Work	89	84	85	83	89	90	90	79	87	91	91	90	88	87	89	87

with low discrimination indexes will very likely have low reliability, and tests with low reliability cannot help but yield results that have low validity. Item differentiation indexes were calculated using the entire normative sample as subjects. The discrimination indexes generated for each of the AAA scales are reported in Tables 8.3 (gender) and 8.4 (race). As can be seen, the scale items satisfy the requirements previously described and provide quantitative evidence of the AAA's item validity.

Delta Scores

To further investigate the AAA adaptive areas for bias, we conducted two studies examining Delta values. This procedure, described by Jensen (1980), was used by Slosson, Nicholson, and Hibpshman (1990) as a way to examine test bias. Jensen noted that the Pearson r between the Delta values of different groups "indicates the degree of group resemblance in relative item difficulties when the rank order of item difficulties is eliminated" (p. 442).

Table 8.3
Median Item Differentiation Statistics
for Males and Females (Decimals Omitted)

Adaptive	Age												
	5-6		7-8		9-10		11-12		13-14		15-16		17-18
Area	M	F	M	F	M	F	M	F	M	F	M	F	M	F
Communication	62	62	63	57	59	59	67	72	63	57	63	58	64	64
Self-Care	61	51	58	58	59	70	58	66	63	59	57	57	50	57
Home Living	45	36	43	50	54	57	49	57	57	45	53	67	61	58
Social	49	51	51	49	51	58	51	55	50	45	51	57	56	53
Community Use	48	56	45	48	56	62	50	58	60	54	58	54	53	56
Self-Direction	58	60	59	56	61	59	54	62	51	48	58	60	67	54
Health & Safety	69	70	66	68	68	70	76	74	72	62	73	65	69	59
Functional Academics	51	56	59	58	65	67	70	66	67	61	67	64	70	68
Leisure	42	44	60	44	54	57	58	51	51	47	59	55	56	54
Work	46	50	53	42	54	51	49	55	49	45	54	55	44	53

Table 8.4
Median Item Differentiation Statistics
for Whites and Non-Whites (Decimals Omitted)

Adaptive Area	5-6		7-8		9-10		11-12		13-14		15-16		17-18	
	W	N	W	N	W	N	W	N	W	N	W	N	W	N
Communication	54	63	61	50	59	51	66	64	65	60	63	54	66	34
Self-Care	61	56	59	43	64	60	63	58	60	59	55	59	55	24
Home Living	40	51	48	29	60	60	50	54	48	60	58	60	57	59
Social	51	39	50	32	54	47	53	35	48	49	53	54	51	10
Community Use	42	49	48	20	58	63	56	53	56	60	52	61	54	46
Self-Direction	61	59	59	59	57	62	60	50	55	53	59	60	65	6
Health & Safety	75	58	68	52	67	72	74	72	68	62	68	72	64	61
Functional Academics	48	53	62	44	63	65	67	46	67	63	66	66	69	60
Leisure	45	39	59	45	53	56	54	45	47	55	56	54	57	60
Work	52	39	52	43	52	59	55	34	45	58	60	50	46	45

Table 8.5
Delta Values for Each Adaptive Area by Gender and Race

Adaptive Area	Gender	Race
Communication	.99	.99
Self-Care	.99	.99
Home Living	.99	.99
Social	.97	.99
Community Use	.99	.99
Self-Direction	.99	.99
Health & Safety	.98	.98
Functional Academics	.99	.99
Leisure	.99	.99
Work	.98	.99

In the first study, Delta values for items in each subtest were computed for the two gender groups. These Delta values for each of the 10 adaptive areas were correlated, and the results are shown in Table 8.5. In the second study, Delta values for items in each subtest were computed for two racial groups, White and non-White. These Delta values were correlated between each racial group on each subtest, and the resulting coefficients are also shown in Table 8.5.

Table 8.6
Item Response Theory Data for Gender

Adaptive Area	Median	Range	Number (%) of Biased Items
Communication	0.960	.04 to 3.30	2 of 44 (4.5)
Self-Care	0.960	.02 to 2.65	14 of 80 (17.5)
Home Living	0.850	.02 to 2.77	1 of 11 (9.0)
Social	1.320	.03 to 3.55	11 of 43 (25.6)
Community Use	1.675	.09 to 21.20	15 of 38 (39.5)
Self-Direction	0.770	.06 to 3.13	6 of 28 (21.4)
Health & Safety	1.020	.25 to 3.50	2 of 11 (18.2)
Functional Academics	0.875	.02 to 2.43	3 of 44 (6.8)
Leisure	1.370	.15 to 2.89	2 of 13 (15.4)
Work	0.990	.09 to 3.51	5 of 20 (25.0)

Item Response Theory

As one means for investigating the bias associated with the AAA scores, we calculated item characteristics curves (ICCs) for each AAA item. Using the ICCs, standardized indexes of bias (SIB) were calculated. According to Muraki and Engelhard (1988), SIBs meeting or exceeding 2.0 are biased items. Unfortunately, there are no criteria for determining how many biased items are needed to result in a biased adaptive area. Thus, we report the median ICC for each scale and the percentage of items that are biased for each adaptive area in Table 8.6 (gender) and Table 8.7 (race).

Table 8.7
Item Response Theory Data for Race

Adaptive Area	Median	Range	Number (%) of Biased Items
Communication	0.900	.04 to 3.90	6 of 44 (13.6)
Self-Care	0.920	.02 to 3.76	12 of 80 (15.0)
Home Living	0.980	.10 to 1.89	0 of 11 (0.0)
Social	0.680	.01 to 2.31	1 of 43 (2.3)
Community Use	1.255	.04 to 28.17	14 of 38 (36.8)
Self-Direction	1.355	.02 to 3.11	8 of 28 (28.6)
Health & Safety	0.640	.32 to 1.61	0 of 11 (0.0)
Functional Academics	0.870	.02 to 4.32	4 of 44 (9.1)
Leisure	0.540	.02 to 2.78	1 of 13 (7.7)
Work	0.900	.03 to 2.27	2 of 20 (10.0)

To further examine the effects of bias on the different groups studied (i.e., males and females; Whites and non-Whites), we calculated standard scores for all members of our sample. To do this, we computed means and standard deviations for three age groups: young—ages 3 to 8; middle—ages 9 to 12; and old—ages 13 and up. We then used these data to generate z-scores for each raw score total at the three age clusters and converted the z-scores to standard scores reported by the AAA (i.e., those having a mean of 10 and standard deviation of 3). We eliminated the biased items, summed the raw scores for the nonbiased items that remained, and generated standard scores for those items not biased with regard to gender and race. Thus, each member of our sample had two standard scores for each adaptive area—one based on all items and the other based on only those items that were empirically demonstrated to be without bias. Separate analyses were run for race and gender biased items; the means and standard deviations are reported in Table 8.8 (gender) and Table 8.9 (race). Subsequently, the difference scores were compared to identify the extent to which the sample's scores differed from one another; the results are also reported in Tables 8.8 and 8.9. We also correlated the results of the two sets of scores; the resulting coefficients also appear in Tables 8.8 and 8.9.

Table 8.8
Item Response Data for Gender

	Male				Female			
	Mean 1	Mean 2			Mean 1	Mean 2		
Adaptive Area	(SD)	(SD)	ƒ	r	(SD)	(SD)	ƒ	r
Communication	10.87 (2.7)	10.86 (2.6)	1.77	.99	10.92 (2.6)	10.93 (2.6)	-.50	.99
Self-Care	10.86 (2.7)	10.70 (2.6)	5.58*	.98	11.01 (2.7)	10.81 (2.6)	6.25*	.97
Home Living	10.53 (2.7)	10.54 (2.9)	-.53	.97	11.00 (2.8)	10.97 (2.9)	.91	.98
Social	10.68 (2.7)	10.67 (2.6)	.28	.98	11.04 (2.6)	11.04 (2.6)	-.28	.98
Community Use	10.86 (2.9)	10.78 (2.8)	2.37	.95	10.69 (2.7)	10.61 (2.7)	1.80	.95
Self-Direction	10.57 (2.8)	10.67 (2.7)	-3.93*	.97	10.89 (2.8)	10.88 (2.7)	.29	.97
Health & Safety	10.96 (3.2)	10.95 (3.2)	.70	.99	10.96 (3.2)	10.93 (3.16)	1.40	.99
Functional Academics	10.85 (2.88)	10.87 (2.87)	-1.48	.99	10.68 (2.77)	10.72 (2.78)	-2.50	.99
Leisure	10.66 (2.9)	10.77 (2.8)	-3.96*	.97	10.54 (2.70)	10.76 (2.68)	-6.1*	.96
Work	10.42 (2.9)	10.48 (2.9)	-2.25	.97	10.98 (2.9)	11.05 (2.9)	-1.98	.97

*$p < .01$

Discussion

An examination of the statistics associated with our analyses demonstrates that, although there is reason to believe that bias is limited with respect to the AAA, there is cause for further exploration and careful interpretation with the AAA scores. We examine each data set in turn.

Reliability and Validity

Tables 8.1 and 8.2 show the reliability coefficients are quite high. Hammill et al. (1992) called for reliability coefficients to meet or exceed .80 for reliability to be considered acceptable. Coefficients of .90 or higher are deemed good. The average coefficients across ages are either acceptable or good for all

Table 8.9
Item Response Data for Race

	Male				Female			
Adaptive Area	Mean 1 (SD)	Mean 2 (SD)	ƒ	r	Mean 1 (SD)	Mean 2 (SD)	ƒ	r
Communication	10.9 (2.7)	10.8 (2.6)	1.38	.99	10.91 (2.6)	10.92 (2.6)	-.80	.99
Self-Care	10.68 (2.6)	10.66 (2.6)	.984	.99	10.81 (2.6)	10.85 (2.6)	-2.0	.99
Home Living	NA	NA	NA	NA	NA	NA	NA	NA
Social	10.71 (2.7)	10.71 (2.7)	-.46	.99	11.06 (2.7)	11.08 (2.7)	-1.6	.99
Community Use	10.86 (2.9)	10.86 (2.7)	.15	.94	10.69 (2.7)	10.60 (2.6)	1.81	.94
Self-Direction	10.57 (2.8)	10.64 (2.7)	-2.0	.96	10.89 (2.8)	10.91 (2.7)	-.68	.96
Health & Safety	NA	NA	NA	NA	NA	NA	NA	NA
Functional Academics	10.85 (2.9)	10.84 (2.9)	.58	.99	10.68 (2.8)	10.68 (2.8)	-.35	.99
Leisure	10.76 (2.9)	10.86 (2.9)	-6.5*	.99	10.59 (2.7)	10.74 (2.7)	-6.7*	.99
Work	10.42 (2.9)	10.45 (2.9)	-1.3	.97	10.98 (2.9)	10.98 (2.9)	-.07	.97

*$p < .01$
NA = Not applicable (no items were deemed biased).

adaptive areas across all groups studied, which would be expected based on the large numbers of items provided for most of the scales.

Examination of the item validity coefficients depicted in Tables 8.3 and 8.4 is also of interest. The median reported coefficients uniformly meet criterion set forth by Hammill et al. (1992) for evidence of item validity.

In the case of reliability and validity, there is evidence that the constructs associated with the 10 adaptive areas can be assessed reliably and with some degree of validity across gender and race categories. This is encouraging when considering the possible implementation of the adaptive areas criterion for mental retardation diagnosis.

Delta Scores

The Delta scores depicted in Table 8.5 are very high. Thus, there is a dramatic degree of group resemblance in relative item difficulties among the adaptive areas. This is the case across genders and racial groups.

Item Response Theory

The median ICCs reported in Tables 8.6 and 8.7 are uniformly low, which means that the majority of items in each adaptive area are nonbiased. Yet the percentages reported for community use are of concern. About 1 in 3 items contains some element of bias for race, which would seem quite high. Closer examination shows that 10 of the items are biased in favor of Whites; 4 are biased in terms of non-Whites. For gender, the number of biased items increases to 15 of 38. In this instance, 11 items are biased in favor of males, and 4 are biased in favor of females.

The importance of bias analyses is not restricted to the identification of items that have bias toward one group or another. The important issue is to identify the extent to which bias results in scores that are not valid indicators of performance. Because the total scores for each adaptive area yield valid results, the examination focuses on the extent to which the scores obtained on only those items without bias compares to the scores of the total set of items.

Coefficients reported in Tables 8.8 and 8.9 are exceedingly high and demonstrate the strong relationship between the sets of scores. Further, the check of mean differences between the sets of scores, with few exceptions, demonstrates that what differences exist between performance are not significant at the .01 level of confidence.

It is interesting to examine the instances where the mean scores are significantly different (gender: self-care, self-direction—for males only, & leisure; race: leisure). In all

cases, the mean differences were less than three tenths of a point. This, coupled with the reliability and validity data and the Delta scores, would cause one to seriously question the extent to which bias plays a deleterious role in adaptive behavior assessment.

In conclusion, the results of these analyses are important in that they begin to provide empirical evidence that can be added to the debate about bias associated with adaptive behavior assessment. Yet limitations associated with this study prevent broad generalizations. First, this study used the AAMR ABS-S:2 and the AAA to collect data. Although the scales have been demonstrated to be reliable instruments that yield valid results, the scales in no way assess all the behaviors associated with its constructs (e.g., leisure, community use). Thus, the results of this study should be interpreted only with respect to the content assessed by the AAA, and generalizations to adaptive behavior should be made with caution.

A second limitation involves the use of item response theory in respect to bias examination. Because there are no criteria for interpreting just how many biased items a scale can have before its results are deemed biased, we were left simply to examine the data and draw our own conclusions. We chose to recalculate scores after we eliminated items that were deemed biased; we found that the biased items had little practical effect on relative performance (i.e., mean standard scores were similar with or without the biased items). Other approaches to analyzing scores for bias may yield different results. Clearly, the need for further study remains. At the very least, all assessment results should be interpreted with caution. This is particularly true when the measurement scale is being used to diagnose disabilities. The dictum "Tests don't diagnose, people do" is always worth considering.

References

Adams, J., McIntosh, E. I., & Weade, B. L. (1973). Ethnic background, measured intelligence, and adaptive behavior scores in mentally retarded children. *American Journal of Mental Deficiency*, 78(1), 1-6.

Anastasi, A., & Urbina, S. (1997). *Psychological testing* (7th ed.). Upper Saddle River, NJ: Prentice-Hall.

Artiles, A. J., & Trent, S. C. (1994). Overrepresentation of minority students in special education: A continuing debate. *The Journal of Special Education*, 27(4), 410-437.

Baca, L. M., & Cervantes, H. T. (1989). *The bilingual special education interface* (2nd ed.). Columbus, OH: Merrill.

Boroskin, A., & Giampiccolo, J. S. (1971). Effect of staff ethnocentrism on the rating of self-help skills of minority group mentally retarded patients. *American Journal of Mental Deficiency*, 76(2), 249-251.

Brown, F. G. (1983). *Principles of educational psychology* (3rd ed.). New York: Holt, Rinehart, & Winston.

Bryant, B. R., Mathews, S. C., Ammer, J., Cronin, M., Mandlebaum, L., & Quinby, S. (in press). *American school psychoeducational assessment batteries: Technical manual*. Austin, TX: Pro-Ed.

Bryant, B. R., Taylor, R. L., & Rivera, D. P. (1996). *Assessment of adaptive areas*. Austin, TX: Pro-Ed.

Cohen, R. J., Swerdlik, M. E., & Smith, D. K. (1992). *Psychological testing and assessment*. Mountain View, CA: Mayfield.

Doll, E. A. (1965). *Vineland social maturity scale; condensed manual of directions*. Circle Pines, MN: American Guidance Service.

Ebel, R. L. (1972). *Essentials of educational measurement* (2nd ed.). Englewood Cliffs, NJ: Prentice-Hall.

Fine, M. A., Tangeman, P. J., & Woodard, J. (1990). Changes in adaptive behavior of older adults with mental retardation following deinstitutionalization. *American Journal of Mental Retardation*, 94(6), 661-668.

Flaugher, R. L. (1978). The many definitions of test bias. *American Psychologist*, 33, 671-679.

Garrett, H. E. (1965). *Testing for teachers* (2nd ed.). New York: American Book.

Guilford, J. P., & Fruchter, B. (1978). *Fundamental statistics in psychology and education*. New York: McGraw-Hill.

Hammill, D. D., Brown, L., & Bryant, B. R. (1992). *A consumer's guide to tests in print* (2nd ed.). Austin, TX: Pro-Ed.

Hammill, D. D., Pearson, N., & Wiederholt, J. L. (1996). *Comprehensive test of nonverbal intelligence*. Austin, TX: Pro-Ed.

Heber, R. (1961). A manual on terminology and classification on mental retardation (2nd ed). *American Journal of Mental Deficiency Monograph*, 65.

Jensen, A. R. (1980). *Bias in mental testing*. New York: Free Press.

Kaplan, R. M. (1985). The controversy related to the use of psychological tests. In B. B. Wolman (Ed.), *Handbook of intelligence: Theories, measurements, and applications* (pp. 465-504). New York: John Wiley.

Lambert, N. M. (1979). Contributions of school classification, sex, and ethnic status to adaptive behavior assessment. *Journal of School Psychology*, 17(1), 3-16.

Lambert, N. M. (1981). AAMD *Adaptive Behavior Scale*. Monterey, CA: Publishers Test Service.

Lambert, N. M. (1986). Evidence of age and ethnic status bias in factor scores and the comparison score for the AAMD Adaptive Behavior Scale—School Edition. *Journal of School Psychology*, 24, 143-153.

Lambert, N., Nihira, K., & Leland, H. (1993). AAMR *adaptive behavior scale—School Version* (2nd ed.). Austin, TX: Pro-Ed.

Lambert, N. M., Windmiller, M., & Cole, L. J. (1975). AAMD *adaptive behavior scale—Public school version*. Washington, DC: American Association on Mental Deficiency.

Leland, H. (1996). *Adaptive behavior scale for young children: Field test manual*. Unpublished manuscript. Austin, TX: Pro-Ed.

Luckasson, R., Coulter, D. L., Polloway, E.A., Reiss, S., Schalock, R. L., Snell, M. E., Spitalnick, D. M., & Stark, J. A. (1992). *Mental retardation: Diagnosis, classification, and systems of support* (9th ed.). Washington, DC: American Association on Mental Retardation.

MacMillan, D. L., Gresham, F. M., & Siperstein, G. N. (1993). Conceptual and psychometric concerns about the AAMR definition of mental retardation. *American Journal on Mental Retardation, 98*, 325-335.

McGloughlin, J. A., & Lewis, R. B. (1991). *Assessing special students* (3rd ed.). Columbus, OH: Merrill.

Mercer, J. R., & Lewis, J. F. (1977). *System of multicultural pluralistic assessment* (SOMPA). New York: Psychological Corp.

Muraki, E., & Engelhard, G. (1988, April). *Examining differential item functioning with BIMAIN.* Paper presented at the annual meeting of the American Educational Research Association, San Francisco.

Nihira, K., Leland, H., & Lambert, N. (1993). AAMR *Adaptive Behavior Scale—Residential and Community Version* (2nd ed). Austin, TX: Pro-Ed.

Oakland, T., & Feigenbaum, D. (1980). Comparisons of the psychometric characteristics of the Adaptive Behavior Inventory for Children for different subgroups of children. *Journal of School Psychology, 18*(4), 307-316.

Oakland, T., & Parmelee, R. (1985). Mental measurement of minority-group children. In B. B. Wolman (Ed.), *Handbook of intelligence: Theories, measurements, and applications* (pp. 699-736). New York: John Wiley.

Oosterhof, A. C. (1976). Similarity of various item discrimination indices. *Journal of Educational Measurement, 13*, 145-150.

Pyrczak, F. (1973). Validity of discrimination index as a measure of item validity. *Journal of Educational Measurement, 10*, 227-231.

Reschly, D. J. (1987). Assessing educational handicaps. In A. Hess & I. Weiner (Eds.), *Handbook of forensic psychology*. New York: John Wiley.

Reynolds, C. R., & Kaiser, S. M. (1990). Test bias in psychological assessment. In C. R. Reynolds & T. B. Gutkin (Eds.), *The handbook of school psychology* (pp. 496-525). New York: John Wiley.

Ross, R. T. (1970). *Manual for the Fairview Self-Help Scale.* Sacramento, California: State of California.

Salagaras, S., & Nettleback, T. (1983). Adaptive behavior of mentally retarded adolescents attending school. *American Journal of Mental Deficiency, 88*(1), 57-68.

Sattler, J. M. (1988). *Assessment of children* (3rd ed.). San Diego: Author.

Scott, L. S., Mastenbrook, J. L., Fisher, A. T., & Gridley, G. C. (1982). Adaptive Behavior Inventory for Children: The need for local norms. *Journal of School Psychology, 20*(1), 39-44.

Shepard, L., Camilli, G., & Williams, D. (1985). Validity of approximation techniques for detecting item bias. *Journal of Educational Measurement, 22*, 77-105.

Slate, N. M. (1983). Nonbiased assessment of adaptive behavior: Comparison of three instruments. *Exceptional Children, 50*(1), 67-70.

Slosson, R. L., Nicholson, C. L., & Hibpshman, T. H. (1990). *Slosson intelligence test for children and adults.* East Aurora, NY: Slosson.

Springer, N. N. (1941). The social competence of adolescent delinquents: A comparative study of white and negro first offenders and recidivists. *Journal of School Psychology, 14,* 337-348.

Taylor, R. L. (1997). *Assessment of exceptional students* (4th ed.). Boston: Allyn and Bacon.

U.S. Bureau of the Census. (1990). *Statistical abstract of the United States.* Washington, DC: Author.

Weber, D. B., & Epstein, H. R. (1980). Contrasting adaptive behavior ratings of male and female institutionalized residents across two settings. *American Journal of Mental Deficiency, 84*(4), 397-400.

Witt, J. C., Elliott, S. N., Gresham, F. M., & Kramer, J. J. (1988). *Assessment of special children.* Boston: Scott, Foresman.

CHAPTER 9

Critical Issues in the Cross-Cultural Assessment of Adaptive Behavior[1]

MARC J. TASSÉ
Université du Québec à Montréal

ELLIS M. CRAIG
Texas Department of Mental Health and Mental Retardation

Introduction

Adaptive behavior is included in all major classification systems (i.e., American Association on Mental Retardation [AAMR; Luckasson, et al., 1992]); *Diagnostic and Statistical Manual of Mental Disorders* [DSM-IV; American Psychiatric Association, 1994]; *International Classification of Diseases* [ICD-10; World Health Organization, 1992]) as one of the essential criteria in diagnosing mental retardation. So it is important to be able to assess the adaptive behavior of individuals of all cultural and linguistic backgrounds.

Leland (1983), when explaining the concept of adaptive behavior, frequently referred to the degree of "visibility" of the individual. The more the individual with significant deficits in intellectual functioning is skilled in adapting to his or her social context and its demands, the more "invisible" the individual becomes. Society takes notice of individuals who have difficulty conforming to its demands and expectations. Each different society or culture imposes different demands and has different expectations for its members.

Thus, whether or not an individual has a deficit in adaptive behavior is in part determined by societal or cultural factors. Cultural differences may become cultural disadvantages when one's ability is measured on the metric of a cultural group different from that person's own (Anastasi, 1988; Mercer, 1976).

A number of issues in cross-cultural assessment of adaptive behavior are critical as we move toward a multicultural society. Mercer (1979), for example, noted a wide range of opinion regarding cultural pluralism in assessment practices (e.g., socioculturally sensitive approaches), with some in the field being highly supportive and others being vehemently opposed. Mercer argued in favor of cultural pluralism, noting that criterion performance should be established by members of the social system, not the test designers.

This chapter examines some of the more critical issues involved in completing and interpreting adaptive behavior assessments of individuals from diverse cultural groups. The chapter begins with a brief historical perspective of the role that cultural stereotypes and biases may have played in the conception and definition for mental retardation. We then discuss culturally related critical issues, including special-education placement, criminal liability, maladaptive behaviors, assessment strategies, cultural communication styles and informant interviews, and culturally competent assessments. In the final sections we address translating and adapting adaptive behavior scales into other languages or cultures.

[1]The writing of this chapter was supported in part by grant No. 98-NC-1734 from FCAR (Fonds pour la formation de Chercheurs et l'Aide à la Recherche).

Historical Perspective

The importance of adaptive behavior in definitions of mental retardation was recognized by the originator of intelligence testing, Alfred Binet, who in 1905 stated:

> An individual is normal if he is able to conduct his affairs of life without having need of supervision of others, if he is able to do work sufficiently remunerative to supply his own personal needs and finally if his intelligence does not unfit him for the social environment of his parents (as cited in Coulter, 1980, p. 67).

Horn and Fuchs (1987) completed an interesting historical analysis of the role of adaptive behavior in views on mental retardation. They pointed out that, prior to the introduction of intelligence testing early in the 20th century, mental retardation was identified primarily by the existence of observable physical defects or unusual behaviors. The concept of mild mental retardation was apparently not even considered. After intelligence testing became established in the early 1900s, cognitive skills were the focus of attention in the diagnosis of mental retardation, with relatively little attention given to assessment of a broader range of adaptive behaviors. The widespread and unreserved reliance on IQ scores during this era led to one of the earliest examples of biased cross-cultural assessment. This was the infamous period when most mental retardation was assumed to be genetic and large nationality groups of immigrants were labeled as "feeble minded" on the basis of very suspect testing procedures.

Cronbach (1975) provided an insightful historical discussion of the public and scientific attitudes toward mental testing. Initially, researchers thought that such objective methods would lead to more efficiency and fairness with respect to a variety of social issues. However, both scientists and the general public were often guilty of "incautious interpretations" of test results. This has resulted in charges of racist motives, ranging from the eugenics movement of the 1920s to "Jensenism" in the 1960s, and even the recent "bell-shaped curve" controversy.

Although the primary focus of concern in the diagnosis of mental retardation has been with intelligence tests, the analysis of cultural differences in adaptive behavior should take into account history and its lessons. Baumeister and Muma (1975) provided a thoughtful discussion of the interaction between cultural differences and the diagnosis of mental retardation. They decried the tendency to regard categorically many disadvantaged people as mentally retarded because they had not adapted "appropriately." They argued that the functional context of the person's life must be considered.

Cole and Bruner (1971) saw the most common interpretation of ethnic and social class differences in intellectual performance as being a deficit hypothesis. The hypothesis assumes that groups living in poverty are disorganized, resulting in various forms of performance deficit. The authors provided a review of data and theory argue against this position; they especially criticized the concept of linguistic deprivation in minority and poverty groups. But their principal point, was that cultural differences arise primarily from a different history of situations to which a person must adapt, rather than from any innate group differences in ability to adapt. Nevertheless, such differences are often labeled as deficits because the standard has been based on Anglo, middle-class expectations.

DeVault and Long (1988) argued that the distinction between cultural deprivation and cultural differences has not been adequately taken into account in many cross-cultural studies. In a 1979 article, Mercer argued that racially and culturally nondiscriminatory assessment is based on the assumption that the different groups have the same average potential for learning culturally valued skills, and that any group differences on standardized tests are a result of differential exposure to the culturally related skills measured by a scale.

There is not universal agreement that the concept of adaptive behavior has been a positive addition to the field of mental retardation. Clausen (1972), for example, argued against the addition of adaptive behavior measures in the definition of mental retardation. Although agreeing that social problems have historically been what have brought attention to this group, he suggested that the causes of social incompetency have their roots in intellectual limitations.

Baumeister and Muma (1975) also acknowledged that usually some problem of adaptive behavior initially leads to a diagnosis of mental retardation. Nevertheless, they argued that adaptive behavior remained a vague and ill-defined concept. Further, they considered it unlikely that adaptive behavior instruments could be developed that would adequately sample the various situations in which one might have to adapt. With the high correlations between scores on adaptive behavior scales and intelligence tests, any such test might well come to be considered a "poor man's intelligence test."

Zigler, Balla, and Hodapp (1984) attacked the imprecision of adaptive behavior measures relative to intelligence tests and suggested focusing only on the latter in defining mental retardation. Others have also pointed out the lack of consensus among professionals as to the exact nature of the construct (Bailey & Harbin, 1980). Examples include the varying content and lack of correlation among scales. In fact, Bailey and Harbin suggested that the rationale for use of adaptive behavior in diagnosing mental retardation may be more political than evidentiary.

Lynch and Hanson (1992) indicated that cultural bias is often more evident in the assessment process than in other services. In certain ethnic groups, children may not have had the opportunity to practice certain behaviors contained on a scale. And yet efforts to take into account cultural differences can in themselves be problematic. For example, there is often very wide variance in performance among individuals and subgroups of any cultural or ethnic grouping. Attempting to characterize a group on the basis of a few broad traits may be simplistic and misleading (Park, Pullis, Reilly, & Townsend, 1994).

For a number of years, colleagues in the field have recommended that ethnic and sociocultural factors in the assessment of adaptive behavior be considered as a part of the various diagnostic and classification systems. Exactly what should be considered and what adjustments made is not clear. An attempt to begin filling this gap is a major purpose of this monograph. The cross-cultural literature emphasizes a number of critical issues that should be considered in the cross-cultural assessment of adaptive behavior. The following review summarizes some of the most important publications.

Culturally Related Issues

Special-Education Placement

Special attention should be focused on the area of special education, as this is where cross-cultural issues frequently present a significant problem. Brady, Manni, and Winikur (1983) discussed the government's efforts to address disproportionate minority representation in special-education placement through the Education of all Handicapped Children Act of 1975 regulations. A section of those regulations, "Protection in Evaluation Procedures," specifies practices and procedures that should ensure nonbiased assessment. Key components of the newly required procedures include adaptive behavior assessments and multidisciplinary teams for evaluation and decision making. Reis (1986) described a model assessment process to address overrepresentation of minority ethnic groups in special-education placement. This process included evaluation of the learning environment, evaluation of a broad array of intelligence tests, evaluation of community-oriented adaptive behavior assessments, determination that the goals of special-class placement could not be as readily achieved in a regular class, and ongoing assessment of the appropriateness of the special-class placement.

Reschly (1981, 1988) provided an extensive review of the litigation associated with special-education placement. There have been two major types of litigation: right to education and placement bias. The right-to-education cases focus on access to public schools and appropriate educational services, especially for students with severe disabilities. The placement-bias cases, on the other hand, have emphasized the need for less, rather than more, special-education services by focusing on the overrepresentation of minorities in the special-education classes. Results of the latter litigation have included a sharp decline in the number of students classified as mentally retarded (especially the mild group), more stringent IQ cutoffs, and increased emphasis on adaptive behavior. Early (pre-1975) litigation resulted in the establishment of due process rights in the placement process and assessment reforms including translations of tests, increased emphasis on adaptive behavior, and decreased emphasis on IQ. Subsequently, the most well known litigation, *Larry P. v. Riles* (1984), led to a ban on the use of intelligence tests with African American students. However, later judicial decisions (e.g., *Pace v. Hannon, Marshall v. Georgia,* & *S-1 v. Turlington*) allowed the continued use of IQ as a criterion as long as the assessment reforms were in place.

Koegel and Edgerton (1982) tested the validity of the concept of the "six-hour retarded child." This concept assumes that many minority children, while doing poorly in academic subjects, are indistinguishable from their peers in community living skills. Additionally, they are unlikely to be identified as having mental retardation outside of the school environment. The authors conducted a follow-up study of African American special-education students and found that the majority did have significant difficulties in daily life. Lack of academic skills was a major factor.

A number of studies were conducted on the impact of the use of the Mercer and Lewis (1978) *System of Multicultural Pluralistic Assessment* (SOMPA) and in particular its *Adaptive Behavior Inventory for Children* (ABIC) on minority overrepresentation. Reschly (1981) examined the impact of adding ABIC scores as a criterion in addition to IQ to determine the prevalence of mild mental retardation in a sample of children of four different ethnic groups. Use of the IQ alone (-2 SD cutoff) resulted in a disproportionate number of minority children identified as mildly retarded (2% of the Anglos as compared to 9% of the African Americans, 9% of the Latinos, and 18% of the Native Americans). Requiring the IQ and ABIC scores both to be two standard deviations below the mean reduced the prevalence to 0.7% in the Anglo group and 0.8% in the Latino group. No African or Native American children were identified under the dual criterion. It was concluded that a dual criterion measure (especially if using the ABIC) would lower the prevalence of diagnosed mild mental retardation to less than 0.5% rather than the 2% figure accepted generally. Childs (1982) explored the impact of using ABIC scores below the third percentile as a criterion for continuing special-education eligibility. The results indicated an 80% declassification rate and 88% for minority children.

Reschly and Ward (1991) addressed the factors involved in the overrepresentation of African American students in special-education placements. Although representing only about 16% of all students nationally, they constitute about 35% of the group identified in the schools as mildly mentally retarded. A key question is whether these placements have been based primarily on IQ scores, or if adaptive behavior deficits were routinely a part of the decision. The authors studied this issue in a random sample of special-education students in Iowa. They found that only half of the students had been assessed with a standardized, normed adaptive behavior assessment scale and that about a third had been placed without any adaptive behavior deficits being identified. However, there was not differential treatment between Anglo and African American students in this regard.

A book edited by Peterson and Ishii-Jordan (1994) contains a review of multicultural issues in special-education programs for the seriously emotionally disturbed (or behaviorally disordered). The issues of concern with this population overlap with those of concern with people diagnosed with mental retardation. The impact of cross-cultural influences and the need for culturally sensitive assessment are especially marked in the educational setting.

Criminal Liability

Some have questioned whether mental retardation is overdiagnosed in criminal populations. Benton (1956), for example, indicated that a misdiagnosis of mental retardation is most commonly made with children exhibiting delinquent or antisocial behavior. Further, some of the conditions (i.e., poverty and ethnic minority status) associated with crime rates also have been associated with intellectual mild retardation (Nelson & Pearson, 1994).

There are unique assessment issues associated with this population. DeVault and Long (1988), for example, proposed indicators of malingering (purposely performing poorly on intelligence tests) in criminal trials. A decline in functional skills, especially in practice rounds, is a key indicator of malingering. Further, historical assessment of adaptive functioning in a variety of areas may well indicate the possibility of malingering.

Baroff (1990) discussed the diagnostic issues involved in assessing individuals suspected of mental retardation who are charged with crimes. He noted, for example, criminal courts' readiness to suspect malingering if there had been no previous diagnosis but the person's current scores suggest mental retardation. Practice effects from repeated testing need to be weighed along with real scores. With regard to adaptive behavior, the

author suggested that most individuals with IQs above 60 should be able to function adequately in the major adult roles and therefore would not meet the criteria for a diagnosis of mental retardation.

In a 1991 article, Baroff discussed the issues surrounding the diagnosis of mental retardation in capital cases. With regard to competency to stand trial, the key issues are understanding the charges and the legal process, ability to give information about the alleged crime, and the ability to assist a lawyer in one's own defense. The author noted that a finding of incompetence is usually made only for individuals with IQs below 50. But he also pointed out that the Miranda rights against self-incrimination are presented at about a 7th-grade reading level, higher than that for most individuals with mild mental retardation. Baroff also explored the relevance of adaptive behavior measures in capital cases. He stressed that most serious crimes reflect behaviors not captured on typical adaptive behavior scales. Further, he rejected the notion that criminal behavior per se is evidence of an adaptive behavior impairment. Yet Baroff did suggest a modification of current diagnostic procedures to allow a diagnosis of mental retardation even if an adaptive behavior deficit is not present—if the individual is unable to weigh the consequences of his or her actions.

Sensitivity to cross-cultural influences on both intellectual and adaptive behavior functioning of individuals accused of criminal offenses is extremely important. Protection of the rights of the individuals involved, as well as making accurate diagnoses of mental retardation in this population, merit much more attention and study.

Maladaptive Behaviors

The inclusion or exclusion of maladaptive behavior as an essential element in the construct of adaptive behavior remains controversial. Some scales, such as the *Vineland Adaptive Behavior Scale* (VABS; Sparrow,

Balla & Cicchetti, 1984), made no reference to it, and assessment in school settings has focused on the development of adaptive skills. The more widely used scales usually have sections addressing maladaptive behavior, but the scoring is separate, with no attempt to combine the measures (*Inventory for Client and Agency Planning*; Bruininks, Hill, Weatherman, & Woodcock, 1986, being one exception). In fact, the 1992 AAMR diagnosis and classification system (Luckasson et al.) does not formally include the maladaptive element in the diagnosis of mental retardation (except in a general sense as part of the social adaptive skills area). Instead, maladaptive behaviors are part of a psychiatric classification system in an assessment dimension called "psychological/ emotional considerations." The point has been made that most of the maladaptive behaviors included in various scales also occur in individuals without mental retardation, so are not diagnostic of it but merely represent an overlying psychiatric disorder. The Editorial Board for the American Psychological Association *Manual of Diagnosis and Professional Practice in Mental Retardation* (Jacobson & Mulick, 1996) has taken the position that presence of maladaptive behaviors, without significant limitations in adaptive skills, does not meet the criteria for a diagnosis of mental retardation.

Assessment Strategies

There are three primary strategies for obtaining the information necessary to complete an adaptive behavior assessment: verbal interviews with the individual being assessed, direct naturalistic or controlled observation of the person being assessed, or verbal interviews with a third-party informant who knows detailed information about the assessee. Most adaptive behavior scales rely on parent, teacher, or other third-party interviews rather than direct observation. Reliance on direct interviews with the assessee are relatively rare.

Although the interview approach is efficient, the information gathered may be of questionable validity (Bailey & Harbin, 1980). McCarver and Campbell (1987) noted, for example, that the reliance on third-party informants in adaptive behavior measurement stands in marked contrast to the procedures used with most other psychological and educational tests, where direct observation is more the norm. Regardless of potential problems, such as having biased or uninformed informants, the third-party interview approach will probably continue in part because of the emphasis in the field on measuring typical rather than optimal performance. Nevertheless, the authors called for increased use of direct observation and development of veracity measures. For instance, the ABIC (Mercer & Lewis, 1978) contains a veracity scale that identifies in parental reports gross exaggeration of a child's functioning.

Harrison (1987) warned that caution should be used in selecting informants, as several studies have found significant differences between the reports of parents and teachers. Higher adaptive behavior ratings by parents than by teachers were reported by MacMann and Barnett (1984) and Heath and Obrzut (1986).

Wolfensberger and Kurtz (1971) obtained developmental age estimates of children from the parents' perspectives and compared these to professional assessments. Parental estimates in general were relatively similar to the professional developmental age findings, although the parents tended to estimate lower self-help skill levels and higher communication skills than the professionals. No significant differences were observed between the estimates of fathers and mothers.

Mealor and Richmond (1980) compared adaptive behavior ratings by parents and teachers of Anglo and African American children with mental retardation. No significant differences were found between the two ethnic groups, but the parents gave higher ratings than the teachers in the self-help dimension (independent functioning, physical development, and economic, domestic, and vocational activity). It was noted that the higher parental ratings occurred primarily in areas where the parents were likely to have more experience with the children than did the teachers.

Voelker et al. (1990) compared the VABS (Sparrow et al., 1984) scores of adult group-home residents serving as self-informants with the information provided by the residents' counselors. For the adaptive skills, the results were very similar, although the counselors gave slightly higher ratings. On the maladaptive scales, however, the self-reports indicated significantly less problem behavior than reported by the counselors. It was suggested that this might be due to defensiveness regarding problem behaviors.

An evaluation of the optimal assessment strategy for various items on the *Adaptive Behavior Scale* (ABS; Nihira, Foster, Shellhaas, & Leland, 1974) was reported by Taylor and Ivimey (1982). On 9 of 10 domains of Part 1 of the scale (adaptive skills), raters preferred a naturalistic observation approach over interviewing an informant. For severe maladaptive behaviors, informant interviewing was preferred. For certain behaviors (e.g., economic and domestic activity) controlled observation (setting up a specific testing situation) was the preferred mode. The authors suggested that all three modes of assessment are probably necessary for valid assessment.

Keller (1988) also emphasized the importance of a multitrait, multimethod assessment strategy, especially with minority group individuals. He noted that the individual being assessed should be the primary source of data for cognitive and communication skills; independent functioning and social responsibility are most efficiently assessed through informants such as parents and teachers. Identified problem areas should be addressed more directly through observation and task analysis. In summary, especially for ethnic minorities, Keller strongly recommended that a multimethod assessment strategy be used.

Cultural Communication Styles and Informant Interviews

For an extremely valuable review of the values, beliefs, and communication styles of the major ethnic groups in the United States, see *Developing Cross-Cultural Competence*, edited by Lynch and Hanson (1992). Miranda (1993) discussed communication styles in the context of completing assessments of culturally diverse families. Special care needs to be taken if the family is bilingual. For example, when using a translator, one should make periodic checks of understanding by asking the person to repeat what has been communicated. In high-context cultures such as African American and many other minority groups, precise verbal communication may be less important than use of examples. Nonverbal communication styles should also be noted, including degree and type of eye contact, facial expressions, personal space, and gestures. Finally, it is important to understand the family structure, including how decisions are made and the roles of various family members.

In a review of racial "experimenter effects" on performance, Sattler (1970) reported inconclusive findings with regard to performance on intelligence tests when the examiner was of a different race than the testee. In interview situations, however, respondents appear to either inhibit or give socially conforming responses, especially if the interviewer is Anglo and the respondent African American. For communicating and working with African Americans Willis (1992) recommended including extended family members, using informal support networks (e.g., churches and friends), being familiar with the resources in the African American community, and expressing respect by addressing family members formally.

Joe and Malach (1992) provided some important recommendations on how to develop good communication with Native American families. For example, the parents of a child being assessed should be asked who they want to have present, because extended family members may be even more involved than the parents in the rearing of the child. If so, communication should be directed at the entire group. Proceed at a pace that is comfortable for the family. Further, if an interpreter is needed, that person should be chosen by the family if possible.

The high-context communication style of Asian cultures has been described by Chan (1992). Respect for authority and polite, deferential interactions with those outside the family are important values; thus, a parent might give a positive answer to a professional's question that is not fully understood if the parent thinks that is the polite thing to do. Similarly, smiling and direct eye contact with strangers is considered inappropriate, and Asians may maintain of a larger personal space when talking to others. There may be marked distrust or suspicion of outsiders, so professional staff working with such families need to ensure that respected authorities in the community have provided some sanction of the activity. Initiating frank discussions of problem areas may be overwhelming until a more trusting relationship has been established. Even then, indirect approaches to the problem may be necessary. Flexibility regarding the site and pace of assessment activities is also important.

Sharifzadeh (1992) described a necessary strategy for communicating with immigrant families from the Middle East. If an assessment is being made of a child with a suspected disability, the interaction should customarily be with the father. This may be problematic because the father may not know the details of the child's developmental history. If sufficient information cannot be obtained, it may be necessary to enlist the aid of a friend or relative of the family to assist with the assessment.

Zuniga (1992) recommended the cultural practice of *platicando* in communicating with Latino individuals and families. This involves an atmosphere of relaxed and informal conversation, rather than a more formal interview style. Although this might be viewed as an inefficient approach, it probably leads to more valid assessment results.

Culturally Competent Assessments

Lynch and Hanson (1992) provided several recommendations regarding culturally competent assessments. In summary:

- Select valid instruments for the language and culture of the individual and the family.
- Use a trained interpreter proficient in the language and cultural cues.
- Conduct the assessment at a time when people important to the family can be present.
- Conduct the assessment at a location comfortable for the family
- Collect information in areas of family concern.
- Explain every step and purpose of the assessment.

Translation or Adaptation of Adaptive Behavior Scales

The literature is replete with examples demonstrating the influence of cultural variables on measuring traits and constructs (cf. Dana, 1993; Helms-Lorenz & Van de Vijver, 1995). Because the criterion for successful measurement of adaptive behavior is performance and not capability (i.e., we do not assess whether the person is capable but rather whether the person emits the behavior), it is crucial to assess only culturally appropriate skills. For example, we do not ask, "Can the person eat with a fork and knife," but rather, "*Does the* person eat with a fork and knife?" This particular item question is laden with cultural bias. In some cultural groups, individuals are neither taught nor expected to perform certain skills (e.g., eating with chop sticks vs. using a fork). Each culture and subculture encourages and fosters the mastery of certain skills, while discouraging or minimizing the importance of mastering other skills (Hinkle, 1994). To adequately assess adaptive skills across cultural and linguistic groups, one must be sensitive both to group differences and the following four specific issues: intralingual adaptations, translation, translation equivalence, and bias.

Intralingual Adaptations

Adaptive behavior scales sometimes need to be adapted when cultural expectations differ, even when the language of the scale remains unchanged. A ficitious example of an intralingual translation or adaptation might be a British Adaptive Behavior Scale developed, field-tested, and normed in Great Britain. Although it would be written in English, an American clinician or researcher would need to validate or adapt the wording of the items before using it. For example, an item in the "Use of Community Resources" section might state, "Purchases needed supplies at the chemist." Left unmodified, this item could cause confusion and inaccurate responses as American respondents might not know that a chemist in England is what Americans call a pharmacist. A similar item might be "Uses the lift unassisted," which could be interpreted as using a fork-lift rather than an elevator. Intralingual adaptations could pertain to item stems tapping country-specific resources. Canadians and Europeans might be at a loss when trying to use a fictitious Adaptive Behavior Scale of America unless an item such as the following were adapted: "Shops for, and purchases, his or her own managed-care plan." Geographical adaptations are also important; test items involving snow removal may be an appropriate adaptive skill in Vermont or Minnesota but would need to be eliminated when assessing individuals living in southern states.

Investing time, effort, and thought in a careful initial translation will inevitably result in greater validity and cross-cultural equivalence. Test translation or adaptation should not be viewed as an economical way of delivering a test to a new population. Translating a test into a different language or adapting it for a different cultural group demands as much work and empirical validation as

constructing a new test (Jackson, 1991). Why then, if it is as much work as developing a new test, do we often prefer to translate or adapt an existing test? Hambleton and Kanjee's (1995) answer may be the most plausible: because there is a sense of security and potential for better marketing success in translating or adapting an established test that has withstood the test of scrutiny.

Translation

Translating a phrase or text requires more than merely transcribing words into another language. Wilss (1990) defined translation as the process of reproducing both content and style. When translating or adapting test items from one language or culture to another, the test developer must attempt to reproduce the *meaning* of the stem and not render a mere literal transformation.

Translators must be fluent in both languages and know well the target culture. It is generally preferable that they translate to their stronger language. It is a distinct advantage throug not essential that translators possess an expertise in the construct the scale purports to measure. Translators and content experts should work collaboratively to ensure a reliable and accurate translation or adaptation of the scale; important insight into the test items' meaning can be provided by working closely with the developers of the scale.

Translating or adapting a test is but the first of a long elaborate process of developing a scale to be used with a different cultural or lingual group. Literal translation may work well if translating a technical manual, but it is not always recommended and may, especially in the case of testing, compromise the validity of the translated document. Consider translating the *Scales of Independent Behavior* (Bruininks, Woodcock, Weatherman, & Hill, 1996) from English to Italian, Item 8 of the "Money & Value/Adaptive Behavior" section, "Gives the exact amount of money to buy something that costs less than $1.00." It would be erroneous for the Italian translator to use the Italian ". . . un dollaro" to represent the SIB's "$1.00," because there is no such denomination in the Italian currency. The translation or adaptation would best be done using the equivalent Italian denomination of "1,000 lire."

When translating test items, the primary concern should be the meaning (skill that is being assessed) of the items and not a robotic translation of equivalent wording in a different language. Hambleton (1996) provided a clear example of this with a maxim to be translated: "Out of sight, out of mind" when back-translated may result in "blind, insane." Regardless of the method of validation of the translation, this example clearly highlights the importance of closely verifying the equivalence of meaning between the original language items and the translated language items.

The information given to the translators plays an important role in ensuring a quality translation. To facilitate the translation and later adjustments, the translators should be given a brief lesson on the purpose of the scale (i.e., the construct measured, how the test scores are used) and be instructed in the following manner:

- Don't try to make the test harder or more easily understood than the source language version.
- Try to capture the *psychological meaning* of the item stem instead of merely reproducing its semantic meaning.
- Keep the structure and format identical as the one used in the source item.
- When in doubt, fall back on the wording of the source item.

The *Standards for Educational and Psychological Testing* (*Standards*; American Psychological Association, 1985) have a section on testing linguistic minorities. When translating a test from one language to another language or dialect, the translated test's validity and reliability must be established. The *Standards* make no mention of adapting a test for a different cultural group within a common linguistic group (e.g., U.S. to Great Britain);

however, the chapters on technical standards for test construction and evaluation (i.e., validity; reliability and errors of measurement; test development and revision; scaling, norming, score comparability, and equating; and technical manuals and user's guides) certainly apply to test translation and adaptation as they do to any test elaboration process.

Translation Equivalence

Although there exists a plethora of assessment instruments that have been translated into several different languages, the translation equivalence has rarely been empirically established (Okazaki & Sue, 1995). This section discusses three methods used to assess the linguistic or cultural equivalence of two versions (i.e., source and target) of a translated or adapted scale: back-translation, decentering, and committee approach. These methods are designed to translate and verify the quality of the translation or adaptation and represent but one small step in a lengthy validation process.

Back-Translation Method

Back-translation involves one person translating from the original (source) language to the other (target) language and a second person blindly (without having seen the original document) translating the text back to the source language. Adjustments are generally made to the target version, depending on discrepancies identified between the back-translated version and the original version. Back-translation is generally an iterative procedure (see Figure 9.1) employing different translators for each different translation (Brislin, 1986). An example of this would be to have someone translate the proposed *Culturally Individualized Assessment of Adaptive Behavior* (CIABS; Heal & Tassé, in this volume) from English to Spanish, and then have a second translator, who would never have seen the CIABS, translate the Spanish version back to English. This method permits qualitative comparison between the author's original English version and the back-translated

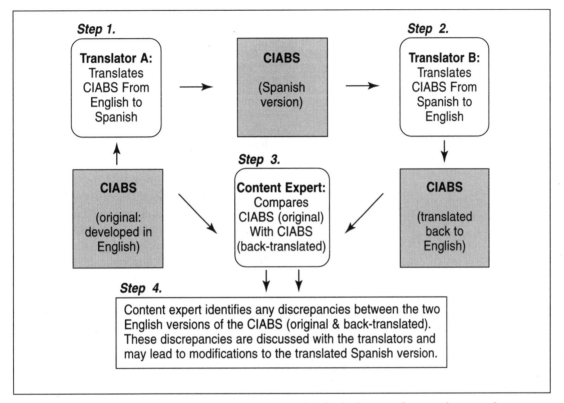

Figure 9.1. *Back-translation procedure.* CIABS = *Culturally Invidivualized Adaptive Behavior Scale, proposed by Heal & Tassé, this volume.*

English. Its obvious advantage is to provide the unilingual test developers (perhaps the author of the original scale) the opportunity to assess the quality of the translation.

When comparing the original version of a scale with the back-translated version, the evaluator looks for any differences in conveyed meaning between the two. Sinaiko and Brislin (1973) proposed six types of meaning errors to look for:

- *Addition*: A word or phrase appears in the back-translation that is not in the original.
- *Omission (minor)*: One or two words are missing in the back-translation that appear in the original.
- *Omission (major)*: Three or more words are missing in the back-translation that appear in the original.
- *Garbling*: Three or more words in the back-translation are incomprehensible.

- *Substitution (minor)*: One or two words from the original have been replaced by a brief phrase (usually when there is no word-for-word equivalent in the target language).
- *Substitution (major)*: Three or more words from the original have been replaced by a brief phrase (usually when there is no word-for-word equivalent in the target language).

Several authors have suggested that back-translation is the procedure of choice when verifying the accuracy of a translation (Brislin, 1986; Haccoun, 1987; Vallerand, 1989). Others have outlined the limitations of this procedure with respect to sacrifices in grammar and meaning in an effort to replicate the exact wording of the original language (Geisinger, 1994; Hambleton, 1993, 1996; Van de Vijver & Hambleton, 1996; Verdier & Laplège, 1995).

Hambleton (1996) demonstrated clearly that discrepancies occur between two groups of translators when one group has been previously informed that their translation would be "back-translated." The informed translators' versions were more literal and less respectful of the sense or meaning of the original items. Hence, when the informed translators' versions were back-translated to the original language, they were quite accurate. But when examined from the perspective of the target language, the items did not always clearly reflect the original item content.

There are pros of the translation to back-translation method: It is relatively inexpensive; it is easy to implement; and the content experts evaluating the translation need not be bilingual. However, discrepancies between the original and back-translated tests may be due to errors introduced by the back-translator rather than the translator. Verdier and Laplège (1995) note that proponents of translation to back-translation methods frequently overlook the fallibility of the back-translator. In the back-translation procedure, the content expert's appraisal of the quality of translation can be compromised in two ways: (a) error can be introduced by the back-translator; or (b) unless specifically instructed otherwise, the back-translator may often correct imperfections in the translated text, thus camouflaging errors of translation. Because verification of translation quality can be compromised by either of these ways, back-translation should not be the sole method employed to verify the equivalence of the original version and the translated version (Sinaiko & Brislin, 1973).

Decentering Approach

A close relative of the back-translation procedure is decentering. In decentering, a scale is translated from the original language to a target language and then back-translated to the original language by a second independent translator. In decentering, identified discrepancies in the original and back-translated versions may lead to changes to either scale (i.e., translated version or original version). Whereas in the basic back-translation method, modifications are made only to the translated

version until equivalence is attained, in a decentering approach both the original and the target versions are important and open to modifications (Brislin, Lonner, & Thorndike, 1973). As shown in Figure 9.2, the decentering technique can be depicted as an iterative process where the original and translated scales are continuously modified until equivalence between the scale's original version and its translated version is attained.

In the example presented in Figure 9.2, the original version of the CIABS 1.0 (English) is given to Translator A (Step 1), who does a translation and produces the CIABS 1.0 (Spanish). The CIABS 1.0 (Spanish) is given to Translator B for a back-translation. The CIABS back-translation (English) is compared to the original CIABS 1.0 (English), discrepancies are noted, and it is determined that they result from difficult wording in the original CIABS 1.0 (English). The CIABS 1.0 (English) is modified in accordance with the observations and produces the CIABS S 1.1 (English). The CIABS 1.1 (English) is given to Translator C for a new Spanish translation (Step 2) that results in CIABS 1.1 (Spanish). The CIABS 1.1 (Spanish) is given to Translator D for a back-translation. The CIABS back-translation (English) is compared to the new source test, CIABS 1.1 (English). Discrepancies are noted, and it is determined that they result from errors in the Spanish translation. The CIABS 1.1 (Spanish) is modified (Step 3) according to the observations, producing the CIABS 1.2 (Spanish). The CIABS 1.2 (Spanish) is given to Translator E for a back-translation. The CIABS back-translation (English) is compared to the source test, CIABS 1.1 (English). No significant discrepancies are noted, and it is decided to keep the last versions as final: CIABS 1.1 (English) and CIABS 1.2 (Spanish). If a term or word survives the decentering process, it is assumed to be culturally unbiased (that is, *etic*), because the word or term has an equivalent in both languages (Brislin, 1986).

The decentering technique is certainly time consuming, may be labor intensive, and may have especially limited use with adaptive

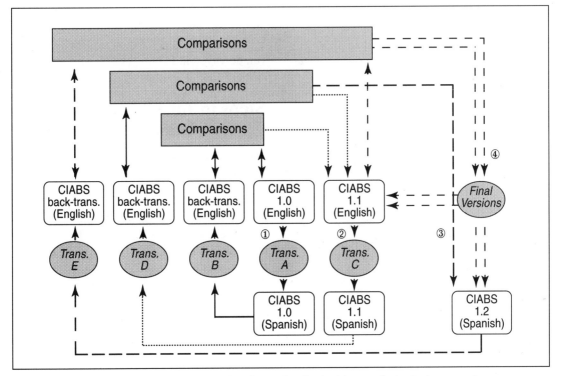

Figure 9.2. *Decentering procedure.* CIABS = *Culturally Invidivualized Adaptive Behavior Scale, proposed by Heal & Tassé, this volume.*

behavior scales that have a long history of use. This technique may be most useful at the initial phases of scale development if versions for diverse lingual or cultural groups are developed conjointly with the original scale or when experimental scales are developed to be used in cross-cultural studies of adaptive skills. Bravo, Woodbury-Farina, Canino, and Rubio-Stipec (1993) used decentering during the initial developmental phases of the *Diagnostic Interview Schedule for Children* (DISC) to translate and adapt the DISC to Spanish.

Committee Approach
The committee approach focuses on obtaining a high-quality initial translation by working with a variety of individuals who are bilingual and/or content experts. This approach employs several translators working individually or in small independent groups. The committee will be most effective if composed of both professional translators and bilingual content

experts (Hambleton, 1993). The team of translators meets to compare and discuss their respective translations. This process of exchange is important in striving to achieve one final consensual translation. Translators debate format using the original scale as the basis for all discussions. It may at times be helpful to invite one or more content experts who were not involved in the translation to participate in the discussions pertaining to the construct or to answer questions about the meaning of the source item stem.

This type of committee approach has gained increasing popularity over the back-translation method (Geisinger, 1994; Hambleton, 1993; 1996; Van de Vijver & Hambleton, 1996; Van de Vijver & Leung, 1997). Geisinger has recommended using translators to perform an initial translation and then a review panel or committee to critique the translation. According to Geisinger, the committee should review the translation by focusing on three essential elements: (a) review and comment on items, (b) share their comments with other committee members, and (c) work out a consensus as to the appropriate final formulation of the translation. Geisinger suggests excluding the translators from the committee's discussions. We believe the involvement of all who work on the translation is valuable throughout the process of translation or adaptation and modification.

Bias

Bias refers to extraneous factors that impinge upon the validity of comparing scores across groups; measurement equivalence is the degree to which scores obtained in different cultural or linguistic groups may be compared (Van de Vijver & Leung, 1997). Bias is an indication of the presence of systematic or consistent error of measurement as opposed to random or chance error (Anastasi, 1988). A test is biased if two individuals from different cultures, but with identical amounts of the trait measured by the test, obtain two significantly different scores. When comparing cross-cultural groups on an identical measure, bias will dampen the comparability of the observed scores. One should not assume that when adapting a test to another language or culture the construct measured by the test will be identical in the other language or culture (American Psychological Association, 1985; Lonner, 1990). There is no guarantee that a construct elaborated within one culture will retain the same functional significance when exported to a different linguistic or cultural group. The Standards (American Psychological Association, 1985) are quite clear on this point: "One cannot assume that translation produces a version of the test that is equivalent in content, difficulty level, reliability, and validity. Psychometric properties cannot be assumed to be comparable across languages or dialects" (p. 73). If test developers and users keep this in mind, perhaps they will avoid slipping into ethnocentric thinking when using measures of adaptive skills with individuals of different cultural and linguistic backgrounds.

For a more in-depth discussion of measurement bias, consult Bryant, Bryant, and Chamberlain (this volume), Osterlind (1983, 1989), Van de Vijver and Leung (1997), and Wainer (1988).

Steps to Take When Validating a Translation or Adaptation

Validating a test is the most crucial element in the appraisal of a test's psychometric qualities (American Psychological Association, 1985). Here we refer to the classic testing definition of validation: the process of accumulating data as to the test's ability to measure the intended construct (Wainer & Braun, 1988). The following two guidelines from the Standards (American Psychological Association, 1985) are of particular interest when it comes to test format and validity of test translations or adaptations:

> When a test user makes a substantial change in test format, mode of administration, instructions, language, or content, the user should revalidate the use of the test for the changed conditions or have a rationale supporting the claim that additional validation is not necessary or possible. (p. 41)

> When a test is translated from one language or dialect to another, its reliability and validity for the uses intended in the linguistic groups to be tested should be established. (p. 75)

Several authors have suggested various procedures for validating a cross-culturally adapted test. Geisinger (1994) recommended the following 10-step procedure: (a) translate or adapt the scale, (b) review the translation or adaptation, (c) revise the scale accordingly (i.e., according to Step b), (d) pilot test the scale (i.e., small sample to validate the comprehension of items and instructions), and revise (e) field test the scale on a large sample, (f) standardize the raw scores, (g) verify the validity and reliability of the scale, (h) develop a user's manual, (i) train users in the administration of the scale, and (j) obtain reactions and feedback from scale users.

A seven-step process has also been presented by Vallerand (1989). Vallerand's steps are the folowing: (a) translate the scale and produce a preliminary version, (b) verify and revise the translated preliminary version, (c) pilot test the translated scale, (d) verify the translated scale's concurrent and content validity, (e) verify the translated scale's reliability, (f) verify the translated scale's construct validity, and (g) collect norms for the translated scale.

Each of these proposed procedures for conducting cross-cultural adaptation of an adaptive behavior scale may invoke an iterative procedure of one or more steps of the process. For example, verifying the interlingual translation of items and scale instructions will lead to revisions. The revised scale's content is then once again evaluated for linguistic, grammatical, or cultural exactitude (be it by back-translation, decentering, and/or a committee process). Further modifications are done accordingly.

Haccoun (1987) presented a validation procedure that requires one group of bilingual participants to complete the adapted scale twice. At Time 1, half of the bilingual group is given the original scale and the other half is given the translated or adapted scale. At Time 2, the procedure is reversed, where the first half of the bilingual group is given the translated or adapted scale; the second half of the bilingual group receives the original scale. Haccoun's procedure has the advantage of permitting an estimation of the scale's (source and target) stability while assessing the equivalence (concurrent validity) of the two versions (original version and adapted version) of the scale. This procedure is shown graphically in Figure 9.3.

Based on the literature reviewed, we feel the basic approach to translating and adapting an adaptive behavior scale must include the following seven steps (summarized in Figure 9.4).

1. *Translations/adaptations*. A strenuous effort needs to be made by committee members to develop a good initial translation and adaptation for the target culture. This first committee is the main group, usually composed of test developers and others interested in the test translation or adaptation. These members translate individually, or in pairs, the entire source scale. The committee should include translators and bilingual content experts.

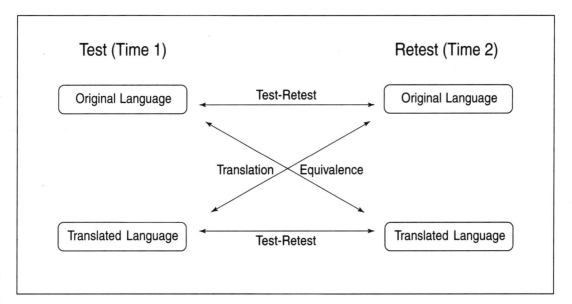

Figure 9.3. Haccoun's single bilingual group test-retest model.

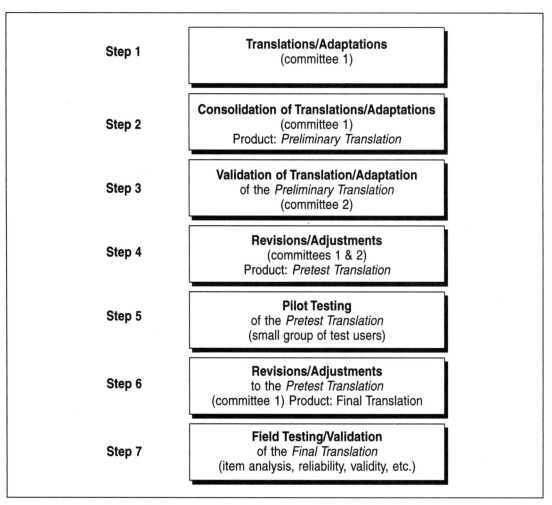

Step 1	**Translations/Adaptations** (committee 1)
Step 2	**Consolidation of Translations/Adaptations** (committee 1) Product: *Preliminary Translation*
Step 3	**Validation of Translation/Adaptation** of the *Preliminary Translation* (committee 2)
Step 4	**Revisions/Adjustments** (committees 1 & 2) Product: *Pretest Translation*
Step 5	**Pilot Testing** of the *Pretest Translation* (small group of test users)
Step 6	**Revisions/Adjustments** to the *Pretest Translation* (committee 1) Product: Final Translation
Step 7	**Field Testing/Validation** of the *Final Translation* (item analysis, reliability, validity, etc.)

Figure 9.4. *Seven steps for translation or adaptation of an adaptive behavior scale.*

2. *Consolidation of translations.* The committee meets and compares their different translations. All parts of the translated scale are thoroughly examined and discussed by the committee members. A consensus translation (preliminary translation) results from this meeting.

3. *Validation of translation.* The preliminary translation is then given to a second smaller group of bilingual content experts and translators. This second committee is asked to verify the translation of the preliminary translation by comparing it to the original scale. They verify translation equivalence, grammatical structure of translation, and cultural appropriateness.

4. *Revisions and adjustments.* Both committees meet to discuss any questions, comments, or suggestions from the second committee regarding the preliminary translation. The first committee generally has the final say, but committee members should strive to reach a consensus with all members of both committees. All modifications deemed justified are made to the preliminary translation, resulting in the version called the pretest translation.

5. *Pilot testing.* The pretest translation is then piloted with a group of potential scale consumers. This phase of validation aims at verifying the clarity and appropriateness

of the test instructions, items, scoring scale, and scale presentation. It may be useful to give an evaluation with a five-point Likert scale to rate clarity and appropriateness.

6. *Revisions.* The members of the first committee meet to evaluate the data collected during the pilot study and make necessary revisions to the scale instructions, item stems, and scale presentation that have been identified as unclear or problematic. The resulting translation (final translation) is now ready for field testing.

7. *Field testing and validation.* The final step of the validation process is field testing, when the final translation is completed by large numbers of scale users. The data are collected to determine the scale's psychometric properties: item analysis, parameter estimation (if using item response theory), factor analyses (exploratory or confirmatory), internal consistency, reliability, validity, and norms.

Standards and Guidelines

The joint effort of the American Educational Research Association, American Psychological Association, and National Council on Measurement in Education is revising the 1985 American Psychological Association's *Standards for Educational and Psychological Testing.* Plans include a chapter dedicated to cross-cultural adaptations and testing. In the interim, an excellent set of guidelines has been produced by a blue-ribbon committee established by the International Test Commission (ITC). In 1993, the ITC formed a committee of psychologists from around the world to develop guidelines for adapting educational and psychological tests. The ITC committee's 22 guidelines for adapting educational and psychological tests are summarized in Table 9.1 (see Van de Vijver & Hambleton, 1996, for a more detailed explanation of each guideline).

Table 9.1

Guidelines for Adapting Educational and Psychological Tests

1. Effects of cultural differences that are not relevant or important to the main purposes of the study should be minimized as much as possible.

2. The amount of overlap in the constructs in the populations of interest should be assessed.

3. Instrument developers or publishers should ensure that the translation or adaptation process takes full account of linguistic and cultural differences among the populations for whom the translated or adapted versions of the instrument are intended.

4. Instrument developers should provide evidence that the language use in the directions, rubrics, and items themselves as well as in the handbook is appropriate for all cultural and language populations for whom the instrument is intended.

5. Instrument developers or publishers should provide evidence that the testing techniques, item formats, test conventions, and procedures are familiar to all intended populations.

6. Instrument developers or publishers should provide evidence that the item content and stimulus materials are familiar to all intended populations.

7. Instrument developers or publishers should implement systemic judgmental evidence, both linguistic and psychological, to improve the accuracy of the translation or adaptation process and compile evidence on the equivalence of all language versions.

Continued on following page

8. Instrument developers or publishers should ensure that the data collection design permits use of appropriate statistical techniques to establish item equivalence between the different language versions.

9. Instrument developers or publishers should apply appropriate statistical techniques to (a) establish the equivalence of the different versions of the instrument, and (b) identify problematic components or aspects of the instrument that may be inadequate to someone in the intended population.

10. Instrument developers or publishers should provide information on the evaluation of the validity in all target populations for whom the translated or adapted versions are intended.

11. Instrument developers or publishers should provide statistical evidence of the equivalence of questions for all intended populations.

12. Nonequivalent questions between versions intended for different populations should *not* (emphasis in the original) be used in preparing a common scale or in comparing these populations. However, they may be useful in enhancing content validity of scores reported for each population separately.

13. Instrument developers and administrators should try to anticipate potential problems and take appropriate actions to remedy these problems through the preparation of appropriate materials and instructions.

14. Instrument administrators should be sensitive to a number of factors related to the stimulus materials, administration procedures, and response modes that can moderate the validity of the inferences drawn from the scores.

15. Aspects of the environment that influence the administration of an instrument should be made as similar as possible across populations for whom the instrument is intended.

16. Instrument administration instructions should be in the source and target languages to minimize influence of unwanted sources of variations across populations.

17. The instrument manual should specify all aspects of the instrument and its administration that require scrutiny in operation in a new cultural context.

18. The administration should be unobtrusive with minimal administrator-examinee interaction. Explicit rules described in the manual for the instrument should be followed.

19. When an instrument is translated or adapted for use in another population, documentation of the changes should be provided, along with evidence of equivalence.

20. Some differences among samples of populations to whom the instrument is administered should *not* (emphasis in original) be taken at face value. The researcher has the responsibility to substantiate the differences with other empirical evidence.

21. Comparisons across populations must be made only at the level of invariance that has been established for the scale.

22. The instrument developer should (a) provide specific information on the ways in which the sociocultural and ecological contexts of the populations might affect performance on the instrument and (b) suggest procedures to account for these effects in the interpretation of results.

Conclusion

The interaction between adaptive skill development and cultural factors has long been of interest to students of mental retardation. The theory that certain cultural environments actually cause mental retardation has been widely asserted. On the other hand, other theorists have cautioned that cultural differences do not equate to cultural deficits, and that most of our assessment instruments are culturally biased.

In analyzing the effects of culture on mental retardation, several measurement issues must be addressed. One concerns the criteria used in diagnosing mental retardation. Where the cutoff scores are set (if at all) for both IQ and adaptive behavior measures has an enormous impact on service eligibility and prevalence, especially for many minority groups. The content and psychometric properties of adaptive behavior scales can also have a major influence on the number of minority individuals identified as having mental retardation. This is especially true with scales that emphasize academic skills or maladaptive behaviors.

Assessment approaches are obviously important. Relying on third-party informants may be time honored, but the validity of such information in contrast to naturalistic and controlled observation has been questioned. Sensitivity to cultural communication styles is also essential if culturally competent assessments are to be attained. Professional training in assessment practices must address these areas more adequately. This is especially true when diagnostic results will have a major impact on an individual's life, such as consideration of special-education placement or criminal liability.

An adaptive behavior test developed and normed on one cultural group may need to be adapted to be used with other groups. Translating or adapting an adaptive behavior scale should not be viewed or approached as a quick and easy way of creating a scale for diverse groups. A systematic methodology is the only sure way of ensuring a proper scale translation or adaptation; this requires as much expertise and empirical effort as developing an entirely new scale.

The easiest way to translate or adapt a test is from the test's initial conception. If test developers are sensitive to cross-cultural issues during initial item construction and test development, test translation and cross-cultural adaptation will be significantly simplified. Initial item development strategies are important, because sound techniques will facilitate eventual item adaptation. When developing scale items, several sources should be consulted (see Osterlind, 1989; Roid & Haladyna, 1982). The International Test Commission (see Van de Vijver & Hambleton, 1996) has provided an excellent set of guidelines to aid developers and test users.

Professionals and test consumers must realize that the mere translation of a test's instructions and item stems is insufficient. Ethically, professionals must ensure that the test they are using has been validated for the population with which they plan to use it (American Psychological Association, 1985, 1996). If the validity of the test cannot be ascertained, the professionals must clearly state the limitations of the test's results and their consequent interpretations and recommendations.

Minimally, until the arrival of more culturally sensitive or culturally specific adaptive behavior measures, we need to sensitize test consumers to the difficulties involved in the comparison of test performances across cultural groups. Second, we need to continue sharing within the literature and professional and scientific conferences our systematic observations and empirical and clinical data regarding cross-cultural assessment of adaptive behavior.

References

American Psychiatric Association. (1994). *Diagnostic and statistical manual of mental disorders* (4th ed.). Washington, DC: Author.

American Psychological Association. (1985). *Standards for educational and psychological testing*. Washington, DC: Author.

American Psychological Association. (1996). *Ethics for psychologists: A commentary on the* APA *ethics code*. Washington, DC: Author.

Anastasi, A. (1988). *Psychological testing* (6th ed.). New York: Macmillan.

Bailey, D. B., & Harbin, G. L. (1980). Nondiscriminatory evaluation. *Exceptional Children, 46,* 590-596.

Baroff, G. S. (1990). Establishing mental retardation in capital defendants. *American Journal of Forensic Psychology, 8,* 35-45.

Baroff, G. S. (1991). Establishing mental retardation in capital cases: A potential matter of life and death. *Mental Retardation, 29,* 343-349.

Baumeister, A. A., & Muma, J. R. (1975). On defining mental retardation. *Journal of Special Education, 9,* 293-306.

Benton, A. (1956). The concept of pseudo feeblemindedness. *Archives of Neurology and Psychiatry, 75,* 379-388.

Brady, P. M., Manni, J. L., & Winikur, D. W. (1983). Implications of ethnic disproportion in programs for the educable mentally retarded. *Journal of Special Education, 17,* 295-302.

Bravo, M., Woodbury-Farina, M., Canino, G. J., & Rubio-Stipec, M. (1993). The Spanish translation and cultural adaptation of the Diagnostic Interview Schedule for Children (DISC) in Puerto Rico. *Culture, Medicine, and Psychiatry, 17,* 329-344.

Brislin, R. W. (1986). The wording and translation of research instruments. In W. Kinner & J. Berry (Eds.), *Field methods in cross-cultural research* (pp. 137-164). Beverly Hills, CA: Sage.

Brislin, R. W., Lonner, W. J., & Thorndike, R. M. (1973). *Cross-cultural methods*. New York: John Wiley.

Bruininks, R. H., Hill, B. K., Weatherman, R. F., & Woodcock, R. W. (1986). *Inventory for client and agency planning*. Chicago: Riverside.

Bruininks, R. H., Woodcock, R. W., Weatherman, R. F., & Hill, B. K. (1996). SIB-R: *Scales of independent behavior* (Rev. ed.). Chicago: Riverside.

Chan, S. (1992). Families with Asian roots. In E. W. Lynch & M. J. Hanson (Eds.), *Developing cross-cultural competence* (pp. 181-257). Baltimore: Paul H. Brookes.

Childs, D. E. (1982). A study of the adaptive behavior of retarded children and the resultant effects of this use in the diagnosis of mental retardation. *Education and Training of the Mentally Retarded, 77,* 109-113.

Clausen, J. (1972). The continuing problem of defining mental retardation. *Journal of Special Education, 6,* 97-106.

Cole, M., & Bruner, J. S. (1971). Cultural differences and inferences about psychological processes. *American Psychologist, 26,* 867-876.

Coulter, W. A. (1980). Adaptive behavior and professional disfavor: Controversies and trends for school psychologists. *School Psychology Review, 9,* 67-74.

Cronbach, L. J. (1975). Five decades of public controversy over mental testing. *American Psychologist, 30,* 1-14.

Dana, R. H. (1993). *Multicultural assessment perspectives for professional psychology*. Boston: Allyn & Bacon.

DeVault, S., & Long, D. (1988). Adaptive behavior, malingering and competence to waive rights: A case study. *American Journal of Forensic Psychology, 6,* 3-15.

Education for All Handicapped Children Act of 1975, PL 94-142. (August 23, 1977). Title 20, U.S.C. 1401 et seq: U.S. Statutes at Large, 100, 1145-1177.

Geisinger, K. F. (1994). Cross-cultural normative assessment: Translation and adaptation issues influencing the normative interpretation of assessment instruments. *Psychological Assessment, 6,* 304-312.

Haccoun, R. R. (1987). Une nouvelle technique de vérification de l'équivalence de mesures psychologiques traduites. *Revue Québécoise de Psychologie, 8,* 30-39.

Hambleton, R. K. (1993). Translating achievement tests for the use in cross-cultural studies. *European Journal of Psychological Assessment, 9,* 57-68.

Hambleton, R. K. (1996, August 15). *Adapting psychological tests: Technical guidelines for improving practices.* Paper presentation at the International Psychology Congress. Montréal.

Hambleton, R. K., & Kanjee, A. (1995). Increasing the validity of cross-cultural assessment: Use of improved methods for test adaptations. *European Journal of Psychological Assessment, 11,* 147-157.

Harrison, P. L. (1987). Research with adaptive behavior scales. [Special Issue: Adaptive behavior.] *Journal of Special Education, 21,* 37-68.

Heath, C. P., & Obrzut, J. E. (1986). Adaptive behavior: Concurrent validity. *Journal of Psychoeducational Assessment, 4,* 53-59.

Helms-Lorenz, M., & Van de Vijver, F. J. R. (1995). Cognitive assessment in education in a multicultural society, *European Journal of Psychological Assessment, 11,* 158-169.

Hinkle, J. S. (1994). Practitioners and cross-cultural assessment: A practical guide to information and training. *Measurement and Evaluation in Counseling and Development, 27,* 103-115.

Horn, E., & Fuchs, D. (1987). Using adaptive behavior in assessment and intervention: An overview. [Special Issue: Adaptive behavior.] *Journal of Special Education, 21,* 11-26.

Jackson, D. N. (1991). Problems in preparing personality tests and interest inventories for use in multiple cultures. *International Test Bulletin, 32/33,* 88-93.

Jacobson, J.W., & Mulick, J.A. (Eds.). (1996). *Manual of diagnosis and professional practice in mental retardation.* Washington, DC: American Psychological Association.

Joe, J. R., & Malach, R. S. (1992). Families with Native American roots. In E. W. Lynch & M. J. Hanson (Eds.), *Developing cross-cultural competence* (pp. 89-119). Baltimore: Paul H. Brookes.

Keller, H. R. (1988). Children's adaptive behaviors: Measure and source generalizability. *Journal of Psychoeducational Assessment, 6,* 371-389.

Koegel, P., & Edgerton, R. B. (1982). Labeling and the perception of handicap among Black mildly mentally retarded adults. *American Journal of Mental Deficiency, 87,* 266-276.

Larry P. v. Riles, 793 F.2d 969 (9th Cir. 1984).

Leland, H. (1983). Adaptive behavior scales. In J. L. Matson & J. A. Mulick (Eds.), *Handbook of mental retardation* (pp. 215-225). New York: Pergamon Press.

Lonner, W. J. (1990). An overview of cross-cultural testing and assessment. In R. W. Brislin (Ed.), *Applied cross-cultural psychology* (pp. 56-76). Newbury Park, CA: Sage.

Luckasson, R., Coulter, D. L., Polloway, E. A., Reiss, S., Schalock, R. L., Snell, M. E., Spitalnik, D. M., & Stark, J. A. (1992). *Mental retardation: Definition, classification, and systems of supports* (9th ed.). Washington, DC: American Association on Mental Retardation.

Lynch, E. W., & Hanson, M. J. (Eds.). (1992). *Developing cross-cultural competence.* Baltimore: Paul H. Brookes.

MacMann, G. M., & Barnett, D. W. (1984). An analysis of the construct validity of two measures of adaptive behavior. *Journal of Psychoeducational Assessment, 2,* 239-247.

McCarver, R. B., & Campbell, V. A. (1987). Future developments in the concept and application of adaptive behavior. [Special Issue: Adaptive behavior.] *Journal of Special Education, 21,* 197-207.

Mealor, D. J., & Richmond, B. O. (1980). Adaptive behavior: Parents and teachers disagree. *Exceptional Children, 46,* 386-389.

Mercer, J. R. (1976). Pluralistic diagnosis in the evaluation of Black and Chicano children: A procedure for taking sociocultural variables into account in clinical assessment. In C. A. Hernandez, M. J. Haug, & N. N. Wagner (Eds.), *Chicanos: Social and psychological perspectives* (2nd ed., pp. 183-195). St. Louis: Mosby.

Mercer, J. (1979). In defense of racially and culturally nondiscriminatory assessment. *School Psychology Digest, 8,* 89-115.

Mercer, J. R., & Lewis, J. F. (1978). *System of multicultural pluralistic assessment.* New York: Psychological Corp.

Miranda, A. H. (1993). Consultation with culturally diverse families. *Journal of Educational & Psychological Consultation, 4,* 89-93.

Nelson, C. M., & Pearson, C. A. (1994). Juvenile delinquency in the context of culture and community. In R. L. Peterson & S. Ishii-Jordan (Eds.), *Multicultural issues in the education of students with behavioral disorders* (pp. 78-90). Cambridge, MA: Brookline.

Nihira, K., Foster, R., Shellhaas, M., & Leland, H. (1974). AAMD *Adaptive Behavior Scale* (rev. ed.). Washington, DC: American Association on Mental Deficiency.

Okazaki, S., & Sue, S. (1995). Methodological issues in assessment research with ethnic minorities. *Psychological Assessment, 7,* 367-375.

Osterlind, S. J. (1983). *Test item bias.* Newbury Park, CA: Sage.

Osterlind, S. J. (1989). *Constructing test items.* Boston: Kluwer.

Park, E. K., Pullis, M., Reilly, J., & Townsend, B. L. (1994). Cultural biases in the identification of students with behavioral disorders. In R. L. Peterson & S. Ishii-Jordan (Eds.), *Multicultural issues in the education of students with behavioral disorders* (pp. 14-26). Cambridge, MA: Brookline.

Peterson, R. L., & Ishii-Jordan, S. (Eds.). (1994). *Multicultural issues in the education of students with behavioral disorders.* Cambridge, MA: Brookline.

Reis, E. M. (1986). Minority disproportionality in special placements as an assessment and programming issue. *Journal of Instructional Psychology, 13,* 135-140.

Reschly, D. J. (1981). Evaluation of the effects of SOMPA measures on classification of students as mildly mentally retarded. *American Journal of Mental Deficiency, 86,* 16-20.

Reschly, D. J. (1988). Assessment issues, placement litigation, and the future of mild mental retardation classification and programming. Special Issue: Emerging challenges. *Education and Training in Mental Retardation, 23,* 285-301.

Reschly, D. J., & Ward, S. M. (1991). Use of adaptive behavior measures and overrepresentation of Black students in programs for students with mild mental retardation. *American Journal on Mental Retardation, 96,* 257-268.

Roid, G. H., & Haladyna, T. M. (1982). A *technology for test-item writing*. New York: Academic Press.

Sattler, J. M. (1970). Racial "experimenter effects" in experimentation, testing, interviewing, and psychotherapy. *Psychological Bulletin, 73*, 137-160.

Sharifzadeh, V. (1992). Families with Middle Eastern roots. In E. W. Lynch & M. J. Hanson (Eds.), *Developing cross-cultural competence* (pp. 319-351). Baltimore: Paul H. Brookes.

Sinaiko, H. W., & Brislin, R. (1973). Evaluating language translation: Experiments on three assessment methods. *Journal of Applied Psychology, 57*, 328-334.

Sparrow, S. S., Balla, D. A., & Cicchetti, D. V. (1984). *Vineland Adaptive Behavior Scales*. Circle Pines, MN: American Guidance Service.

Taylor, R. L., & Ivimey, J. K. (1982). Considering alternative methods of measurement on the Adaptive Behavior Scale. *Psychology in the Schools, 19*, 117-121.

Vallerand, R. J. (1989). Vers une méthodologie de validation trans-culturelle de questionnaires psychologiques: implications pour la recherche en langue française. *Canadian Psychology, 30*, 662-680.

Van de Vijver, F., & Hambleton, R. K. (1996). Translating tests: Some practical guidelines. *European Psychologist, 1*, 89-99.

Van de Vijver, F. J. R., & Leung, K. (1997). *Methods and data analysis for cross-cultural research*. Newbury Park, CA: Sage.

Verdier, A., & Laplège, A. (1995). Place des contre-traductions dans la méthodologie d'adaptation en français d'une mesure de qualité de la vie internationale. *Revue Européenne de Psychologie Appliquée, 45*, 265-269.

Voelker, S. L., Shore, D. L., Brown-More, C., Hill, L. C., Miller, L. T., & Perry, J. (1990). Validity of self-report of adaptive behavior skills by adults with mental retardation. *Mental Retardation, 28*, 305-309.

Wainer, H. (1988). *The future of item analysis*. Princeton, NJ: Educational Testing Service.

Wainer, H., & Braun, H. I. (Eds.). (1988). *Test validity*. Hillside, NJ: Lawrence Erlbaum.

Willis, W. (1992). Families with African American roots. In E. W. Lynch & M. J. Hanson (Eds.) *Developing cross-cultural competence* (pp. 121-150). Baltimore: Paul H. Brookes.

Wilss, W. (1990). Cognitive aspects of the translation process. *Language & Communications, 10*, 19-36.

Wolfensberger, W., & Kurtz, R. A. (1971). Measurement of parents' perceptions of their children's development. *Genetic Psychology Monographs, 83*, 3-92.

World Health Organization. (1992). *International classification of diseases* (10th ed.). Geneva: Author.

Zigler, E., Balla, D., & Hodapp, R. (1984). On the definition and classification of mental retardation. *American Journal of Mental Deficiency, 89*, 215-230.

Zuniga, M. E. (1992). Families with Latino roots. In E. W. Lynch & M. J. Hanson (Eds.), *Developing cross-cultural competence* (pp. 151-179). Baltimore: Paul H. Brookes.

CHAPTER 10

The Culturally Individualized Assessment of Adaptive Behavior:

An Accommodation to the 1992 AAMR Definition, Classification, and Systems of Supports

LAIRD W. HEAL
University of Illinois at Urbana

MARC J. TASSÉ
Université du Québec à Montréal

Introduction

This chapter proposes the development of an individualized criterion-referenced system of assessment for adaptive behavior based on the assumptions that lie explicitly and implicitly in the American Association on Mental Retardation (AAMR) definition of mental retardation, revised in *Mental Retardation: Definition, Classification, and Systems of Supports*, by Luckasson et al. (1992). This definition features subtle but profound implications for the definition and assessment of adaptive behavior. What had been regarded as a single, global ability was parceled into 10 broad areas of adaptive skills, and limitation of adaptive behavior was defined as functional limitations in 2 or more of the 10 areas. Limitation in this context requires objective assessment criteria. Luckasson et al. (1992) addressed this requirement by another subtle but profound modification of previous conceptions of adaptive behavior: grading each skill by the "intensity of support" required assured that the individual with mental retardation could exercise the skill—the greater the support, the more limited the skill. The purpose of the present chapter is to address these modifications logically, laying the groundwork for the development of the system of adaptive behavior assessment that they imply.

Definition of Mental Retardation

Since the fifth revision of the American Association on Mental Deficiency (AAMD; now AAMR) classification manual by Heber (1959), the AAMR's sanctioned definition of mental retardation has had three components: (a) origination during the developmental period, (b) subnormal intelligence, and (c) limitations in adaptive behavior. These components have been retained, albeit with some revision, throughout the subsequent editions. This is the definition from the ninth (i.e., latest) edition (Luckasson et al., 1992):

> *Mental retardation* refers to substantial limitations in present functioning. It is characterized by significantly subaverage intellectual functioning, existing concurrently with related limitations in two or more of the following applicable adaptive skill areas: communication, self-care, home living, social skills, community use, self-direction, health and safety, functional academics, leisure, and work. Mental retardation manifests [itself] before age 18. (p. 1)

The nuances of the treatment of these three components by the ninth edition are elaborated below, especially as they affect the assessment proposal that follows.

Developmental Origin

Of the three conditions for defining mental retardation, "developmental origin" is the most arbitrary. When one agrees that there should be a class of conditions labeled "mental retardation," characterized by the preemption or interruption of the unfolding of cognitive ability, one has the problem of establishing the upper age at which cognitive development has ended. Cognitive development, after all, occurs throughout one's life. Legislation (e.g., the Developmental Disabilities Act (1996) and its predecessors; the Individuals With Disabilities Education Act (1997) and its predecessors) has set the upper limit of development at one's 22nd birthday.

This upper limit has been embraced by the editorial board of Division 33 (Mental Retardation) of the American Psychological Association (Jacobson & Mulick, 1996, p. 13). This limit was presumably chosen to coincide loosely with the legal age of majority, at which most individuals assume adult rights and privileges in the United States, unless the court declares them wholly or partially incompetent to conduct their own affairs. Luckasson et al. (1992) sustained Grossman's (1983) position that the developmental period ends at the 18th birthday. The American Psychiatric Association (1994) *Diagnostic and Statistical Manual* also puts the definitional age at the 18th birthday. Luckasson et al. justified this choice by noting that it coincides with the end of public schooling and with many other adult rites of passage for those without disabilities.

Because this part of the definition is completely arbitrary, it does not affect assessment. Indeed, assessment of adaptive behavior must continue lifelong to determine whether an adult's mental retardation has persisted, whether an adult with a history of mental retardation who has been temporarily declassified should be reclassified as mentally retarded, or whether an adult without a history of mental retardation is eligible for other disability services.

Intelligence

Thanks to its venerable tradition, the assessment of intelligence is the most straightforward step in assigning someone the classification of mental retardation. Indeed, many services and scientists (e.g., Clausen, 1972a, 1972b; Conley, 1973) have argued that we should use only an IQ score to define mental retardation. As with selection of an upper age limit for the developmental period, the selection of the upper limit of the IQ range for attribution of mental retardation has varied from one time or source to another.

Most definitions use an IQ of 70 because it lies a convenient two standard deviations below the population mean of 100, placing approximately 2.23% of the population in the IQ range of eligibility. Luckasson et al. (1992, p. 37) raised some controversy (e.g., MacMillan, Gresham, & Siperstein, 1993) by arguing that rather than using the traditional IQ of 70 as a rigid cutoff score for defining mental retardation, professionals should accept a range of 70 plus-or-minus one standard error of measurement of 5 points (i.e., a range of 65 to 75) within which clinical judgment would be used to decide whether low functioning should be attributable to low intelligence or to other causes.

A cutoff of 75 would add about 1.3% to the population eligible for mental retardation classification, which could overtax the service system. However, Heal (1993) has argued that a more flexible cutoff would probably have little effect because very few borderline individuals would choose or be assigned a mental retardation classification. Indeed, Grossman's (1983) definition included an eloquent suggestion that the error of measurement be considered in the classification decision, but the proportion of the population classified as mental retardation has decreased during the past two decades (U.S. Department of Education, 1996).

Adaptive Behavior

Adaptive behavior is the least tractable of the three components of the mental retardation definition. Grossman's (1983, p. 42) definition was cited by Luckasson et al. (1992) as follows:

Adaptive behavior refers to the quality of everyday performance in coping with environmental demands. The quality of general adaptation is mediated by level of intelligence; thus, the two concepts overlap in meaning. It is evident, however, from consideration of the definition of adaptive behavior, with its stress on everyday coping, that adaptive behavior refers to what people do to take care of themselves and relate to others in daily living rather than [to] the abstract potential implied by intelligence. (p. 38)

The ninth edition of the AAMR classification manual (Luckasson et al., 1992) imposed several elaborations on this definition. These are paraphrased from Luckasson et al. as the following six corollaries:

1. A general adaptive skill limitation requires "limitations in two or more of the following *applicable* [italics added] adaptive skill areas: communication, self-care, home living, social skills, community use, self-direction, health and safety, functional academics, leisure, and work" (p. 1). Thus, Luckasson et al. identified specific areas, which set the boundaries of adaptive skills in both an inclusionary and an exclusionary sense. A sanctioned adaptive behavior assessment must consider all 10 of these skill areas and none other. Additionally, the qualification *applicable* permits an assessor to omit any areas that are not applicable to the self-sufficiency needs of any assessed individual in his or her personal setting and/or subculture.

2. While it might be that "as a rule, the person's level of needed habilitation and supports parallels the individual's limitations, . . . many limitations can be overcome by using systems of supports that include people, prosthetics, and/or environmental accommodation. . . . By relating a person's functional limitations to the intensities of needed supports, education and habilitation personnel can use behavioral descriptors associated with the respective skill areas as objectives in the development and implementation of the person's individual plan" (p. 26). Accordingly, the habilitation of the individual is much better served if the assessment of adaptive skills is focused on the intensities of the support required to maximize performance rather than on the unsupported skill limitations directly.

3. "*Specific adaptive limitations often co-exist with strengths and other adaptive skills or other personal capabilities*" (p. 7). In other words, profiles of adaptive skills are not necessarily flat. Limitation must be manifested in "at least two adaptive skill areas, thus showing a generalized limitation and reducing the probability of measurement error" (p. 6).

4. "*With appropriate supports over a sustained period, the life functioning of the person with mental retardation will generally improve. . . . Appropriate Supports* refer to an array of services, individuals, and settings that match the person's needs" (p. 7).

5. "*Valid assessment considers cultural and linguistic diversity as well as differences in communication and behavioral factors*" (p. 6).

6. "*The existence of limitations in adaptive skills occurs within the context of community environments typical of the individual's age peers and is indexed to the person's individualized needs for support*" (p. 7). "'Adaptive behavior [reflects] the ability to fit into a given niche'" (Evans, 1991, p. 34 as cited in Luckasson et al., p. 39).

Thus, the ninth edition of *Mental Retardation* (Luckasson et al., 1992) introduced six interrelated corollaries, which define adaptive behavior not as a global personal ability, but as a *profile of supports*, from none to pervasive, that an *individual* requires to achieve or approximate self-sufficiency in 10 *specific but cumulatively comprehensive skill areas* in his or her *specific subcultures and settings*. These corollaries appear to render obsolete all previously used, norm-referenced adaptive behavior scales, which define adaptive behavior as an array of skills that reside in an individual as a trait and are not ordinarily limited to specific settings as states.

These interpretations of mental retardation should probably be filtered by the *International Classification of Impairments, Disabilities, and Handicaps* (World Health Organization, 1980). Under this classification,

> an *impairment* is any loss or abnormality of psychological, physiological, or anatomical structure or function; *disability* is any restriction or lack (resulting from an impairment) of ability to perform an activity in the manner or within the range considered normal for a human being; *handicap* is a [societally imposed] disadvantage for an individual (resulting from an impairment or disability) that limits or prevents the fulfillment of a role that is normal (…depending on age, sex, and social and cultural factors) for that individual. (pp. 27-29).

Fryers (1993) offered a useful interpretation of these distinctions as they relate to mental retardation. He suggested that "intellectual impairment" be defined strictly in terms of IQ, which admittedly might be fallibly measured. "General learning disability," which most nearly resembles what most educators would call mental retardation, Fryers defined as subnormal performance on learning, memory, and problem-solving tests. Finally, Fryers defined "general dependency handicap," as a "social disadvantage" that is not a necessary concomitant of the disability. Using this filter, an IQ impairment without a corresponding adaptive skill limitation is not sufficient to justify a diagnosis of mental retardation (i.e., in World Health Organization [1980] terms, not sufficient to identify a disability). Luckasson et al. (1992) emphasized functional supports to assure that mental retardation be seen as a disability rather than a handicap; the AAMR definition of mental retardation is one of a functional disability rather than a mere organic impairment or a societally imposed handicap.

Classification of Adaptive Skill Areas, Intensities of Support, and Types of Support

The definitions and corollaries proposed by Luckasson et al. (1992) appear to require three interdependent classification systems: (a) a refinement of the classification of adaptive skills, (b) an elaboration of the intensities of support, and (c) the definition and specification of the types of supports.

Adaptive Skill Areas

Adaptive behavior is a broad, multifaceted construct, facets of which must be specified if it is to be understood and used in practice or research. Two very different approaches have been taken to analyze adaptive behavior in its component parts.

Subjectively Developed Lists of Skill Areas

Luckasson et al. (1992) list of 10 adaptive behavior skills is one of many attempts to specify and organize the activities required for self-sufficiency into areas of competence that can be assessed and subsequently remediated if they are deemed inadequate. Every adaptive behavior scale has a list of behavior categories. Cooper (1996; see also Bryant, Seay, & Bryant) reviewed 32 adaptive behavior scales, and found that only the revised AAMR *Adaptive Behavior Scales* (Lambert, Nihira, & Leland, 1993; Nihira, Leland, & Lambert, 1993) included content in all 10 of the areas specified by Luckasson et al. By Cooper's reading, 24 of the 32 scales covered 5 or fewer of these 10 areas. Thus, the taxonomies of adaptive behavior generated by subjectively organizing important skills have not proven replicable. Because the subjective classification of adaptive behavior has proven so elusive, the AAMR list of adaptive behavior areas will undoubtedly be revised as it is used. Of course, as the areas are revised, their assessment must be revised also.

The committee that created the list of 10 adaptive skills consisted of the nation's leaders in adolescent and adult curricula for individuals with mental retardation. Even so, this list may be the theoretically least defensible feature of the new definition. Would other panels of curriculum specialists arrive at a similar adaptive behavior taxonomy? Why are such disparate subareas, such as health and safety, listed under a single area? Why are some areas (e.g., communication) basic skills, others (e.g., functional academics) advanced skills, and still others (e.g., home or work) settings in which skills are revealed? Finally, to what extent were the area divisions based on the considerable empirical research on existing adaptive behavior instruments?

The Factor Structure of Adaptive Behavior

The alternative to the subjective development of an adaptive behavior taxonomy is application of the factor analysis statistical tool to identify the factor structure of the skills that practitioners have used to assess adaptation to home, community, school, and work settings. Widaman and McGrew (1996; see also Thompson, McGrew, & Bruininks, this volume) have recently reviewed the literature resulting from these analyses. Like subjective analyses, factor analyses have been inconsistent in determining the exact nature and number of more-or-less independent dimensions of adaptive skills. Nevertheless, Widaman and McGrew concluded from their review that four major factors have dominated adaptive behavior scales:

(a) Motor Development, measuring gross and fine motor skills, ambulating, and basic eating and toileting skills; (b) Independent Living Skills, assessing skills in completing household chores, dressing, bathing, making food, and washing dishes; (c) Cognitive Competence, assessing receptive and expressive language, reading and writing skills, handling money, and other cognitive skills; and (d) Social Competence, measuring the formation and maintenance of friendships, interactions with others, and participation in group activities. (p. 105)

Apparently these dimensions are more stable than subjectively constructed dimensions; any adaptive behavior scale should assess these general dimensions as its first requirement.

Comprehensive Assessment of Adaptive Behavior

In spite of the importance of the factor structure of adaptive skills, Heal (1993) argued that adaptive behavior assessment should range beyond factor structure; a comprehensive adaptive behavior scale must address all the skills required for self-sufficiency. Even though community skills such as shopping or taking a bus might be empirically correlated with making one's bed and attending to one's hygiene needs, all these skills are necessary in a comprehensive curriculum to prepare children and youths for independent living. Factorial comprehensiveness is necessary, but not sufficient, for complete adaptive behavior assessment. Accordingly, assessing specific areas of a competency curriculum must be a second, parallel or subordinate, requirement of an adaptive behavior scale. The 10 adaptive skill areas specified by Luckasson et al. (1992) are the bases for the curriculum suggested by the 92 AAMR System by the American Association on Mental Retardation. To be credible, any adaptive behavior assessment must address these 10 areas and no others. Excluding sanctioned areas would make the assessment an incomplete representative of the construct, and including nonsanctioned areas would make it a dilution of the construct; either transgression undermines the content validity of the assessment.

Expanded and Refined Taxonomy of Adaptive Behaviors

In spite of Cooper's (1996) conclusion that the revised AAMR *Adaptive Behavior Scale* (Nihira et al., 1993) and its adaptation, the *Adaptive Areas Assessment* (Bryant, Taylor, & Rivera, 1996), can accommodate the 10 adaptive skill areas specified by Lukasson et al. (1992), these 10 areas include several types and intensities of skills and require some reorganization if they are to make for a comprehensive, internally consistent taxonomy. Table 10.1 shows an adaptation of the list of adaptive skills listed by Luckasson et al. This table features a settings-by-skills arrangement: Each of the three settings (home, work, and community) has its own inherent skills, and each is crossed with 9 other skills, resulting in an expansion of the sanctioned AAMR list of 10 adaptive skills to 30. This expansion of the AAMR list separates communication into *receptive* and *expressive*, separates functional academics into *functional literacy* and *functional mathematics*, and separates health and safety into *health* and *safety*. *Self-care*, *social skills*, and *leisure* are retained as they had been. *Self-direction* is seen not as a specific skill but as a broad "metaskill" used by a person to recruit and apply a specific skill at an appropriate time and place. From the perspective of supports, self-direction forestalls a supervisor from using motivational

supports such as reminding, coaxing, warning, and/or rewarding to elicit an appropriate adaptive behavior. Seen to be the complement of motivational support, self-direction is removed from the list of the skills themselves and reassigned as a type of support.

It is important to note four assumptions in applying this taxonomy. First, with the exception of self-direction, which is assessed with every adaptive skill, each of the 10 adaptive skill areas from Luckasson et al. (1992) should be given approximately the same weight in determining one's overall adaptive skill. Thus, social skills or self-care, which were not subdivided, should have twice as many items as health or functional mathematics, which resulted from subdivisions.

Second, the three settings might not necessarily be weighted equally in determining one's overall adaptive skill level, because the Luckasson et al. (1992) corollaries mandated that these be individualized. The individualization of each assessment described below provides for the selective omission of items

Table 10.1
Taxonomy of 12 Adaptive Skill Areas in Three Settings

Skill Areas	SETTINGS		
	Home	School or Work	Community
Communications, Expressive	X	X	X
Communication, Receptive	X	X	X
Functional Academics, Literacy	X	X	X
Functional Academics, Mathematics	X	X	X
Social Skills	X	X	X
Leisure	X	X	X
Self-Care	X	X	X
Health	X	X	X
Safety	X	X	X
Home Living	X		
Work		X	
Community			X

Note. Cells marked "X" indicate skills to be assessed; cells left blank have no assessed skills.

that are inappropriate for an assessed individual's setting or culture, so each assessed person will have an overall assessment that emphasizes some settings more than others.

Third, some skill areas might be declared inappropriate for an assessed individual's culture or setting. Thus, slightly different profiles of skill areas will ordinarily be used to evaluate the overall adaptive skill of different assessed individuals.

Fourth, in spite of individual variations in profiles, no skill (e.g., clairvoyance, sexual potency, pet care, etc.) should be added to those encompassed by the Luckasson et al. (1992) list of 10, because adding skills, regardless of their cultural validity, would undermine the sanctioned definition of adaptive behavior. Thus, adaptation to an assessed individual's culture is done by eliminating assessed skills, not by adding skills that might be culturally unique to the individual. This feature exposes a major weakness in the foregoing interpretation of the Luckasson et al. corollaries: An individual might be so exceptionally skilled in areas not covered by Table 10.1 as to be highly successful in his or her environment; yet this

same person might need support on all the areas that apply to him or her from Table 10.1. It is logically impossible for Table 10.1 to have such completely comprehensive coverage as to assure the correct classification of all *nondisabled*, impaired individuals.

Intensities of Support

The ninth edition of the AAMR classification manual (Luckasson et al., 1992) featured a major conceptual change from previous characterizations of adaptive behavior: Instead of defining adaptive behavior in terms of skill *deficits*, it emphasized (Corollary 2 above) the *supports* necessary for an individual to perform optimally. Ideally, these supports would permit performance within the normal range, as eyeglasses permit someone with limited vision to see with 20-20 corrected vision or prostheses enable someone to walk with no perceptible limp. In reality, however, some skill limitations are so profound that continuous, pervasive human or prosthetic supports are required for even seriously subnormal functioning. For example, some individuals must be fed pureed food; their swallowing is

Table 10.2
Definition and Examples of Intensities of Support

1. Intermittent Supports
Supports on an "as needed basis." Characterized by episodic nature, person not always needing the support(s), or short-term supports needed during transitions (e.g., job loss or acute medical crisis). Intermittent supports may be high or low intensity.

2. Limited Supports
Supports characterized by consistency over time, time limited but not intermittent; may require fewer staff members and less cost than more intense levels of support (e.g., time-limited employment training or transitional supports when leaving school and starting adult programs or employment).

3. Extensive Supports
Supports characterized by regular involvement (e.g., daily) in at least some environments (such as work or home) and not time limited (e.g., long-term support and long-term home living support).

4. Pervasive Supports
Supports characterized by their constancy, high intensity; provided across environments; potential life-sustaining nature. Pervasive supports typically involve more staff members and intrusiveness than do extensive or time-limited supports.

virtually all they contribute to their being fed. Such support would be termed pervasive by any reasonable assessment. The support intensities that Luckasson et al. proposed appear in Table 10.2. Four intensities (in addition to normal support) were anticipated: *intermittent* supports are occasional supports that are more than would be given a person who has no disabilities; *limited* supports are ongoing but expected to be temporary; *extensive* supports are expected to be long-term in many but not all situations; and *pervasive* supports are intense, long-term, and required in nearly all situations. Several implications of Table 10.2 bear comment.

Normal Support

A fifth intensity of support is implied by the Luckasson et al. classification. This intensity, normal support, is required for individuals whose needed supports are indistinguishable from those who have no mental retardation.

Support in Multiple Settings

By contrasting extensive and pervasive supports in Table 10.2, one finds the implication that an individual's intensity of support is proportional to the number of settings in which that person requires support. This implication is anticipated superficially by Corollary 6 above, which emphasizes the fact that people are more competent in some settings than in others. If one is to score support intensity by counting the number of supported settings, one must start with a standard list of settings so that every evaluated individual has an equal opportunity to get a high-intensity score. This approach undermines culture-fairness, if one assumes that some cultures are more complex than others. If one holds that each individual has a unique cultural background, one makes this assumption. However, if one takes another approach—to score support intensity by counting supports only from settings that an evaluated individual encounters—then a person with a complex environment will tend to score higher than a person with a more

simple environment. Scores will vary with degree of cultural complexity rather than with intensity of supports required by one's unique culture and setting. Thus, it is crucial that supports intensities be referenced to culturally appropriate settings, not totaled over a standard list of settings.

Cost of Support

It seems important to separate the assessment of adaptive skill and its supports from the cost of providing supports to maximize self-sufficiency. Yet Table 10.2 mentions cost directly under limited supports and by implication ("more staff members") under pervasive supports. Performance is performance, and cost is cost; say two people have exactly the same mobility with their wheelchairs; it seems self-contradictory to argue that one is less skilled than the other because his or her wheelchair is more expensive. Each adaptive skill performance should be assessed in its specified setting with its existing supports in place, regardless of their cost. If one wants to evaluate cost of support, one can easily measure and compare costs in two or more individuals who might have identical adaptive skill profiles. Furthermore, cost-effectiveness can be assessed by dividing the overall intensity of support by the cost of support, both of which are arguably measured on ratio scales.

Types of Support

Generically, there are many types of support, including moral encouragement, reward, environmental engineering, prosthetics, verbal reminders, verbal instruction, and physical guidance. How does one decide how much weight to give each of these types of support in computing the total amount of support required by a particular individual for a particular behavior in a particular setting? On reflection, it appears that all types of support can be subsumed under four conceptually distinct, mutually exclusive, categories: (a) nonhuman prosthetic support (including environmental engineering); (b) human motivational support (the complement of self-direction, one of the 10 defining adaptive skill areas); (c) human protective supervision (regarding property, self, or others); and (d) human assistive support (physical or verbal).

Table 10.3 shows the organization of these supports as mutually exclusive categories. First, prosthetic supports and environmental engineering (i.e., adaptations that are under the control of the assessed individual) are distinguished from human supports. Second, human supports are subdivided into *protective supports* (i.e., those required to forestall injury to the assessed individual or to people or property in assessment environment) and *performance supports* (i.e., those required for the actual performance of the assessed skill). Finally, two distinct types of human supports promote performance: *physical or verbal assistance*, helping the assessed individual execute an act that he or she could not execute unassisted, and *motivational support*, encouraging independent performance without providing any verbal instruction or physical guidance to assist its actual execution. Verbal substantive assistance is limited to instruction to help the assessed individual know what action is required to complete a task. Verbal reminding, encouragement, praise, or coaxing are evaluated as motivational supports.

Cultural Fairness

Perhaps the most important and yet unmet challenge that assessors of mental retardation face is to assure that their assessments are based upon limitations of performance and not on cultural differences between the assessment process and the assessed individual. All previous adaptive behavior scales have been norm-referenced; the norms being based imperfectly on some subsample of the U.S. population at large (Cooper, 1996). The major strategy for culture-fair assessment of adaptive behavior or any other characteristic is to assess minority populations and claim that they do not differ significantly from norms gathered on a quota sample from the population at large (e.g., Bruininks & McGrew, 1995).

Table 10.3

Four Types of Supports and Their Weights
for Calculating Overall Intensity of Support for Each Adaptive Skill

Nonhuman	Human		
A. Prosthetic (weight = 1)[a]	Human Protective or Performance		
	C. Protective (weight = 3)[a]	Performance	
		B. Motivational (weight = 2)[a]	D. Assistive (weight = 4)[a]

Note. Detailed definitions of these four types of support are provided in Table 10.4.

[a]The weights are suggested multipliers used to calculate a total score from the four type-of-support scores. For example, a person with A, B, C, and D scores of 0, 3, 1, and 2 respectively would have a weighted total score of $[(1 \times 0) + (2 \times 3) + (3 \times 1) + (4 \times 2)]/10 = 17/10 = 1.7$.

Bryant, Bryant, and Chamberlain (this volume) have presented impressive evidence that adaptive behavior in general and the *Adaptive Areas Assessment* (AAA; Bryant et al., 1996) in particular are remarkably insensitive to differences between males and females or between minority and nonminority U.S. residents. The AAA is an adaptation of the revised, AAMR Adaptive Behavior Scale (Nihira et al., 1993) to assess each of the 10 Luckasson et al. (1992) areas of adaptive skills. Similarly, Bryant (1995) found that Hispanic (both Mexican American and Peruvian) performance was similar to that of the broad American AAA norming group. This approach seems logically flawed. Tests that fail to discriminate among cultural subgroups may simply lack the reliability to do so. It is logically unsound to claim that a scale is culture-fair when cultural subgroups have similar distributions of scores; relatively large errors of measurement could obscure true differences that might exist between the distributions of two different populations. Furthermore, subculture norms are little better than overall population norms in achieving cultural fairness. Any group norms are logically imprecise. Everyone has a *unique cultural heritage*, and the assessment of adaptive behavior requires an individualized assessment system. In conclusion, only an individualized evaluation system, which takes account of the unique cultural heritage and setting requirements of the individual examinee, can address the adaptive skills of an individual in his or her current and anticipated environments, as required by the assumptions articulated by Luckasson et al. (1992).

Quantification of Adaptive Behavior in Terms of Supports Given to Assessed Individuals in Unique Settings and Subcultures

A prior section detailed the three coordinated classification systems to evaluate adaptive

behavior that seem to be required by the 1992 AAMR definition of adaptive behavior: (a) a taxonomy of skills that has fidelity to the 10 skill areas sanctioned by Luckasson et al. (1992) and 5 empirical skill factors identified by Widaman and McGrew (1996); (b) a gradation of levels of support, described in Table 10.2; and (c) a classification of types of support described in Table 10.3. The present section applies the last two of these systems to develop general scoring protocols that can be used to assess any skill at any intensity of support. Following these protocols, we describe their applicability to assessments that are individualized to specific settings or subcultures.

General Scoring Protocols for Assessing Adaptive Skills

The general scoring protocols presented in Table 10.4 embody intensity and type of support described above and thereby form the basis of a scoring system to quantify the amount of support for any adaptive skill and, averaging over skills, in any area of adaptive behavior. These protocols are elaborations of the gradations or intensities of support described in Table 10.2—pervasive, extensive, limited, intermittent (or normal)—for each of the four types of support listed in Table 10.3—prosthetic, motivational, protective, or assistive.

Although the protocols from Table 10.4 satisfy the requirements implied by the six corollaries of Luckasson et al. (1992) for assessing adaptive behavior, they leave unsolved a fundamental quantification problem. The scoring system described in Table 10.4 would provide a score in the range of 0 to 4 for each type of support for each skill assessed, for each skill area, and for all skills combined. Yet Luckasson et al. proposed that mental retardation classification require, in addition to low intelligence, limitations in 2 or more of the 10 adaptive skill areas.

Table 10.4

Scoring Standards for Type and Intensity of Support for a Culturally Individualized Adaptive Behavior Scale (CIABS)

[a]Intensity of Support	Standard for Each of the Four Types of Support
Excluded (0)	The targeted behavior or support type is not appropriate for the assessed individual's culture, setting, and lifestyle. • This code should also be used when one cannot make an informed judgment regarding the performance of the assessed individual regarding the targeted behavior. • All ratings of support intensities should be based on direct observation of the rated behavior or on inferences based on direct observation of very similar behavior. • This code should not be used to avoid assessing individuals who have low ability; culturally appropriate behaviors for low-ability individuals should be evaluated under prosthetic, motivational, protective, and human-assistive supports they require under A, B, C, and/or D, respectively, below. • This code may be used to exclude an entire item or to exclude any type of support selectively: A, B, C, or D.
	A. Nonhuman Support Through Adaptations and/or Prostheses Adaptations to the environment and/or assistive devices that promote the assessed individual's functioning. (Assess human assistance under D below, not here.)
Normal (0)	Performs normally[b] for the culture and setting. Environmental adaptations and/or prostheses, if any, are temporary or inconspicuous.
Intermittent (1)	Performs normally[b] for the culture and setting with adaptations and/or prostheses that provide for independent functioning (at the 4th percentile or above[b]).
Limited (2)	Usually performs below the norms for the culture and setting using optimal environmental adaptations and/or prostheses.
Extensive (3)	Always performs below the norms for the culture and setting using prostheses that may be designed to provide for independent functioning, but never do.
Pervasive (4)	Always performs below the norms for the culture and setting. Prostheses are either precluded by the profoundness of the impairment or are designed for partial enhancement of function or comfort.
	B. Human Motivational Support Support required to prompt, coax, warn, or reward the assessed individual to complete or attempt the behavior with minimal prosthetic supports (A), maximal self-protection (C), and/or minimal human assistance (D). That is, judgments under A, C, and D should reflect the best performance that the assessed individual can give when at his or her highest intensity of motivation. *The intensity of motivational support is ordinarily at least as great as that attributed to D (below), because one can ordinarily do no better than one wants to do.* Moreover, motivational support might exceed human physical and/or verbal support, because one might need extensive reminders even though one performs a task with only intermittent or limited human assistance.

Table 10.4 continued on following page

Normal (0)	Performs with only rare reminders or incentives, if any.
Intermittent (1)	Performs with only occasional reminders or incentives.
Limited (2)	Performs with frequent reminders or incentives, which ordinarily lead to a serious effort to perform the prompted behavior.
Extensive (3)	Despite extensive reminders and/or incentives, the assessed individual usually fails to make a serious effort to perform the prompted behavior.
Pervasive (4)	Despite extensive reminders and/or incentives, the assessed individual rarely makes a serious effort to perform the prompted behavior.

C. Human Protective Supervision

Supervision required to protect the assessed individual or to protect the people or property affected by the targeted performance.

Normal (0)	Requires protective supervision only in new, dangerous circumstances.
Intermittent (1)	Usually requires protective supervision in new situations and seldom otherwise.
Limited (2)	Needs some protective supervision daily, and always has emergency supervision available by telephone.
Extensive (3)	Needs nearly continuous protective supervision, with only brief exceptions during special safe situations.
Pervasive (4)	Needs continuous protective supervision.

D. Human Assistive Support (Physical or Verbal)

Physical or verbal assistance given by a human companion to an assessed individual who is motivated to perform the targeted behavior in the specified setting. (Adaptations or prostheses, reminders or incentives, and/or protective supervision are scored respectively as support types A, B, and C above, not here.)

Normal (0)	Performs normally[bc] (above the 3rd percentile) for the culture and setting with rare human assistance except on new tasks or in new settings. Assistance is always provided by the natural (friends and family) support network.
Intermittent (1)	Performs normally[c] for the culture and setting with occasional human assistance, usually during changes in tasks or settings. Nearly all assistance is provided by the natural (friends and family) support network.
Limited (2)	Occasionally performs normally[bc] for the culture and setting without human assistance; usually performs below normal,[c] even with optimal assistance.
Extensive (3)	Requires extensive assistance to approximate independent[c] performance. Unassisted performance is limited to familiar, routine settings and tasks. Nevertheless, the assisted individual usually contributes more than half the performance effort.[d]
Pervasive (4)	Never approximates independent[c] performance, even with pervasive support. Requires continuous assistance. Unassisted performance, if any, is always closely monitored and is limited to easy routine tasks. The assisted individual always contributes less than half the performance effort.[d]

Table 10.4 continued on following page

Intermittent, limited, extensive, and *pervasive* are the terms chosen by AAMR professionals to represent four intensities of support. Assessors might find it useful to use the following approximate correspondences for the four intensities of support:

> • *Intermittent*: mild mental retardation, educable, educably mentally handicapped, occasional support; performance usually approximates normal[c]

> • *Limited*: moderate mental retardation, trainable, trainable mentally handicapped; frequent support, usually time-limited, but sometimes standby, support; performance seldom approximates normal[c];

> • *Extensive*: severe mental retardation; intensive, constant, continuous, seldom standby support, that usually provides less than half the effort for performance[d]; performance never approximates normal[c];

> • *Pervasive*: profound mental retardation; constant, continuous support that always provides more than half the effort for performance[d].

[b]Normal is defined to be at the 4th percentile (or above) of the assessed person's nondisabled peer reference group; subnormal is at the 3rd percentile or below. That is, a rating of "normal" means that fewer than 4 people in 100 would require as little support for the targeted performance as the individual being assessed.

[c]The grading of "normal" and "independent" performance was not explicit in the Luckasson et al. (1992) formulations. It was adopted for the CIABS as an understandable hierarchy to help distinguish among intermittent, limited, and extensive support.

[d]The distinction between less or more than half of the performance effort was not explicit in the Luckasson et al. (1992) formulations. It was adopted for the CIABS as an understandable distinction between extensive and pervasive support.

The transformation of the proposed 0-to-4 support-intensity scale from Table 10.4 to the Luckasson et al. 2-of-10 limitation standard for the diagnosis of mental retardation can be readily accomplished by applying the following transformations:

- 0.00 - 0.79 = normal supports = less than 20% support
- 0.80 - 1.59 = intermittent supports = 20% to 40% support
- 1.60 - 2.39 = limited supports = 40% to 60% support
- 2.40 - 3.19 = extensive supports = 60% to 80% support
- 3.20 - 4.00 = pervasive supports = 80% to 100% support

Not only does this transformation permit the identification of a quantitative cutoff score (20% support or more) for discriminating between those with or without mental retardation, it provides a quantitative distinction among four intensities of support.

Culturally Individualized Assessment of Adaptive Behavior

A final point with regard to scoring is the ease with which the proposed assessment system lends itself to cultural individualization. Each of the four types of support is scored from an intensity of 0 to an intensity of 4 (normal supports to pervasive supports) for every assessed skill, and the weighted average of the four types indexes the amount of support for each assessed skill. Thus, every skill is scored from 0 to 4; the average of all skill items equals the overall adaptive behavior score, which again may range from 0 to 4. This broad scoring range at all intensities of assessment has remarkable implications for individualization. Because every type of support and every skill is scored from 0 to 4, any type of support that is inappropriate for any item for the assessed individual or the assessment setting may be omitted without affecting the individual's evaluation on the remaining skills and/or types of support, whose intensity-of-support score will always be the average of the types of support and skills that have been applied. Thus, the items selected to assess any individual should be completely individualized and appropriate to that individual's setting and subculture.

Field Test of 32 Participants With 20 Items

To test the feasibility of using the approach described above to evaluate adaptive skills in individuals with mental retardation, 20 broadly ranging items were used to evaluate 32 diverse adults who were receiving services from the major developmental disability service agency in each of two midsized central Illinois cities. Respondents were eight employees of these service agencies who were paid a $20 honorarium for each participant they recruited and from whom they obtained permission to complete an anonymous assessment. The seven who reported their ages ranged from 24 to 51 years, with an average of 37.9 and a standard deviation of 9.6. All eight had had some college; six had degrees; two had graduate degrees. Seven of the eight were female. Respondents were asked to select individuals whose ability varied greatly, so the assessed skills could be evaluated over a broad range of supports. Of the 32 assessed individuals, 19 were assessed by direct care staff, 10 by supervisory staff, and 3 by an agency nurse. Eighteen were female, and 14 were male. They ranged in age from 24 to 63 with an average of 38.8 and a standard deviation of 10.7. Two were classified by their agencies as borderline, 10 as mild, 8 as moderate, 8 as severe, and 4 as profound.

Twelve had a high school diplomas, 2 more had attended high school, and 17 had attended only elementary school. Two of the 32 were called friends rather than clients by their evaluators.

Respondents trained themselves with a self-instructional manual (Heal, 1996). The training asked them to select 2 fictitious individuals from 11 whose "life stories" and situations were described in two-page vignettes. Their vignette selections were to be those that most nearly resembled the clients whom they would rate for the project. They compared their ratings of these fictitious individuals to those made by the research team[1] in order to reconcile any discrepancies that exceeded one support intensity. Respondents based their trial assessments on protocol sheets adapted from Table 10.4 for each of 20 skills (see Table 10.5). Protocol sheets gave specific standards and examples for every intensity of every type of support for every assessed skill.

The assessed skills are listed in Table 10.5; skill numbers correspond to those in Figure 10.1. As shown, they were broadly distributed over the three settings and 12 skill areas. Skill 4, "reads community signs," was repeated as skill 11 to evaluate reliability. Assessments using these 20 items required an average of 54.1 minutes, with a standard deviation of 32.2 minutes and a range of 15 to 120 minutes. It is unlikely that a skilled evaluator can complete a careful evaluation in less than 1 minute per skill.

The results of the field-test assessments appear in Figure 10.1. Intensity of support is shown for each of the four types of support for every item. Ideally, every item would have an

1. Jennifer Mueller was a research assistant on this project. Janell Copher wrote several items, and Neil Barshes and Christi Hillebrand contributed as James Scholars at the University of Illinois at Urbana-Champaign. As a team these four helped refine the concepts reported herein and develop their operational use. Diane Krandel was instrumental in arranging the adaptive behavior skills as they appear in Table 10-1. Ju-Shan Hsieh and Madhab Khoju conducted the MULTILOG item-response analyses for an earlier discarded version of this paper. In addition, we are grateful for helpful comments and suggestions from George Baroff, Ron Berk, P. Helen Heal, Bradley Hill, Diana Krandel, Ruth Luckasson, and Scott Spreat. This chapter was supported in part by the University of Illinois Research Board and in part by the U.S. Office of Special Education and Rehabilitative Services, contract No. 300-85-0160, to the Transition Institute at the University of Illinois at Urbana-Champaign.

Table 10.5
Skills Assessed in Field Study

SKILL AREAS	SETTINGS		
	Home	**Work**	**Community**
Communication, Expressive	6. Expresses feelings.	16. Registers oral grievances or complaints.	
Communication, Receptive	7. Fulfills spoken requests.	17. Follows directions to complete a sequence of tasks.	
Functional Academics, Literacy	8. Follows written directions of a boxed food item.		4., 11. Reads community signs.
Functional Academics, Mathematics		18. Uses clocks and schedules to pace and complete projects at work.	12. Uses money to shop at a familiar store.
Social	2. Engages in interpersonal interactions.		13. Forms and fosters friend ships and loving relationships.
Leisure			
Self-Care	5. Dresses and undresses.	19. Uses a vending machine to obtain a snack or soda.	3. Eats in public places and at public occasions.
Health	9. Maintains a balanced diet.	20. Treats illnesses and injuries on the job.	
Safety			14. Avoids exploitation and/or harassment.
Home Living	10. Uses the telephone.		15. Finds their way home.
Work			
Community			1. Uses a public restroom.

aSkill numbers are listed in the order that the skills were assessed by respondents. These numbers correspond to those in Figure 1.

average support intensity of 2.0, assuming a sampling distribution that was spread equally over the mental retardation range. Although most of the skills required support that averaged between 1.5 and 2.5, four skills clearly required less support. Types of support were highly correlated within skills: If one type of support is low for a skill, so are the others. Nevertheless, the correlations for different skills was nearly as high as those within skills. Correlations for skill-type subscores ranged from .851 for work prosthetics with community protection to .990 for work motivation with work assistance. If support types or skills were truly independent, the correlations among them would be low. Thus these results point to a general adaptive skill dimension that pervaded all the conceptual distinctions that were so carefully drawn above. On the other hand, these high correlations indicate that

these judgments are made with extraordinary reliability, even though the skills varied in difficulty.

The variability in difficulty among skills undermines the logic described above for achieving cultural fairness. This logic held that skills could be dropped from an assessment without affecting the assessed individual's overall support score. However, if skills differ in difficulty despite parallel, full-range, absolute protocols, then adjustments must be made to assure that skill difficulty is considered in assessing overall support intensity. Item response theory (Baker, 1992; Hambleton, Swaminathan, & Rogers, 1991; Lord, 1980; Tassé, 1994) is an excellent tool for scaling the difficulty of skills, but it would necessarily replace the absolute support scale with a relative, standardized scale. This replacement would undermine the entire logic of a scale

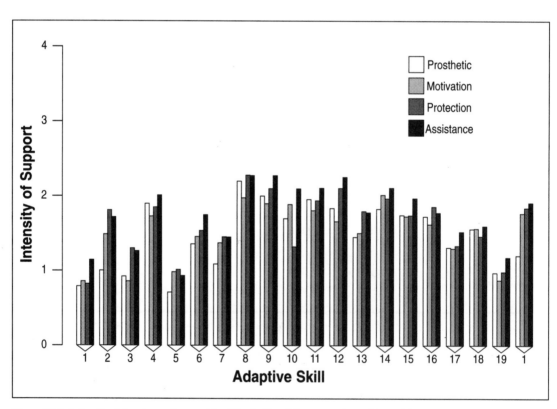

Figure 10.1. Intensity of four types of support for 20 adaptive skills averaged over 32 participants.

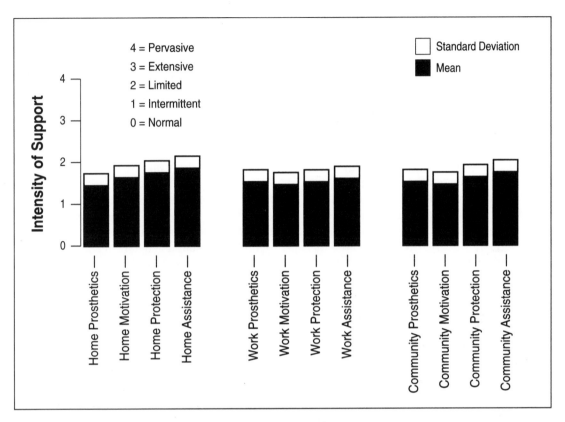

Figure 10.2. *Average intensity of support for four types of support in three settings.*

based on support standards. It would obscure the anchors and intensity thresholds so explicit in the new definition. Perhaps the best tack is to retain only those skills that range equally over the entire five-intensity support range on a standardized national sample.

Figure 10.2 shows the mean and standard deviation for the intensity of each type of support in each of the three settings. This figure reveals a consistency that was difficult to see in Figure 10.1. Supports averaged between 1.0 (intermittent) and 2.0 (limited) for all support types in all three settings. Furthermore, the pattern of increasing intensities was the same for all three settings, rising from about 1.5 for prosthetics to about 1.75 for human assistance. The similarity of these profiles reflects the fortuitous selection of some easy and some difficult skills from each setting. This selection was also responsible for the remarkably small standard deviations. Because standard deviations are the upper limit of standard errors, it is clear that the support estimated for any individual in any setting from this set of skills is within a quarter of an intensity unit.

If Figure 10.2 shows the stability of these assessments over settings, Figure 10.3 shows their sensitivity to differences among individuals. When they were averaged over the 20 items, the reported intensities of support for these individuals ranged from nearly normal (0) to pervasive (4). See Figure 10.2. Using our proposed transformation of support intensity and number of limited adaptive skills with the quantitative cutoff .80 or 20%, described on the previous page, nine of these individuals have support intensities that are too low (i.e. below .80) for classification of mental retardation.

Parallel to Figure 10.1, types of support were highly correlated across individuals. Correlations with agency records of mental retardation level ranged from .802 for home protection to .849 for community motivation. These high correlations among ratings might indicate a halo effect on the part of assessors rather than correlated support needs within assessed individuals. Qualified by this caveat, these results indicate that the strategy described above to assess adaptive skills using absolute standards of support was effective in reliably specifying the intensity of support required by an individual and that this intensity of support was consistently reported for all types of support and in all settings.

Culturally Sensitive Individualized Assessment of Adaptive Behavior

The foregoing chapter features solutions to four challenges for the assessment of adaptive behavior in order to classify a person to some level of mental retardation, if any: (a) the taxonomy of adaptive skills reflects a comprehensive curriculum of skills to assess; (b) the four types of support clarify the meaning of support; (c) the five intensities of support refine the standards for quantifying support and drawing a correspondence between one's intensity of support and one's degree of mental retardation; and (d) the individualization of the assessment maximizes its cultural fairness. It appears that this approach to the assessment of adaptive behavior is uniquely suited to meet the conditions of the revised definition of adaptive behavior sanctioned by the AAMR manual, *Mental Retardation: definition, Classification, and Systems of Supports* (Luckasson et al., 1992).

The results of the pursuit of a culturally sensitive individualized adaptive behavior assessment appear to be extremely promising. Protocols can be constructed for a broad array of adaptive skills; minimal training with these

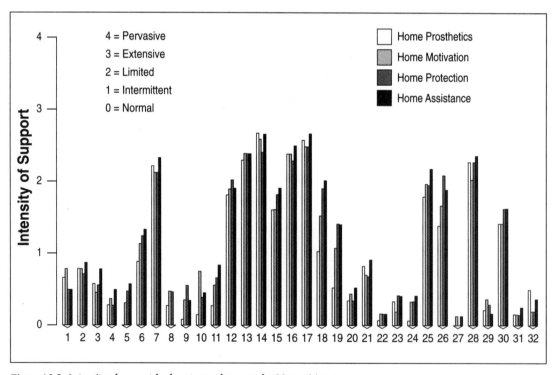

Figure 10.3. *Intensity of support for four types of support for 32 participants.*

protocols enables professional direct care staff and case managers to rate reliably the support required by adults across the entire range of mental retardation. If there is a caveat for this pursuit, it is that these ratings within participants were so highly intercorrelated as to suggest a halo effect. In spite of this caveat, we expect that these findings appear to be sufficiently promising to prompt a national field test to select several skills in each cell of Table 10.1 and to standardize them on a representative population of individuals with adaptive behavior limitations occurring concurrently with low intelligence.

References

American Psychiatric Association. (1994). *Diagnostic and statistical manual of mental disorders* (4th ed.). Washington, DC: Author.

Baker, F. B. (1992). *Item response theory: Parameter estimation techniques.* New York: Marcel Dekker.

Bruininks, R. H., & McGrew, K. S. (1995, May). Adaptive behavior: Definition, uses, and issues. Paper presented at the 119th annual meeting of the American Association on Mental Retardation, San Francisco.

Bryant, B. R. (1995, June). *Report to the AAMR committee on adaptive behavior.* Paper presented at the 119th annual meeting of the American Association on Mental Retardation, San Francisco.

Bryant, B. R., Taylor, R. L., & Rivera, D. P. (1996). *Assessment of adaptive areas.* Austin, TX: Pro-Ed.

Clausen, J. A. (1972a). Quo Vadis, AAMD? *Journal of Special Education, 6,* 52-60.

Clausen, J. A. (1972b). The continuing problem of defining mental retardation. *Journal of Special Education, 6,* 97-106.

Conley, R. W. (1973). *The economics of mental retardation.* Baltimore: Johns Hopkins University Press.

Cooper, P. (1996, May). *Draft format for referent group and psychometric qualities of existing adaptive behavior scales.* Paper presented at the 120th annual meeting of the American Association on Mental Retardation, San Antonio, TX.

Developmental Disabilities Act of 1996 (P.L. 101-496). 42 U.S.C.§ 6001.

Evans, I. M. (1991). Testing and diagnosis: A review and evaluation. In L. H. Meyer, C. A. Peck, & Brown, (Eds.), *Critical issues in the lives of people with severe disabilities* (pp. 25-44). Baltimore: Paul H. Brookes.

Fryers, T. (1993). Epidemiological thinking in mental retardation: Issues in taxonomy and population frequency. In Norman W. Bray (Ed.), *International review of research in mental retardation* (Vol. 17, pp. 176-192). New York: Academic Press.

Grossman, H. J. (Ed.). (1983). *Manual on terminology and classification in mental retardation.* Washington, DC: American Association on Mental Deficiency.

Hambleton, R. K., Swaminathan, H., & Rogers, H. J. (1991). *Fundamentals of item response theory.* Newbury Park, CA: Sage.

Heal, L. W. (1993). Dear editor: An analysis of the tensions engendered by the 1992 AAMR definition of mental retardation. APA *Division 33 Newsletter,* 19(2), 14-17.

Heal, L. W. (1996). *The culturally individualized adaptive behavior scale manual.* Champaign, IL: University of Illinois Department of Special Education.

Heber, R. (1959). A manual on terminology and classification in mental retardation. *American Journal of Mental Retardation Monograph, 64.*

Individuals with Disabilities Education Act (IDEA) of 1997 (P.L.101-476). 20 U.S.C.§ 1400 et seq.

Jacobson, J. W., & Mulick, J. A. (1996). *Manual of diagnosis and professional practice in mental retardation.* Washington, DC: American Psychological Association.

Lambert, N., Nihira, K., & Leland, H. (1993). AAMR *Adaptive behavior scale— School Version.* Austin, TX: Pro-Ed.

Lord, F. M. (1980). *Applications of item response theory to practical testing problems.* Hillsdale, NJ: Lawrence Erlbaum.

Luckasson, R., Coulter, D. L., Polloway, E. A., Reiss, S., Schalock, R. L., Snell, M. E., Spitalnik, D. M., & Stark, J. A. (1992). *Mental retardation: Definition, classification, and systems of supports* (9th ed.). Washington, DC: American Association on Mental Retardation.

MacMillan, D. L., Gresham, F. M., & Siperstein, G. N. (1993). Conceptual and psychometric concerns about the 1992 AAMR definition of mental retardation. *American Journal on Mental Retardation, 98,* 325-335.

Nihira, K., Lambert, N., & Leland, H. (1993). AAMR *Adaptive behavior scale—Residential and community version.* Austin, TX: Pro-Ed.

Tassé, M. J. (1994). *Étude de la stabilité et de la concordance de l'Échelle québécoise de comportements adaptatifs (ÉQCA) et élaboration d'une version testage adaptatif informatisé de l'ÉQCA.* Unpublished doctoral dissertation, Department of Psychology, Université du Québec à Montréal.

Widaman, K. F., & McGrew, K. S. (1996). The structure of adaptive behavior. In J. W. Jacobson & J. A. Mulick (Eds.), *Manual of diagnosis and professional practice in mental retardation* (pp. 97-112). Washington, DC: American Psychological Association.

U.S. Department of Education. (1996). *To assure the free appropriate public education of all children with disabilities: 18th annual report to Congress on the implementation of the* Individuals With Disabilities Education Act. Washington, DC: Author.

World Health Organization. (1980). *International classification of impairments, disabilities, and handicaps.* Geneva: Author.

PART 3

The Future of the Construct of Adaptive Behavior

Introduction

The Spanish philosopher Ortega y Gasset once said that "human life is a constant preoccupation with the future." We now turn to the future of the construct of adaptive behavior. In this concluding chapter, Bob Schalock reviews the five major themes of the preceding 10 chapters and suggests four challenges that the construct of adaptive behavior presents to the field of mental retardation:

- to integrate the concepts of adaptive behavior and intelligence;
- to understand the contextual variables that influence the condition of mental retardation;
- to rethink the definition of mental retardation and its measurement; and
- to address the complex issues involved in the cross-cultural assessment of adaptive behavior.

As discussed throughout this book, the field of mental retardation is currently undergoing significant changes in the way we view both the condition of mental retardation and people with mental retardation. This state of transition is characterized by:

- a changing conception of disability, moving away from a pathology focus to a contextual perspective in which a person's disability results from an interaction among limitations and the person's social and physical environment;
- a supports paradigm that underlies service delivery to people with disabilities and focuses on the individual strengths and limitations in functional skill areas;
- a reconceptualization of intelligence and adaptive behavior based on the consistent findings that both are multidimensional constructs;
- an increasingly multicultural society; and
- the availability and use of prosthetics and technical devices that significantly reduce

the mismatch between people and their environments and consequently enhance their adaptive behavior.

Chapter 11 discusses future challenges and opportunities as we continue to attempt to understand better the construct of mental retardation, its treatment and amelioration, and its three primary defining variables: intelligence, adaptive behavior, and age of onset. Keep in mind these key points in reading chapter 11:

- How is the concept of mental retardation changing as it moves away from a pathology focus to a contextual perspective?
- How are the multidimensional components of adaptive behavior and intelligence merging into a broader conception of personal competence?
- What indicators point to a logical merging of the concepts of adaptive skills, environmental demands, and criterion-referenced assessment?
- How do cultural factors play a critical role in understanding adaptive behavior and its assessment?
- How should future research in the areas of adaptive behavior and intelligence be driven by conceptual models that integrate and expand upon what is currently known about the two areas?
- What role should culture play in the definition of mental retardation?
- What role should supports play in the definition and diagnosis of mental retardation?
- What role should technical aids play in the diagnosis of mental retardation and its amelioration?
- Are the historical criteria used to diagnose mental retardation—deficits in intelligence, limitations in adaptive behavior, and age of onset below 18 (or 21 in some systems)— still appropriate?

Adaptive Behavior and Its Measurement: Setting the Future Agenda

ROBERT L. SCHALOCK
Hastings College

Introduction

I trust readers of this book have responded to a number of questions about the concept of adaptive behavior and considered a number of challenges faced by the field of mental retardation regarding the conceptualization, measurement, and use of the adaptive behavior construct. If the authors of this book have been successful, we have stimulated thought and further discussion about the role of adaptive behavior in the definition of mental retardation, the interrelatedness of adaptive behavior and intelligence, and the measurement of adaptive behavior within a multicultural environment.

By way of review, five major themes emerge from the preceding 10 chapters:

- The concept of mental retardation is changing, moving away from a pathology focus to a contextual perspective in which a person's condition results from an interaction among functional limitations and the person's social, physical, and augmentative environments.
- The multidimensional components of adaptive behavior and intelligence are merging into a broader conception of personal competence.
- There is a logical merging of the concepts of adaptive skills, environmental demands, and criterion-referenced assessment.
- Cultural factors play a critical role in understanding adaptive behavior and its assessment.
- Future research in the areas of adaptive behavior and intelligence should be driven by conceptual models that integrate and expand upon what is currently known about the two areas.

Embedded in these five major themes are four challenges that provide the focus of this final chapter: (a) to integrate the concept of adaptive behavior and intelligence, (b) to understand the contextual variables that influence the condition of mental retardation, (c) to rethink the definition of mental retardation and its measurement, and (d) to address the complex issues involved in the cross-cultural assessment of adaptive behavior. Here I attempt to integrate the major points of each of the preceding chapters, but I take some "poetic license" in the spirit of stimulating dialogue and future research.

Challenge: To Integrate the Concepts of Adaptive Behavior and Intelligence

Two recurring themes throughout Part 1 relate to the multidimensional and hierarchical aspects of adaptive behavior and intelligence and to the merging of these two constructs into the broader concept of personal (or overall) competence.

Multidimensional and Hierarchical Nature

As discussed throughout this book, there has been interesting parallel historical debate about the unidimensional versus multidimensional nature of both intelligence and adaptive behavior. In regard to intelligence, Spearman's (1923) conception of a general factor of intelligence (called *g*) dominated early theories of intelligence and can still be found today in the most recent revision of the *Stanford-Binet Intelligence Scale* (Thorndike, Hagen, & Sattler, 1986), which groups its 15 subtests into a composite IQ that is reflective of g. Similarly, the earlier conception of adaptive behavior provided for a general factor that accounted for the most variance (see Bruininks, McGrew, & Maruyama, 1988; Thompson, McGrew, & Bruininks, this volume; Widaman & McGrew, 1996).

Today, there is a strong trend to view both intelligence (Carroll, 1993; Daniel, 1997; Gardner, 1993) and adaptive behavior (Widaman & McGrew, 1996) as multidimensional and hierarchically arranged. In regard to intelligence, for example, Carroll, in a thorough review of the significant theoretical and empirical work on intelligence, identified three levels of cognitive factors varying in breath and generality: (a) many narrow, first-level stratum factors that represent greater specialization of abilities (analogous to Cattell's "fluid intelligence"); (b) a smaller number of broad second-stratum factors that represent general abilities (analogous to Cattell's "crystallized intelligence") and includes abilities related to visual perception and psychomotor movement; and (c) a single broad third-stratum factor that represents general ability. The results of Carroll's meta-analysis are similar to Cattell's (1971) triadic theory of abilities, Thurstone's (1947) vectors of mind, and Vernon's (1961) hierarchical theory of intelligence.

In regard to adaptive behavior, Widaman and McGrew (1996) state that "a hierarchically organized, multi-factorial approach to adaptive behavior appears to hold the most promise" (p. 109). Similarly, Thompson et al. (this volume) state:

In sum, important lessons can be gleaned from the rich history of attempts to define an empirically based (largely factor analytic) taxonomy of cognitive abilities. Foremost is the need to evaluate the breadth or degrees of generality of dimensions identified in adaptive behavior and maladaptive behavior factor analytic research. Furthermore, it is particularly important that the results of factor analytic studies be interpreted within hierarchical adaptive and maladaptive frameworks,

which in turn could be embedded in even larger frameworks (e.g., Greenspan's model of personal competence) that include other important human competencies (e.g., intelligence). (p. 45)

There are advantages to viewing adaptive behavior and intelligence from a multidimensional, hierarchical perspective. First, it allows us to agree on concepts and terminology and thereby better integrate assessment and diagnostic processes; second, it is consistent with current theoretical and empirical work in the areas of intelligence and adaptive behavior.

Personal Competence

In the future, we need to better integrate the constructs of adaptive behavior and intelligence within the larger construct of overall or personal competence. This suggestion is consistent with that made earlier in this volume by Greenspan (see Figures 4.1 and 4.2), Thompson et al. (Figures 2.4, 2.5, & 2.6), and Schalock (Figure 3.2).

As discussed in chapters 2 and 3, integrating the constructs of adaptive behavior and intelligence into a broader construct of personal competence might logically progress in the following four steps. First, work within the framework of overall (or personal) competence, as this concept allows the delineation of those skills or achievements in the major life domains that are most important in describing how a person is adapting to his or her environment. Second, complete exploratory factor analysis of a three-factor model of overall competence composed of (a) conceptual intelligence (comprised of cognitive, communication, and academic skills); (b) practical intelligence (comprised of those independent living skills that allow one to deal with the physical and mechanical aspects of life); and (c) social intelligence (comprised of those skills deemed necessary to understand and deal effectively with social and interpersonal relations, responsibility, emotional competence, and social competence). Third, determine the appropriate stratum within the respective hierarchical structure, paying very close attention to the obtained patterns of convergent and discriminant validity. Fourth, complete confirmatory factor analyses of the results of Steps 2 and 3 for the purposes of theory building, measurement development, and the generation of hypotheses for testing.

There are advantages to integrating the constructs of adaptive behavior and intelligence within the construct of overall competence:

- It would provide the framework for the construction of criterion-referenced assessments of overall competence.
- It is consistent with the current emphasis on dynamic assessment and integrating the assessment intervention or habilitation process.
- It would help reduce the confusion among terms, constructs, and measures in both adaptive behavior and intelligence.
- It would allow the field to incorporate better an ecological model that focuses on a person-environmental analysis of specific skills required within that environment and strategies to reduced mismatches.
- It would allow the field to focus on a broader range of functional conceptual and social skills.
- It would allow researchers and scholars in the field of mental retardation to cast a much wider net for important ideas and concepts emanating from other behavioral sciences.
- It would provide a productive platform for conceptually driven research and scholarly discourse.

Challenge: To Understand Contextual Variables

The recent changes in our conception of adaptive behavior has occurred as the field of mental retardation has increasingly embraced the notion of contextualism. If we continue to move toward a contextually based, multidimensional concept of overall or personal competence, there will be a corresponding need for the field to do two things: (a) shift from a trait to a functional or ecological approach in our definition, assessment, and (re)habilitation efforts; and (b), understand better the role of mediating variables in the condition of mental retardation.

Trait Versus an Ecological or Functional Approach

Moving from a trait to an ecological or functional approach to mental retardation will not be easy, for it involves accepting the notion that

> mental retardation is not something you have . . . nor is it something you are . . . it is not a medical disorder . . . or a mental disorder. Mental retardation refers to a particular state of functioning that begins in childhood and in which limitations in intelligence coexist with related limitations in adaptive skills. . . . As a statement about functioning, it describes the "fit" between the capabilities of the individual and the structure and expectations of the individual's personal and social environment. The level of functioning in mental retardation may have a specific etiology . . . but mental retardation is not synonymous with the etiology. (Luckasson et al., 1992, p. 9)

It is very apparent to this author that we will experience considerable debate during the next decade within the field of mental retardation as to which approach (trait vs. functional or ecological) the field takes. If we take a trait approach, for example, we will continue to employ a psychometric model of assessment, and continue to rely on standardized instruments for the assessment and diagnosis of mental retardation. Furthermore, we will likely see more reliance on etiology and level of impairment as central in the diagnostic process (Haywood, 1997; Zigler, Balla, & Hodapp, 1984). Conversely, if we take a functional or ecological approach, we will (a) see the use of more functional assessments; (b) accept clinical judgment along with the results of functional assessments as part of the diagnostic process; (c) focus on person-environmental matches and mismatches and their amelioration; (d) define disability and mental retardation within the context of environments, cultures, and support factors; (e) shift from what people are to what they need; and (f) consider the dynamic role that both cognition and motivation play in mental retardation. Furthermore, we will consider people with mental retardation as affected significantly by variables such as physical well-being, psychological and behavioral factors, and family and community supports (Polloway, 1997; Switzky, 1997).

Three significant questions and issues need to be addressed whether the field adopts a trait or an ecological or functional approach.

• What role should etiology play in the diagnosis of mental retardation? If one accepts Haywood's (1997) suggestion, then mental retardation would be limited primarily to those with clearly discernible etiological conditions and groupings. If, however, one accepts Greenspan's (1997) definition, then the role of etiology would be minimized and the role of environments and supports emphasized.

• How does one align the multidimensional concept of mental retardation with the measurement thereof? Although the understanding of intelligence and adaptive behavior has changed over time, old measurement approaches and standards have not. As discussed by Crossen (1997) in reference to IQ tests, there are disincentives to changing from our current psychometrically focused approach, including: (a) A single number is concrete and therefore very easy to defend in court and elsewhere; (b) creating new tests is very costly, because they require 3 to 6 years for their development; and (c) current IQ tests such as the *Weschler* (1981) and *Stanford-Binet* (Terman & Merrill, 1973) are deeply entrenched in the minds of Americans and in the psychological and educational bureaucracies.

• What will be the basis of classification and categorization? The central question here is whether people will be classified based on intellectual deficits, functional behavioral limitations, level of support needs, or some combination of the three.

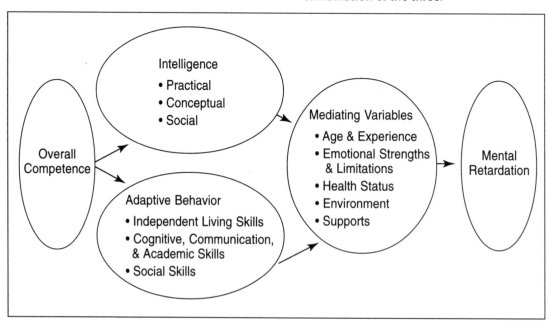

Figure 11.1. *A heuristic model of mental retardation.*

Role of Mediating Variables

Mental retardation is present when specific intellectual and adaptive limitations affect the person's ability to cope with the ordinary challenges of everyday living. This statement suggests the critical role that ecological or contextual variables play in mental retardation. As shown in Figure 11.1, at least five contextual variables act as mediating variables in the expression of mental retardation: (a) age and experience, (b) emotional strengths and limitations, (c) health status, (d) environment, and (e) supports. Each of the mediating variables listed in Figure 11.1 might be included in a definition of mental retardation and/or determine whether or not a person receives a diagnosis of mental retardation.

How might these mediating variables impact the condition of mental retardation? In integrating these mediating variables into subsequent definitional and diagnostic endeavors, the field of mental retardation needs to address a number of questions posed by each of the contextual variables. These questions are discussed briefly in reference to each mediating variable.

Age and Experience

Should there be an age of onset criterion for mental retardation, and if so, what should it be? Currently, there is consensus that there should be such a criterion, but no consensus as to whether the age should be 18 or 21 (Schalock, Stark, Snell, Coulter, & Polloway, 1994). Also, can a person move "in and out" of the condition of mental retardation? Experiences of many suggest that this may be the case, which is consistent with the fourth assumption of the 1992 System, that "with appropriate supports over a sustained period, the life functioning of the person with mental retardation will generally improve" (Luckasson et al., p. 5). Thus, age and experience can be either inclusionary or exclusionary variables in any diagnosis of mental retardation.

Emotional Strengths and Limitations

What is the best way to incorporate the concept of emotional intelligence (Goleman, 1995) or emotional competence (Greenspan & Granfield, 1992) into the concept of mental retardation? Should it be subsumed within the area of social intelligence, social skills, or as a mediating variable that is common to both? In this regard, a significant question is whether the concept of maladaptive behavior is relevant to the definition and/or diagnosis of mental retardation. Although it is critical to the provision of services and supports, and historically has been a part of many scales of adaptive behavior, its relevance can be questioned in the definition and diagnostic process.

Health Status

What role should one's health status (including medication level) play in the diagnosis of mental retardation, and how can we best integrate the influence of health and functioning into the diagnosis of and amelioration of mental retardation? For example, for people with mental retardation, the person's health status impacts assessment, response to (re)habilitation strategies, and the type and intensity of needed supports. I foresee an increasingly strong research need to determine the relations among health status, health care needs, provision of resources, and the achievement of desired health-related and adaptive behavior outcomes.

Environment

To what degree should the discrepancy between the person's strengths and limitations and the environment's performance demands be incorporated into the conceptualization of mental retardation? Similarly, what is the best way to incorporate the environment's facilitory and inhibitory factors into a definition and/or diagnosis of mental retardation?

Supports

What role should needed supports play in a definition and/or diagnosis of mental retardation? Analogously, what role should the availability and use of assistive technology play in the conceptualization, definition, and diagnosis of mental retardation?

These questions related to the role of mediating variables on the condition of mental retardation are critical to address and resolve, because they are involved significantly in answering the ultimate question: What is mental retardation? The following section discusses the need to rethink the definition of mental retardation and its measurement.

Challenge: To Rethink the Definition of Mental Retardation and Its Measurement

If we integrate the concepts of adaptive behavior and intelligence and understand better the contextual variables that influence the condition of mental retardation, then the future requires that we rethink the definition of mental retardation and its measurement. To this end, H. Carl Haywood (1997), in his keynote address to the 121st annual conference of the American Association on Mental Retardation, challenged the field to

> begin a quest for new concepts and new definitions of mental retardation, recognizing the inadequacy of present concepts and definitions to incorporate what is known about the behavior and development of persons with mental retardation, and the inadequacy of present concepts and definitions to incorporate both the cultural relativism and the physical absolute—that is, cultural constancy—perspectives. (p. 5)

It is apparent that the quest has begun, and that a number of conceptual shifts have already occurred that should influence our rethinking the condition of mental retardation. Among the most important:

- The concept of disability has shifted from pathology to a condition resulting from the interaction of the person and his or her environment.
- There is a trend to define disability—and by inference mental retardation—in terms of functional limitations in practical, conceptual, and social skills.
- Assistive technology is providing people with mental retardation opportunities for increased independence, productivity, community integration, and satisfaction.
- Public policy now examines disability with respect to external barriers that limit a person's access to educational, economic, and social opportunities and strategies used to reduce the mismatch between individuals and specific environmental demands.
- Successful education and (re)habilitation strategies demonstrate that acquiring adaptive skills permits an individual to cope better with environmental demands and thus participate in societal activities to a greater extent.
- The supports paradigm has shifted the focus of intervention from the person only to the role that various support systems and the natural environment can play in reducing functional limitations.

Each of these changes has been discussed at some length earlier in this monograph. I now address the impact these changes might have on the definition and measurement of mental retardation.

Definition of Mental Retardation

The integration of adaptive behavior and intelligence and the movement toward a more contextual definition of mental retardation is reflected in the 1992 AAMR System (Luckasson et al.) that defines mental retardation as

> [referring] to substantial limitations in present functioning. It is characterized by significantly subaverage intellectual functioning, existing concurrently with related limitations in two or more of the

following applicable adaptive skill areas: communication, self-care, home living, social skills, community use, self-direction, health and safety, functional academics, leisure, and work. Mental retardation manifests before age 18. (p. 5).

In the four assumptions of this definition one finds the impact of the conceptual shifts listed above. The following four assumptions are essential to the application of the 1992 AAMR definition: (a) valid assessment considers cultural and linguistic diversity as well as differences in communication and behavioral factors; (b) the existence of limitations in adaptive skills occurs within the context of community environments typical of the individual's age peers and is indexed to the person's individualized needs for supports; (c) specific adaptive limitations often coexist with strengths in other adaptive skills or other personal capabilities; and (d) with appropriate supports over a sustained period, the life functioning of the person with mental retardation will generally improve.

With the shift toward a more functional, context-related conception of mental retardation, it is no surprise that alternative definitions of mental retardation are being offered for discussion and debate within the field (Greenspan & Switzky, in preparation). Within this movement, one finds the following key points:

- The definition of mental retardation should incorporate what is known about the behavior and development of people with mental retardation.
- The key to devising an adequate definition of mental retardation is to base it on the broader cognitive underpinnings of the condition while using a model that gives equal emphasis to social and practical competence and captures the essence of mental retardation by more closely aligning the condition with deficits in everyday intelligence.
- The definition of mental retardation should

include skills domains effected by a mix of cognitive and noncognitive abilities, de-emphasizing intelligence and recapturing the natural basis of mental retardation reflective of earlier constructs.
- People with mental retardation have demonstrated deficits in everyday (that is, social and practical) intelligence.
- Social deficits account for many of the problems that people with mental retardation experience at work, in the community, and in school.
- The construct of mental retardation is embedded in a historical-contextualist perspective.

What might be the logical consequence of basing one's definition of mental retardation on the integration of the concepts of adaptive behavior and intelligence and a better understanding of the contextual variables that influence the condition of mental retardation? While not necessarily advocating for the following definition, I note that it does reflect the logical consequence of integrating the constructs of adaptive behavior, intelligence, and contextual variables into the definition of mental retardation. As proposed by Greenspan (1997), mental retardation refers to:

persons widely perceived to need long-term supports, accommodations or protections due to persistent limitations in social, practical, and conceptual intelligence and the resulting inability to meet the intellectual demands of a range of settings and roles. These limitations are assumed, in most cases, to result from abnormalities or events occurring during the developmental period, and which have permanent effects on brain development and functioning. Persons with mental retardation may be divided into three sub-categories that indicate degree of overall disability: limited, extensive, and pervasive. These levels are determined by the intensity and pervasiveness of supports needed rather than by degree of intellectual impairment. (p. 186)

Any system by which a person is diagnosed as having mental retardation and is classified according to some criterion consists of a series of formalized rules specifying the characteristics a person must have to be so diagnosed and classified. Over the years, these rules have changed in response to consumer, professional, political, and social forces. Since its publication, we have noted a number of concerned discussions about the the 1992 AAMR System (Luckasson, et al.). Concerns include its impact on: the diagnostic process (Greenspan, 1994, 1997; Jacobson, 1994; Jacobson & Mulick, 1992, 1996; MacMillan, Gresham, & Siperstein, 1993); prevalence rates (Greenspan, 1994; MacMillan et al.); classification based on level of supports rather than on [intellectually based] severity level (Borthwick-Duffy, 1994; Greenspan, 1994; MacMillan et al.); research (Borthwick-Duffy; Greenspan, 1994); and educational practices (Smith, 1997).

Despite these concerns, a number of factors will continue the movement away from a definition and classification system that is overly reliant on tested intelligence to one that reflects better the integration of adaptive behavior, intelligence, and contextual variables. Chief among these are (a) the merging of the constructs of intelligence and adaptive behavior; (b) the ecological conception of disability; (c) the contextual model of assessment, intervention, and outcomes-evaluation; (d) the demonstration of the effectiveness and efficacy of appropriate supports, (re)habilitation programming, and assistive technology; (e) the increased use of assessment for intervention planning; and (f) the transformed vision of the life possibilities of people with mental retardation.

Measurement of Mental Retardation

In chapter 3 (Figure 3. 2,) I suggested that, based on a model of personal competence, the focus of assessment in the field of mental retardation should be related to the performance domains of practical, conceptual, and social skills. I suggested further that develop-ing this approach to assessment would involve: (a) selection of behaviorally based or performance indicators that represent the measurable components of practical, conceptual, and social skills; and (b) use of standardized instruments and/or functional assessments to document a person's functioning across the overall competence domains.

Despite the attractiveness of the suggested approach, there are potential impediments to focusing assessment on the performance domains of practical, conceptual, and social skills. For example, although the understanding of intelligence and adaptive behavior has changed over time, old measurement approaches die hard. As discussed by Crossen (1997) and Sternberg, Wagner, Williams, and (1995), there are disincentives to changing from our current psychometrically focused approach to intelligence testing: (a) a single number is concrete and therefore easy to defend in court and elsewhere; (b) creating new tests is very costly as they require 3 to 6 years for their development; and (c) current IQ tests are deeply entrenched in the minds of Americans and in the psychological and educational bureaucracies.

Additionally, there are still disagreements in the literature regarding the best approach to use in assessing intelligence and whether one should assess psychometric abilities, neuropsychological-processing variables, or more dynamic aspects of intellectual behavior. Differences among these three approaches are important. For example, if one focuses on psychometric abilities, assessment will be based on a model of the structure of abilities such as the multifactorial model of intelligence (Daniel, 1997). The neuropsychological-process approach, however, stresses the need to replace the concept of IQ with the concept of cognitive processing and replaces the model of intelligence based on content, modality, or method of presentation with a theoretical model describing the cognitive processes required to solve the task (Naglieri, Das, Stevens, & Ledbetter, 1991). Using a dynamic assessment approach, the structure of abilities is minimized, and one focuses on cognitive processes and the teachability of those processes (Feurerstein, Rand, & Hoffman, 1979; Haywood, Brown, & Wingenfield, 1990).

With the measurement of adaptive behavior, the impediment to change is primarily the lack of understanding (until recently) of the factor structure of adaptive behavior. As reviewed by Thompson et al. (this volume), research on adaptive behavior is still in an early stage of development. However, there is both good news and bad news as we think about the future of adaptive behavior assessment. The good news is that we are beginning to develop conceptual models that should result in major advances in the measurement of adaptive behavior around the natural problems critical to adaptation in the real world (Ceci, 1996; Ford, 1994). The bad news is that we still have not resolved the issue of using a norm versus a criterion-referenced assessment approach (see Heal and Tassé, this volume), and we have yet to address adequately the complex issues involved in the cross-cultural assessment of adaptive behavior.

Challenge: To Address Issues of Cross-Cultural Assessment of Adaptive Behavior

As discussed by Craig and Tassé (this volume), the literature is replete with examples demonstrating the influence of cultural variables on measuring traits and constructs. Because the criterion for success in the measurement of the construct of adaptive behavior is performance and not capability, it is critical to assess only culturally appropriate skills. Thus, if we are to assess adequately adaptive skills across cultural and linguistic groups, it is important to address the following four critical and complex issues: (a) determining the primary purpose of adaptive behavior assessment, (b) validating cross-cultural assessments, (c) reducing test bias, and (d) developing cross-cultural competence.

Purpose of Adaptive Behavior Assessment

As discussed by Spreat (this volume) and Nihira (this volume), adaptive behavior assessment instruments have been developed and marketed for many purposes in addition to the diagnosis and classification of mental retardation. Major purposes include identification of personal strengths and weaknesses, diagnosis, individual goal setting, documentation of progress, assessment of communication, administration of programs, and research. As stated by Spreat:

> A major problem for any instrument proposed for such a wide range of uses is this: To obtain sufficient information to support individualized programming, the test must be quite detailed and, in the case of the multifaceted construct like adaptive behavior, quite lengthy. An instrument of sufficient length to permit individual programming is simply unwieldy for the clinician conducting a diagnostic classification. (p. 107)

Thus, developers of adaptive assessment measures should address simultaneously the depth and breadth of the assessment in order to have a test that links clearly the purpose of assessment to the nature of the assessment. With a broad construct like adaptive behavior, I agree with Spreat (this volume) that it is unrealistic to think that the same test can be used for program evaluation, diagnosis, classification, and individual programming. So what should be the primary purpose for adaptive behavior assessment? It seems reasonable that the primary purpose of adaptive behavior assessment should be on the diagnostic decision, especially if mental retardation is defined in reference to significant limitations in practical, conceptual, and social skills.

Cross-Cultural Validation

Adaptive behavior differs across cultural and linguistic groups. Using an adaptive behavior test developed and normed on one cultural group will undoubtedly need to be adapted for use with other groups. Thus, test validation becomes a critical issue to address in the cross-cultural assessment of adaptive behavior. Two validation standards are critically important to test format and determine the validity of test translations or adaptations (American Psychological Association, 1985):

> When a test user makes a substantial change in test format, mode of administration, instructions, language, or content, the user should revalidate the use of the test for the changed conditions or have a rationale supporting the claim that additional validation is not necessary or possible.(p. 41)

> When a test is translated from one language or dialect to another, its reliability and validity for the uses intended in the linguistic groups to be tested should be established. (p. 75)

A systematic methodology is the only sure way to ensure a proper scale translation or adaptation, which requires as much know-how and empirical effort as developing an entirely new scale. As discussed by Tassé and Craig (this volume), there are several procedures for validating a cross-culturally adapted test. Common to these procedures is the 10-step procedure recommended by Geisinger (1994): (a) translate or adapt the scale, (b) review the translation or adaptation, (c) revise the scale according to the preceding step, (d) pilot test the scale and revise as necessary, (e) field test the scale on a large sample, (f) standardize the raw scores, (g) verify the validity and reliability of the scale, (h) develop a user's manual, (i) train users in the administration of the scale, and (j) obtain reactions and feedback from scale users.

In addressing the complex issues of adaptive behavior assessment, we need to sensitize test consumers to the difficulties involved in the comparison of test performances across cultural groups. In addition, as stated so well by Tassé and Craig (this volume),

Professionals and test consumers must realize that the mere translation of a test's instructions and item stems is insufficient. Ethically, professionals must ensure that the test they are using has been validated for the population with which they plan to use it, [and if] the validity of the test cannot be ascertained, the professionals must clearly state the limitations of the test's results and their consequent interpretations and recommendations. (p. 181)

Test Bias

A test is biased if its contents, procedures, or use result in a systematic advantage or disadvantage to members of certain groups over other groups and if the basis of this differentiation is irrelevant to the test purpose (Brown, 1983). As discussed by Bryant, Bryant, and Chamberlain (this volume), there are a number of sources of test bias, including background and orientation of the examiner, tester attitudes about different cultural groups, the working relation between the examiner and the examinee, the manner in which test results are interpreted, the examines background and expectations, and educational or habilitation personnel.

One of the biggest issues to be resolved in the cross-cultural assessment of adaptive behavior is how to reduce test bias. As discussed by Bryant, Bryant, and Chamberlain (this volume) and Hammill, Pearson, and Wiederholt (1996), the following four techniques should be used by test authors to control their tests for bias: (a) describe the content of their tests in terms of potential bias; (b) include targeted demographic groups (that is, identifiable groups that differ from the "mainstream" population in their normative samples) in the same proportion as the groups occur at each age level in the most recent census data; (c) provide separate reliability and validity information for the targeted groups; and (d) show that their test items are as appropriate for the targeted groups as for the mainstream population.

Cross-Cultural Competence

The next decade will undoubtedly be a "decade of ethnicity." Thus, it is apparent that the cross-cultural assessment of adaptive behavior involves not just the understanding of cultural or ethnic differences, but the ethnic competence of evaluators as well. Greene (1982) defines ethnic competence as "being able to conduct one's professional work in a way that is congruent with the behavior and expectations that members of a distinctive culture recognize as appropriate among themselves" (p. 52). Summarizing work in this area (e.g. Ibrahim, 1995; Keith, 1996; Lynch & Hanson, 1992; Marsella, 1990), ethnic competence includes: (a) an awareness of one's own cultural limitations; (b) an openness, appreciation, and respect for cultural differences; (c) the ability to interact and communicate in a sensitive fashion; (d) a view of intercultural interactions as learning opportunities; (e) the ability to use cultural resources in the assessment process; (f) an acknowledgment of the integrity and value of all cultures; and (g) an ability to reach consensus regarding the appropriate adjustments that should be made in adaptive behavior assessment findings when clear evidence exists of a strong cultural difference among groups.

The Future

It is an exciting time in the field of mental retardation. The trends and factors discussed in this book are beginning to coalesce into a new approach to the conceptualization, measurement, and use of the adaptive behavior construct. What makes the future so exciting and full of opportunities is that this new approach is occurring simultaneously with other conceptual shifts in how we view intelligence, contextualism, behavior assessment, supports, and the life possibilities of people with mental retardation.

What the future field of mental retardation will be like is anyone's guess. Whatever that future, it will be influenced significantly by how well we resolve the challenges addressed in this chapter—integrating the concepts of adaptive behavior and intelligence, understanding the contextual variables that influence the condition of mental retardation, rethinking the definition of mental retardation and its measurement, and addressing the complex issues involved in the cross-cultural assessment of adaptive behavior. In the significant work that lies ahead, we might well be guided by the sage advice of Benan (1991), that "behind all scientific studies there is not only the drive to understand, but the compulsion to persuade. All scholarship, including science, uses argument, and argument uses discourse" (p. 478).

References

American Psychological Association. (1985). *Standards for educational and psychological testing.* Washington, DC: Author.

Benan, W. (1991). A tour inside the onion. *American Psychologist, 46*(5), 475-483.

Borthwick-Duffy, S. (1994). [Review of *Mental retardation: Definition, classification, and systems of supports*]. *American Journal on Mental Retardation, 98,* 541-544.

Bruininks, R. H., McGrew, K., & Maruyama, G. (1988). Structure of adaptive behavior in sample with and without mental retardation. *American Journal on Mental Retardation, 93*(3), 265-272.

Brown, F. G. (1983). *Principles of educational psychology* (3rd ed.). New York: Holt, Rinehart & Winston.

Carroll, J. B. (1993). *Human cognitive abilities: A summary of factor analytic studies.* New York: Cambridge University Press.

Cattell, R. B. (1971). *Abilities: Their structure, growth, and action.* Boston: Houghton Mifflin.

Ceci, S. J. (1996). *On intelligence: A bioecological treatise on intellectual development* (Expanded ed.) Cambridge, MA: Harvard University Press.

Crossen, C. (1997, June 5). Mind fields: Think you're smart? Then just try to sell a new kind of IQ test. *Wall Street Journal* (pp. A1, A12).

Daniel, M. H. (1997). Intelligence testing. *American Psychologist, 52*(10), 1038-1045.

Feuerstein, R., Rand, Y. J., & Hoffman, M. (1979). *The dynamic assessment of retarded performers: Learning potential assessment device, theory, instruments, and techniques.* Baltimore: University Park Press.

Ford, M. E. (1994). Social intelligence. In R. J. Sternberg (Ed.), *Encyclopedia of human intelligence* (Vol. 2, pp. 974-978). New York: Macmillan.

Gardner, H. (1993). *Multiple intelligences: The theory in practice.* New York: Basic Books.

Geisinger, K. G. (1994). Cross-cultural normative assessment. Translation and adaptation issues influencing the normative interpretation of assessment instruments. *Psychological Assessment, 6,* 304-312.

Goleman, D. (1995). *Emotional intelligence.* New York: Bantam.

Greene, J. W. (1982). *Cultural awareness in the human services.* Englewood Cliffs, NJ: Prentice-Hall.

Greenspan, S. (1994). [Review of *Mental retardation: Definition, classification, and systems of supports*]. *American Journal on Mental Retardation, 98,* 544-549.

Greenspan, S. (1997). Dead manual walking? Why the 1992 AAMR definition needs redoing. *Education and Training in Mental Retardation and Developmental Disabilities, 32*(3), 179-190.

Greenspan, S., & Granfield, J. M. (1992). Reconsidering the construct of mental retardation: Implications of a model of social competence. *American Journal on Mental Retardation, 96*(4), 442-453.

Greenspan, S., & Switzky, H. N. (in preparation). *What is mental retardation?* Washington, DC: American Association on Mental Retardation.

Hammill, D. D., Pearson, N. & Wiederholt, J. L. (1996). *Comprehensive test of nonverbal intelligence.* Austin, TX: Pro-Ed.

Haywood, H. C. (1997, May 28). Global perspectives on mental retardation. Keynote address, 121st annual meeting of the American Association on Mental Retardation, New York.

Haywood, H. C., Brown, A. L., & Wingenfield, S. (1990). Dynamic approaches to psychoeducational assessment. *School Psychology Review, 19,* 411-422.

Ibrahim E. A. (1995). Multicultural influences on rehahilitation training and services: The shift to valuing nondominant cultures. In O. C. Karan & S. Greenspan (Eds.), *Community rehabilitation services for people with disabilities* (pp. 145-168). Boston: Butterworth-Heinemann.

Jacobson, J. W. (1994). [Review of *Mental retardation: Definition, classification, and systems of supports*]. *American Journal on Mental Retardation, 98*, 539-541.

Jacobson, J. W., & Mulick, J. A. (1992). A new definition of mentally retarded or a new definition of practice. *Psychology in Mental Retardation and Developmental Disabilities, 18*(2), 9-14.

Jacobson, J. W., & Mulick, J. A. (1996). *Manual of diagnosis and professional practice in mental retardation*. Washington, DC: American Psychological Association.

Keith, K. D. (1996). Measuring quality of life across cultures: Issues and challenges. In R. L. Schalock (Ed.), *Quality of life: Vol. 1. Conceptualization and measurement* (pp. 73-82). Washington, DC: American Association on Mental Retardation.

Luckasson, R., Coulter, D. L., Polloway, E. A., Reiss, S., Schalock, R. L., Snell, M. E., Spitalnik, D. M., & Stark, J. A. (1992). *Mental retardation: Definition, classification, and systems of supports*. Washington, DC: American Association on Mental Retardation.

Lynch, E. W. & Hanson, M. J. (1992). *Developing cross-cultural competence: A guide for working with young children and their families*. Baltimore: Paul H. Brookes.

MacMillan, D. L., Gresham, F. M., & Siperstein, G. N. (1993). Conceptual and psychometric concerns about the 1992 AAMR definition of mental retardation. *American Journal on Mental Retardation, 98*, 325-335.

Marsella, A. J. (1990). Ethnocultural identity: The new independent variable in cross-cultural research. *Focus (American Psychological Association), 4*(2), 14-15.

Naglieri, J. A., Das, J. P., Stevens, J. J., & Ledbetter, M. F. (1991). Confirmatory factor analysis of planning, attention, simultaneous and successive cognitive processing tasks. *Journal of School Psychology, 29*, 1-17.

Polloway, E. A. (1997). Developmental principles of the Luckasson et al. (1992) AAMR definition of mental retardation: A retrospective. *Education and Training in Mental Retardation and Developmental Disabilities, 32*(3), 174-178.

Schalock, R. L., Stark, J. A., Snell, M. E., Coulter, D., & Polloway, E. (1994). The changing conception of mental retardation: Implications for the field. *Mental Retardation, 32*(1), 25-39.

Smith, J. D. (1997). Mental retardation as an educational construct: Time for a new shared vision? *Education and Training in Mental Retardation and Developmental Disabilities, 32*(3), 167-173.

Spearman, C. (1923). *The nature of "intelligence" and the principles of cognition*. London: Macmillan.

Sternberg, R. J., Wagner, R. K., Williams, W. M.,& Horvath, J. A. (1995). Testing common sense. *American Psychologist, 50*(11), 912-927.

Switzky, H. N. (1997). Mental retardation and the neglected construct of motivation. *Education and Training in Mental Retardation and Developmental Disabilities, 32*(3), 194-200.

Terman, L. M., & Merrill, M. A. (1973). *Stanford-Binet intelligence scale: 1972 norms ed.* Boston: Houghton-Mifflin.

Thorndike, E. L., Hagen, E. P., & Sattler, J. M. (1986). *The Stanford-Binet intelligence scale: Technical manual* (4th ed.). Chicago: Riverside.

Thurstone, L. L. (1947). *Multiple factor analysis: A development and expansion of the vectors of mind.* Chicago: University of Chicago Press.

Vernon, P. E. (1961). *The structure of human abilities* (2nd ed.). London: Methuen.

Wechsler, D. (1981). Manual for the Wechsler adult intelligence scale-revised. New York, NY: Psychological Corporation.

Widaman, K. F., & McGrew, K. S. (1996). The structure of adaptive behavior. In J. W. Jacobson & J. A. Mulick (Eds.), *Manual of diagnosis and professional practice in mental retardation* (pp. 97-110). Washington, DC: American Psychological Association.

Zigler, E., Balla, D., & Hodapp, R. (1984). On the definition and classification of mental retardation. *American Journal of Mental Deficiency, 89,* 215-230.

Subject Index

A

Acculturation (*see* cross-cultural assessment issues)

Adaptations
  assistive technology
    adaptations, 88, 89, 91
  nontechnological adaptations, 88
  selection, 90
  training, 90

Adaptive behavior
  assessment of, 99, 141, 166
  concept of, 1, 15
  controversy concerning, 15, 207
  cross-cultural assessment of, 119, 163, 217
  definition, 103, 187
  developmental age norms, 113
  factor analytic studies of, 19
  factor structure, 25, 189
  hierarchical/structural model, 32, 35
  history of, 7
  measurement of, 99
  multidimensional and hierarchical, 30, 33
  multidimensionality, 49
  relation to mental retardation, 162, 187, 213
  psychometric standards and, 103, 106
  research on, 16

Adaptive behavior and intelligence
  merging of, 43
  integration of, 44, 209

Adaptive behavior measures
  expectation, 105
  measures, 120
  scales, 120
  translation or adaptions of, 168, 174

Adaptive behavior measurement (*see also* cross-cultural assessment, cross-cultural issues, cultural comparisons, factor analysis, gender, ethnicity, race)

Adaptive skill areas, 86, 188, 190

Assistive technology
  definition, 81, 84
  evaluation of effectiveness, 92
  use in task-person matches, 89

B

Back translation method, 170

C

Classification
  1992 AAMR System, 15

Competence (*see also* personal competence)
  cross cultural, 221
  domains, 46
  functional capabilities, 87

Contextualism
  and mental retardation, 61, 63, 211
  definition, 53, 61
  focus, 53
  setting, 61
  contextual variables, 211

Credulity
  assessment of, 71
  core deficit in mental retardation, 69

Criminal liability (*see also* credulity, cross-cultural assessment issues, gullibility)

Criterion-referenced assessment
  definition, 113
  examples of, 194

Cross-cultural assessment issues
  competence, 167
  cultural fairness, 193
  cultural factors, 126
  culture and development, 161
  interlingual adaptations, 169
  translation methods, 168
  validation, 174

Cross-cultural assessment of adaptive behavior
  culturally related issues, 127, 163

N

Norms
    role of, 113
    use of, 145

P

Personal competence
    definition, 46, 49, 210
    models of, 46, 65
Performance domains, 51
Performance indicators, 31, 51
Psychometric standards (*see also* reliability
  and validity)

R

Race/ethnicity
    assessment in adaptive behavior, 121,
     141
    relationship between adaptive
     behavior and race/ethnicity, 143, 146
Reliability
    definition, 106
    internal consistency (Cronbach's alpha),
     108
    interobserver, 107
    test-retest, 106

S

Service eligibility (*see* cross-cultural
  assessment issues [factors])
Setting (*see* contextualism)
Setting demands, 85

Social adaptation, 72
Social effectiveness
    action model of, 73
Social processes/contexts (*see* contextualism)
Special-education placement (*see*
  cross-cultural assessment issues [factors])
Standardized assessment instruments (*see*
  also reliability and validity)
    critical components, 52
Supports
    as part of the 1992 AAMR System, 188
    definition, 191
    intensities and levels, 191
    types, 192, 193

T

Test
    characteristics, 104
    definition, 104
Test bias
    definition, 144, 218
    controlling for, 144
Test interpretation
    test fairness, 112
    norms, 113
Trait vs. functional approach, 211

V

Validity
    definition, 110
    concurrent, 111
    content, 110
    construct, 110
    criterion and predictive, 111